Jesus and the Transformation of Judaism

Jesus and the Transformation of Judaism

JOHN RICHES

The Seabury Press · New York

1982
The Seabury Press
815 Second Avenue
New York, N.Y. 10017

Printed in the United States of America

Library of Congress Cataloging in Publication Data

Riches, John Kenneth.
    Jesus and the transformation of Judaism.

    Bibliography: p. 227
    Includes indexes.
    1. Jesus Christ—Relation to Judaism.   I. Title.
BT590.J8R53   1982   232.9′5   81-13629
ISBN 0-8164-2361-X   AACR2

Contents

Introduction

In the course of the history of critical investigation of the life and teaching of Jesus of Nazareth a host of questions have been thrown up and considered by scholars. By way of introduction I should like to give some account of which questions have seemed to me of greatest urgency. In so doing I am aware of the extent to which I am in debt to certain figures of the past as well as to teachers and colleagues.

For me the most pressing question about Jesus was put by Reimarus when he asked what was Jesus' *purpose*. What, as a man belonging to a particular community with a particular history, aspirations, etc., was he about? This is where we shall start and where, somewhat reformulated in terms of Jesus' 'role', we shall end. This does not mean that questions about Jesus' 'person', his divinity, etc., are unimportant, or indeed less important. But I would argue that unless we ask ourselves very seriously what he was up to, and ask that question as historically as we can, we shall all too easily slip into dogmatic abstractions which mask the reality of Jesus and which insulate our dogmatic traditions and their attendant ecclesiastical practices from criticism both from within and without. These latter points were impressed on me forcibly as a student by Professor Donald MacKinnon against the school theology of the 50s which too easily separated the Jesus of history from the Christ of faith. Subsequent reading in the history of biblical criticism and theology has only served to reinforce the view that this question must constantly be put and is still largely silenced in the courts of orthodox theologians and ecclesiastics. Here I acknowledge an obvious debt to Albert Schweitzer's great work, *The Quest of the Historical Jesus* and also to the independent spirit of G. E. Lessing who first gave this question to the public world of theology. Of all this more in Chapter 1.

Of course such a question is very broad, one might say 'fecund'. It spawns hosts of other questions which become urgent and pressing if one is to give it the answer it deserves. Of these, two are for me of greatest importance. The first is a question about language. Put simply, how is it possible to say new things in a particular given—natural—language? How does language change and grow? How do we take account of this in interpreting the utterances of figures of the past? Of course there is here a cluster of complex questions and I have said something about its history in Chapter 1. What I have to say substantively on the matter will be found in Chapter 2 and it has provided, as far as was possible, the framework for the account of Jesus' teaching in the later chapters. As it stands Chapter 2 owes a very great deal indeed to Alan Millar of Stirling University. In so saying, however, I should stress that the views in Chapter 2 should not be simply identified with Millar's. Those who would like to discover more of Millar's own views are invited to write to him at the Department of Philosophy, Stirling University.

Clearly on the answers to such questions depends how one will interpret the ways in which Jesus took the religious vocabulary of his day and reworked it for his purposes. How, it is sometimes asked, could Jesus formulate great theological truths in the religious clichés of first-century Palestine? Not all originality perhaps involves an original use of language, but certainly in the case of Jesus I will argue that his use of certain key terms, viz. 'Kingdom of God' *is* original and that the better we understand the manner of that originality the better we shall be able to trace the relations between his various utterances and between his views and the views of his contemporaries. This, of course, also sheds light on the vexed question of the authenticity of Jesus' sayings, which is so much bound up with the questions of distinctiveness and coherence. Chapter 3 is particularly concerned with this.

The second kind of question concerns the relation between theology and its social, political, 'attitudinal' implications. If we are to see Jesus as a man of his time, then we have to know how his fairly explicitly religious theological utterances related to the broad range of social and political questions which concerned Jews of the first century. This kind of question was raised very sharply by the answers which Reimarus gave to his question about Jesus' purpose. It is also one which has not often been satisfactorily answered in subsequent studies of Jesus. Of all these Bultmann's *Jesus the Word* stands out in its attempt to spell out the kinds of attitudes Jesus wished to encourage, but it deals little with questions of society and politics. My own reflections on the matter were initially much stimulated by reading social anthropologists' accounts of the relation of religious beliefs to social practice and attitudes in primitive societies. In particular I was greatly interested in Mary Douglas's work on the interpretation of religious symbols. However for reasons given briefly in Chapter 2 I am persuaded that there are serious difficulties with Mary Douglas's account of religious language, while again the account offered by A. Millar offers alternative ways of tracing the interrelation between theological, social and political utterances as well as enabling one to talk about the social and political effects—the *force*—of such utterances.

At this point I would declare an interest other than purely academic. The actual decision to write this book was taken when, as well as teaching New Testament in Glasgow, I was working in a Glasgow church in a downtown area. Questions about the relation of Christian preaching and theological utterance to social and political attitudes and actions are obviously pressing in such areas and I hope that indirectly at least this study may help to shed light on them. If so, it would be some return for the real friendship I have been shown at St George's, Maryhill.

Of the many other debts I have incurred in the writing of this book some at least must be acknowledged. Mrs M. Balden has typed the various drafts with amazing patience, speed and skill. My good fortune in this respect can hardly be exaggerated. David Weston has succeeded in composing a genuinely analytic index. Ernest Best and Robert Carroll and Jim Davies have generously commented on sections of the book at various stages, though my mistakes are not theirs. William Barclay first asked me to lecture on 'Jesus' theology' and generously encouraged me to go my own way.

I have attempted to detail further debts in the notes which do not pretend to offer exhaustive bibliographies, but to indicate my major sources where appropriate.

I have argued in the body of the book that Jesus advocated powerfully and originally the virtues of patience, forgiveness and long-suffering love. If this book were to have a dedication it would be to those whom I know who have shown me most of such virtues.

1

Putting the Questions

In any inquiry it is the questions one asks which determine the kind of results one may get. This is as true of studies of Jesus' life and preaching as it is of any field of inquiry. 'The quest for the historical Jesus' as a term for nineteenth- and twentieth-century studies of this kind is not a little misleading in that it masks the very different questions which men in fact sought to answer about Jesus. The questions I want to examine are first raised in the eighteenth century and have their origins both in rationalist criticism of the Bible and Christianity and in other more historical and political interests. They are then largely lost to view until raised again by the History of Religions school at the end of the nineteenth century. At the present time there is renewed interest in the work of such scholars after the long silence imposed in the era following the dialectical theology of the early 1920s.

Let us start with Reimarus (1694–1768),[1] the Hamburg school-master of whose manuscript a series of fragments was published anonymously (after Reimarus' death) by Lessing in the last years of his life. Reimarus was a Deist and a philologist. While he was perhaps deficient in moral courage, he was more generously endowed with linguistic skills and a historical sense for the odd, the significant, the obvious which others overlook. He was known to the world at large for his scholarly works[2] and his defence of natural religion against atheism,[3] but his own desk concealed darker secrets: his *Apology for Rational Worshippers of God*.[4] Much of the manuscript was fairly typical of the work of the Deists, and contained criticisms of the moral character of Old Testament figures, of miracles, of the resurrection accounts, and of any religion requiring belief in a

1

particular revelation as necessary for salvation. Even if it was in a sense typical, it was powerfully expressed and supported by detailed philological work on the biblical texts. Lessing's selections[5] from this material provoked a fairly vehement response from the orthodox of his day who sprang to the defence of revealed religion in general and of the resurrection in particular. This in turn provided Lessing with the pretext for publishing the last of the fragments: *Of the Purpose of Jesus and his Disciples.*[6]

What is so remarkable about this section of the manuscript?[7] It starts by repeating the results of his inquiry so far. The Old Testament teaches no doctrine of immortality, though in subsequent generations Jews, under the influence of pagan philosophy, attempted to read the doctrine into it. In this respect the Pharisees in Jesus' day attempted to rework the legalistic elements in Judaism to bring them more into accord with the proper end of religion, but in so doing they succeeded only in marring their efforts by laying stress on the external ceremonial requirements of the law. Jesus by contrast attacked the hypocrisy of the Pharisees and preached a 'better righteousness', while agreeing with them on the question of immortality and blessedness. Thus his teaching is superior to that both of the Pharisees and of the Old Testament. Jesus does not entirely exclude from the hope of immortality the heathen who are still in the darkness of their ignorance.

Thus broadly and acceptably—at least to the more enlightened of Lessing's contemporary theologians—Reimarus sets Jesus in the context of the development of the Jewish religion. The next section, however, shows clearly that this is not to be conceived of simply as an apologetic device for demonstrating the superiority of Jesus' teaching over all other religious teaching, but rather merely a preliminary sighting shot prior to a more thoroughgoing *historical* inquiry into Jesus' teaching.

For it is now that he puts the question which Lessing singled out for the title of this fragment. Disarmingly, as if it were a final detail to be tidied up, he writes: 'Just as after this there can be no doubt that Jesus in his teaching pointed men to the true great purpose of any religion, viz. eternal blessedness, so we are left only with the question *what purpose Jesus himself had for himself in his teaching and actions.*'[8] The question is slipped in almost as if he himself had hardly grasped its significance, its originality. For he turns immediately to the question of the historical sources for Jesus' views, to the possibility of distortion in the Gospel records.[9] We are engaged on an historical inquiry: 'We want to know what Jesus' teaching actually was, what he said and preached; and this is a question of *res facti*, a question of something that occurred; and therefore something that has to be drawn out of the reports of those who wrote the histories.'[10] And undoubtedly it is this concern with *res facti*, rather than with the philosphy of rationalism that constitutes the true offence and interest of Reimarus's work.[11]

Like Locke before him,[12] Reimarus settles his attention on two points in Jesus' teaching: Repent and believe the gospel. But whereas Locke was able to find in this an enlightened, reasonable version of the Protestant doctrine of the atonement, Reimarus is guided by a much firmer historical sense to inquire what exactly Jesus' gospel of the coming of the Kingdom and the Messiah might have meant to a Jew of the first century. Before he can tackle this task he must clear two prevalent views out of the way: first, that Jesus came above all to reveal the mysteries of the incarnation and the Trinity; second, that Jesus came to found a new religion with its own rites and ceremonies. The first point had already been treated extensively by the Socinians, but the second required a detailed attack on the view that Jesus came to institute baptism and communion as the new rites of a new religion. Reimarus attacks such a view in order to insist that Jesus' work—at least as far as its 'positive'[13] aspects are concerned—must be seen as an attempt to reform Judaism from within.

Once he has established this to his satisfaction then he can turn, freed from the weight of traditional interpretation of Jesus, to examine the meaning of Jesus' preaching and actions in the context of the Judaism of Jesus' day. The results of his inquiry are familiar enough. Jesus' teaching about the Messiah and the Kingdom was related simply to current beliefs in a future political saviour who would free the Jews from foreign rule and re-establish the Jewish Kingdom. Jesus believed that he was destined to fulfil this role; he sent his disciples out to proclaim this, performed miracles to accredit

3

himself and then set out for Jerusalem at Passover to carry out his purpose. Such popular support as there was at his entry into Jerusalem, however, soon waned; Jesus was forced into hiding, was betrayed and summarily executed as an insurgent. Later, however, his disciples gave it out that he had risen from the dead and thus founded a new religion.

It would be tempting to follow Reimarus further into his work, to see how often he raised questions which have continued to engage the attention of serious scholars of the New Testament, or which indeed they have put out decades later as new and original questions, little suspecting that the Hamburg schoolmaster had already set them down in the privacy of his study. But it is no part of my purpose to trace in detail the history of the quest for the historical Jesus, simply to trace the emergence of the key questions. With Reimarus we have already seen the sharpness with which he posed the question about Jesus' place within the development of Judaism, how he pointed straightway to the need for a critical sifting of the texts in order to distinguish the authors' views from those of Jesus himself, the insistence that positive theology is historical, concerned to establish the *res facti*.

All this flows naturally from his question about Jesus' purpose, though we may marvel at the clarity of mind and resoluteness of spirit which enable him to draw these conclusions with such sureness. What might almost escape our attention is the remarkable nature of the original question: *what purpose Jesus himself had for himself in his teaching and actions*. For centuries, as Schweitzer argues at the beginning of his great work,[14] theologians had paid tribute to the victory of Alexandrian Christology over the Antiochenes. The manhood of Jesus was conceived of as little more than the instrument of the divine Logos, and what sense there might have been of co-operation or co-inherence between the Logos and his assumed flesh was largely excluded by the doctrine of the impersonal manhood of Christ. Questions about Jesus' own intentions were simply not put. Even when men like Locke set themselves to discover the true nature of Christian doctrine by an examination of what Jesus actually taught, there is something strangely lifeless about the inquiry: it is an inquiry into the meaning of the sayings of Jesus, yes, but one remarkably divorced from any interest in the context in which those sayings were uttered. Neither the wider context of contemporary Judaism, nor the context of Jesus' own experience, plans and actions seriously claims his attention. Yet once the question was out—and it required someone of Lessing's courage and cunning to unleash it—it could not be suppressed. No matter how the orthodox might rue it and rail against the anonymous author and his editor, the question would goad them into reply, while bolder spirits would soon rush into the quest for an answer.

Among the immediate reactions to Reimarus's questions many were ill-considered and beside the point, but one stands out both because of the distinction of its author and because it lays the foundation for all future prevarication on the subject. Of it Schweitzer says that it inaugurates the 'Yes-But' theology which dominated the nineteenth century.[15] The book is Johann Salomo Semler's *Answer to the Fragments*.[16] He concedes that Jesus indeed used on occasion the terms in which his contemporary Jews expressed their national, material and political hopes and aspirations. But—and there follows a stream of 'buts'—Jesus taught in one way to the *sarkikoi*, in another to the *pneumatikoi* (he has the teaching of the fourth Gospel and the private explanations to the disciples in mind).[17] There were two doctrines of the Messiah current in Judaism, one of a political figure, the other a suffering spiritual Messiah, and it was to the latter, spiritual conception that Jesus attempted to lead men of his time.[18] While Jesus may have used the language of the Kingdom and the Messiah, the heart of his preaching was of a more spiritual conception and worship of God.[19] As if his attempts to distinguish the spiritual from the material sense or content of Jesus' teaching were not tortuous enough, Semler proceeds to apply the same principle to Jesus' ministry. While the Jews may have been tempted to see in Jesus a political Messiah, Jesus took every opportunity to convince them by his actions that the true Messiah was to be of a different kind. Thus when Semler comes to consider the question of Jesus' arrest and trial, he asks the fragmentist why, if Jesus had intended to provoke a revolt at Passover, he did not then flee when he saw it fail. Because, he replies triumphantly, he went to Jerusalem not to cause a revolt but to

5

teach the Jews a more spiritual religion, and when arrest appeared imminent he simply could not miss the chance of teaching them a more spiritual Messiahship by allowing himself to be crucified.[20]

Semler's reply is, of course, painfully inadequate. He squirms on the hook of Reimarus's question in a series of vain and often ridiculous attempts to avoid taking seriously Jesus' involvement with his contemporary world, its religious and political aspirations. And Schweitzer is right in seeing him as the father of all subsequent attempts to avoid the offence of Jesus' Jewishness, of his roots in the culture, religion and politics of a particular age and place. For Semler's talk of 'Jesus' double mode of teaching' effectively presents a blank cheque to all those who will come after. However men may describe and account for the specific 'material' references to contemporary beliefs and hopes, and for his death at the hands of the authorities, they may still fill in the 'spiritual' sense of Jesus' teaching at their pleasure. It was this device above all which accounts for the phenomenon, so often noted, that liberal lives of Jesus reflected more of the spiritual ideals of their authors than of Jesus himself.[21]

But at one significant point Semler scores off Reimarus. He seizes on the fragmentist's distinction between Jesus' general and positive teaching. If Jesus pointed men to the true end or purpose of all religion, viz. eternal blessedness, then what sense does it make to speak also of 'his purpose *for himself*'? What is this doctrine of double purpose? It is clear that here he has put his finger on the weak point in Reimarus's position, which was also noticed by Lessing when he pointed to the uneasy relationship between the Wolffian principles of the first book and the paths down which the material of the subsequent books led him (see note 11). That is, when Reimarus talks of Jesus' general teaching of immortality he is, in common with other Rationalists, simply identifying part of Jesus' teaching with certain doctrines of eighteenth-century natural theology. Reimarus's achievement lies in noticing that this by no means does justice to all that is recorded of Jesus, but his characterization of the remainder as 'positive theology' effectively separates it from Jesus' other teaching and so enables him to treat it as purely political, non-theological teaching.

6

Yet to concentrate on what Reimarus said about Jesus' 'general' and 'positive' teaching would be to miss altogether the achievements of his book. These lie firmly in his raising the question of Jesus' *own* intentions. It was this question which set men on the quest for a Jesus who could speak to them from beyond the authoritative dogma of the Church. Men set out, says Schweitzer, to find the historical Jesus in the belief that they could then transport him, as he was, into their own times as teacher and saviour.

> The quest loosed the bands by which He had been riveted for centuries to the stony rocks of ecclesiastical doctrine, and men rejoiced to see life and movement coming into the figure once more, and the historical Jesus advancing, as it seemed, to meet it. But He does not stay; but passes by our time and returns to his own.[22]

Why was this question about Jesus' own intentions so important? Why did Lessing, the great dramatist, philosopher, man of letters devote so much of his last years to this question and to the defence of Reimarus? Not simply in order to challenge the orthodoxy of his day, nor to provide some apologetic for a more enlightened Christianity.[23] Lessing does not divulge his own motives easily, but we may surmise an answer on two levels. In the first place, Lessing was possessed by a genuine desire to understand religion as a phenomenon in its own right. The options which his own age provided for understanding religion were two. Either you pressed religion into the straitjacket of a particular kind of philosophy of a more or less rationalist kind; or you identified it, as did the orthodox of the various confessions, with a series of traditional dogmas which had to be accepted unquestioningly. The fascination of Reimarus's work is that, for all that he accepted rationalism as an adequate account of religion, his own inquiry into Jesus' intentions raises the possibility that great religious insight and truth may be expressed in language which is neither that of metaphysics nor of traditional Christian orthodoxy. How then for example is such language to be *understood*? How can important religious truths be expressed, for example, in terms of first-century Jewish beliefs about the kingdom?

7

In the second place, Lessing saw Reimarus's question as a weapon in his own political struggle for the emancipation of the middle classes.[24] It represented an attack on elements in church life which reinforced the authoritarian despotism of the petty princedoms of his day by inculcating attitudes of total, unreasoning obedience in matters of faith. The claim that Jesus did not propose mysteries which had to be believed, as well as the content of the fragment *Of the Denunciation of Reason from the Pulpit*, lies along this line. Lessing, it is true, recognized that to some extent such attitudes had been modified since Reimarus wrote; but equally he believed that Semler and the Neologists had achieved only an uneasy compromise between reason and authority. They allowed reason a certain role in the reception and understanding of revelation, even in providing proofs for it! This was simply to subordinate reason to authority, while decking authority out with the robes of reason. Lessing had long lost his taste for the Berlin enlightenment with its mixture of Prussian authoritarianism and French philosophy and culture. Thus it was of great importance to Lessing that Reimarus's question, by concentrating attention on the purposes, plans and actions of Jesus 'for himself' gave, or opened up the possibility of giving a real and independent significance to human reasoning and planning in the quest for and discovery of truth.

One may develop this point a little further. For Lessing, we may surmise from his *Education of Mankind*,[25] religion is not only the means by which men have been held in bondage to despotism as in Lutheran orthodoxy, it is also the means by which men have been brought from a state of barbarism to a gradually deepening understanding of the truth. Philosophy may be the way to truth for a few individuals, but for the vast mass of people advances in the truth are brought through religious truths and doctrines. If this is so, then a number of points follow. First, religious teaching must by nature be couched in terms that are intelligible to the people in the community to whom it is addressed, not in terms of 'timeless, necessary truths of reason'. Secondly, because religion is a constant process of *education*, the great religious teachers will be concerned to deepen the religious understanding of their people, to express new truths in terms of their existing religious vocabulary. Change and

8

development are an essential party of any true religion. Thirdly, religion properly is a means of mankind's education, which is to say of its emancipation from subservience to ignorance and despotism. Each of these assertions, however, may equally well be put in the form of questions: How can religious truths be expressed in terms of myths, stories, prophecies of coming saviours, etc.? How does the religious teacher deepen and modify the tradition which he inherits? What is the relation of theological doctrine, of specifically religious discourse to social and political beliefs and practice?

We may do well as we follow the history of the examination of these questions to take Schweitzer's hint[26] and to pass quickly over the next three generations of scholars. For despite all the labours of rationalists, Schleiermacherians, Hegelians, Ritschlians and others it is effectively only with the History of Religions School that the full force of the questions again begins to be perceived. This is not to say that important contributions to the inquiry were not made during the period up to the publication of Johannes Weiss's *Jesus' Preaching of the Kingdom of God*,[27] and we shall notice some of these retrospectively. The real achievement of these years was to centre attention on Jesus' personality, his 'self-consciousness' as the locus of revelation, his gift to men in which they too might share and sharing find faith, courage, hope and love. It was in the light of Jesus' personality that his words were to be interpreted and the key to that personality was to be found in the story of his life as well as in the impact it made upon his disciples and subsequent followers. Jesus' words and teaching were but the contemporary expression of the eternal gospel of his own 'God-consciousness', his own living faith.[28] This on the one hand; on the other the nineteenth-century lives of Jesus, notably in the work of Albrecht Ritschl, emphasized strongly Jesus' ethical preaching of the Kingdom as a task set before men to be realized through their own 'self-activity'.[29]

It may sound unduly harsh to say that the representative scholars of this period lacked historical rigour; but while they certainly lacked nothing in energy and application they failed to set the question about Jesus' intentions and plans fully in the context of the development of contemporary Judaism. This, perhaps, above all because the question about Jesus' intentions still evoked from the majority of scholars a defensive, apologetic response which precluded a truly historical answer. The real historical break-through came in the work of the History of Religions School. This work on the contemporary setting of Jesus' teaching, together with the form-critical studies of the synoptic tradition of the next generation, still provides the indispensable basis for an historical study of Jesus' life and teaching.[30]

The History of Religions School arose by way of reaction to the Liberal theologians' isolation of primitive Christianity from its contemporary religious context. Men like Hausrath demanded that the attempt be made: 'to insert New Testament history back into the historical nexus in which it originally stood; to contemplate it . . . as a part of a general historical process.'[31] What this called for was in the first instance a thorough examination of contemporary religious movements and of the similarities and connections beteeen them and Christianity. In this respect the important work done by this school lay in the field of Jewish apocalyptic, of Gnosticism and of the Hellenistic mystery religions. The application of such ground-work to the New Testament was made above all in two books: J. Weiss's book which we have just mentioned and W. Bousset's *Kyrios Christos*. Weiss's book is written with a deliberate polemical purpose. It was to show the great gap that existed between Jesus' use of the notion of the Kingdom of God, which he believed was rooted in contemporary Jewish apocalyptic, and the use of the same term by his father-in-law, Albrecht Ritschl, which was rooted in the critical philosophy of Immanuel Kant. If Ritschl saw the Kingdom as an ethical task, a community of men in brotherly love, set up by Jesus' teaching and growing steadily through history as a result of men's 'self-activity', Jesus saw the Kingdom as something which comes independently of men's efforts, as the harvest springs 'of itself', from the seed. It was something moreover which would come to put an end to this world, this order of things which now stands under judgement. The force of Weiss's work however, apart from the death-blow it dealt to Ritschlianism,[32] was to raise very sharply a question which has since dominated the inquiry: namely that of the relation between Jesus' apocalyptic and ethical teaching. If this world is to pass away, what is the point of present ethical endeavour? Is not the wise thing to prepare for the coming day, to repent and to watch?

Bousset's work in *Kyrios Christos* is of more importance in relation to the development of New Testament Christianity than specifically in relation to Jesus' preaching. He indeed wrote a reply to Weiss's book: *Jesus' Preaching in contrast to Contemporary Judaism*[33] where he praised the way that Jesus transcended contemporary Judaism and its empty speculations about the end of the world. However, in his study of the development of Christology in primitive Christianity he showed the extent to which that Christology was the product of a generation of Christian writers who owed a deep debt to the beliefs and practices of the Hellenistic world. This alerted scholars like Bultmann to the possibilities of Hellenistic influences in the Gospels themselves and led them to discern the influence of the Hellenistic cult on the passion narrative.[34] Bousset's work well exemplifies two aspects of the History of Religion School's work. In the first place, it shows how they were eager to plot the *development* of Christianity through the New Testament period, a task which had been pioneered indeed by Baur and Ritschl and to which Bousset had made a major contribution in his exploration of pre-Pauline Hellenistic Christianity. In the second place, it shows the stress they laid on the relation between religious beliefs and the practice of the community which held them. The institutions, rites, activities of the community are so closely interrelated to its expressed beliefs that the one can scarcely be understood without the other. This view of New Testament studies was well set out by W. Wrede in his programmatic essay 'The Task of New Testament Theology'.[35] The New Testament is to be considered not as a source-book for Christian doctrine but as the literary deposit of the developing religion of the Christian communities of the New Testament era, starting with Jesus and his followers through to the catholicizing communities of the second century.

The implications of this approach to the study of the New Testament for the examination of the religion of Jesus are primarily twofold. First it means, if the New Testament records are deposits of the developing religion of the New Testament period, that we must distinguish as carefully as we can in the synoptic tradition between the different layers of community belief which it contains and the original utterances and actions of Jesus in so far as they are still contained in it. Wrede himself pursued this task to some purpose in his book *The Messianic Secret*[36] by attempting to discern theological motifs in the Gospels which were attributable to the Christian community or the evangelists, rather than to Jesus himself. Wellhausen in his commentaries on the synoptic Gospels[37] began the work of paring away the editorial work of the evangelists from the tradition which they received. This task was then taken up in earnest by the 'Form-Critics' who published their findings after the First World War. We shall consider these matters further in Chapter 3. Secondly, it means that where Jesus is concerned we must also attempt to relate his uttered beliefs, as far as we can recover them, to his own practice and the practice of his followers during his ministry. This task however was not taken up, largely as we shall see, because it was felt that the sources did not provide adequate evidence for it. More precisely it was thought, rightly I believe, that the sources provide only slender evidence for a reconstruction of the course of Jesus' ministry, the causes of his arrest, etc., and it seems that it was therefore assumed that there was nothing of real significance which could be learnt about his ministry. Hence the matter was dropped. One interesting exception to this is provided by Rudolf Otto's *The Kingdom of God and the Son of Man*,[38] where Otto contrasts the ascetic figure of the Baptist with the charismatic Jesus, the glutton and the wine-bibber. The influence of this book can be seen in C. H. Dodd's *The Parables of the Kingdom*[39] but the methodological insight has not been pursued further. The task remains and will be returned to later in this book.

So far we have considered the growth within the History of Religion School of an awareness of new tasks confronting the historian of the New Testament period, tasks which relate directly to the sifting of sources, to the desire to plot the development of Christianity in its earliest period in relation both to its own various stages and to the surrounding world of religious belief and practice. But behind these particular tasks, which are, of course, of fundamental importance to the inquiry, lies a task of a different order, namely the task of *understanding* Christianity, once we have set it back into the historical nexus in which it originally stood. What is it to 'contemplate it . . . as part of a general historical process'?

Certainly where the rise of Christianity in the teaching of Jesus of Nazareth is concerned this meant trying to assess Jesus' place in and contribution to Jewish sectarianism of the first century A.D. It proved however easier to show similarities and connections between Jesus and his contemporary Jews than to grasp the significance of these similarities. At one level it was possible to discount unhistorical readings of Jesus, as Weiss was able to attack Ritschl's understanding of Jesus' preaching of the Kingdom. But when he himself suggested that for Jesus it referred to an imminent future event which would put an end to this world, did he go too far towards *equating* Jesus with contemporary Jewish apocalyptic?[40] Bousset[41] in his reply to Weiss certainly thought so. He agrees with Weiss that it is right to make a thorough study of the similarities between the religious ideas and atmosphere of 'late Judaism' and Jesus, if we are to understand the 'historical phenomenon of Jesus'. But he equally objects to the attempt to understand Jesus 'from the start within the framework of Judaism' because 'such an approach does not allow an unbiased comparison and truly historical appreciation of the figure of Jesus. Jesus' piety was related to the piety of late Judaism only in its external form, in the expectation of an early end to the world', but 'this is not to say that the whole figure of Jesus was held under the spell of Judaism.' Rather it remains true that 'the Gospel develops hidden elements in the Old Testament, but it protests against the ruling direction of Judaism.'[42]

The options which this early debate opens up are harshly contrasted. Either to see Jesus purely as a man of his time, 'within the framework of Judaism', or to see him as a religious genius, who, even if he makes use of contemporary ideas and expressions, so far transcends them as to produce a religion of a quite different kind. There seems little room within such a conception of things for modification and adaptation of contemporary beliefs and practice in such a way as to produce something interestingly and importantly new. A man either remains within the framework of his time and culture or he transcends it.

At one level the reason for this harsh disjunction is methodolog-

13

ical. For all that scholars of this period were aware of the need to relate the expressed beliefs of the community to its religious practice, they nevertheless categorized religious communities and movements principally in terms of their distinctive ideas and concepts. Now the problem of defining 'Judaism' and 'Hellenism' and their various subdivisions by reference to the ideas and terms used within them is fairly evidently that of overlooking the diversity of *use* which may be made of religious ideas within different *systems* of religious belief. It is seriously misleading to do isolated word studies of religious concepts or terms, for such will fail to take into account the pattern of terms of which they form a part and that it is this overall pattern which determines their meaning. However, I think it is fairly clear that many members of this school regarded religious ideas as having an independent, timeless value of their own, at least when they were the product of the spontaneous reason of a religious genius, just as they believed that there were religious systems which were void of all true originality, whose ideas and concepts simply failed to attain to any real level of religious insight and truth.

A perceptive analysis of the reasons for this dichotomy at an epistemological level was offered by Ernst Troeltsch:

Present-day science of religion labours under the same major difficulty as all other studies of culture, viz. that the decisive fundamental assumption which will determine its treatment of the subject must be made at the outset and that this assumption then dominates the whole subsequent treatment in all its aspects. The question which has to be decided is how to view the great cultural creations of the human spirit: whether to see in them *independent* dispositions and forces of the spirit which give form to their own ideas and values *on the basis of their own internal necessity*, or whether to see in the spirit nothing but the formal power which orders positive facts, when they have been apprehended as objectively as possible, into a coherent system of generalizations and then makes this system serve the human goals of self-preservation and the progress of the species.[43] (My italics.)

On the one hand the mysterious, irreducible wonders of reason, *spontaneously* producing the great cultural monuments of the family, state, society, law, art, science, religion, morality; on the other merely the orderly regulating of such facts as can be known in the cause—as it is understood—of the advancement of mankind.

Troeltsch's analysis of the state of religious studies at this time is illuminating in a number of respects. In the first place the fundamental problem for a thoroughgoing historical explanation of Jesus' teaching is not simply how to plot the relationship between his teaching and the beliefs of contemporary Judaism, but rather how to understand any religious beliefs at all, once we have attained a historical perspective of man's cultural achievements, their diversity, their comings and goings. Thus the problem where Jesus' teaching is concerned is to understand the religious phenomenon of Jewish apocalyptic; then perhaps Jesus' teaching may appear in its own light, both contrasted and compared with it. The work of scholars like Weiss, Bousset and indeed Schweitzer was vitiated by the fact that none of them had any real *understanding* of apocalyptic. Whatever view they took of Jesus' teaching, they all agreed that, if he were primarily an apocalyptic teacher, then his message would be strange and largely unintelligible to us.

Secondly, it is interesting to note that the alternatives which Troeltsch holds out for the understanding of religion relate rather surprisingly to the actual work of New Testament historians of his day. Few of them opted for the second view of religion to the complete rejection of the first. Perhaps Schweitzer comes nearest to such a course when he portrays the development of Christianity from John the Baptist through Jesus and Paul to the mysticism of John as a series of adaptations of Jewish apocalyptic hopes and expectations in the light of the events of Jesus' ministry, death and resurrection and the subsequent fading of the hope of an early end to the world.[44] Even then Schweitzer sees in Jesus' ethical teaching the spontaneous work of the practical reason which, while in Jesus' eyes it is subordinated to his apocalyptic beliefs, is nevertheless of infinite value. The tension between Troeltsch's two options is however much more marked in the work of Bousset. For him the beliefs of religious *communities* are subject to iron laws of causal necessity. Hellenistic Christianity with its sacramental Kyrios-cult was the form which Christianity had to assume when it moved into the Hellenized world beyond Palestine.[45] But when it comes to considering the beliefs of Jesus or Paul then we are in a different world altogether. Here we encounter the free, independent working of the human spirit which produces ideas of eternal value. It is in Jesus' case a spiritualizing, a purging of contemporary Jewish ideas which Bousset can portray as a triple liberation, from the national character of Jewish religion, from the ceremonial element in religion and from the letter of the law.[46] Similarly Paul, though indebted to the sacramentalism of Hellenistic Christianity, attains a higher, individualistic mysticism; 'a mysticism of a more personal note struggles free and flies upward with freer strokes of the wings'.[47] Such a lack of decisiveness about one's understanding of religion can easily lead to a false apologetic which contrasts Christianity understood in one way, namely as a pure product of the spontaneous reason, and other religions, notably Jewish apocalyptic, understood in a quite different way.

But the very alternative which Troeltsch sets out stands in need of critical appreciation. The contrast he draws between two possible conceptions of religion is based on the view that human reason may function in one of two possible ways: either spontaneously, producing ideas of its own, independently of the information it may receive through the senses; or by way of reaction to the information it receives which it orders and classifies in accordance with certain fundamental aims and purposes, hopes, fears and aspirations. One might say that the first view sees the religious leader as an artistic genius who, at least on a romantic view of artistic creation, produces his work out of the pure springs of the human spirit; while the second view sees him more as a great chess-player, making the most of a particular position, where 'most' means seeking to assert himself, to achieve certain goals within the limits which he is set by the game he is playing.

Already this analogy might suggest that the disjunction Troeltsch makes is in important respects unsatisfactory. For it obscures significant similarities between the artist's creativity and the wit of the really good chess-player. The artist does not work wholly independently of an artistic tradition of techniques, forms, conventions, etc., though clearly his use of such forms may be surprising and unexpected; similarly, for all that a really good chess-player can only make certain moves, his 'wit' in seeing the unexpected and surprising is what marks him out from the merely competent performer.

More specifically, Troeltsch's disjunction, as applied to the study of religion leads, I think, to a number of *aporia*. In the first place the relation of the religious innovator to his tradition is hardly illuminated by talk of *independent* dispositions and forces of the spirit which *give form* to their own ideas and values *on the basis of their own internal necessity*. The question here is in what relation does the innovator stand to the language, forms and conventions which he inherits? While indeed new forms may be created, it is very rare that such forms bear no relation whatsoever to those that have gone before. Similarly, if he uses terms and sentences which bear no relation to previous uses, he will simply not be understood. Such an understanding of religious originality, that is to say, raises enormous difficulties for the historian who is, perhaps, attempting to trace the historical development of Christianity out of Judaism. Bousset's solution to this difficulty is to see the *community* as being bound by rigid laws determining its development, while the *individual* is free to develop his own spirituality. Yet this hardly clarifies, for example, Paul's relation to his community and its faith, which remains no more than a spring-board for his personal mysticism. Alternatively, one might concentrate as did Bultmann in his *Jesus and the Word* and Barth in his *Epistle to the Romans*[48] on the utterances of the prophet or writer himself seeing in these the work of religious inspiration or revelation and seeking to understand them in such a way that they speak to us with the same freshness and originality with which they spoke to Jesus' or Paul's contemporaries. But this is effectively to abandon the search for a coherent account of the *development* of Christianity.

If on the other hand one takes the second half of Troeltsch's disjunction and sees religious developments as being fundamentally determined by developments in the social, economic, technological and political situation of a group then one is not only opting for a view of religion which is quite other than that which the religionist himself has of it, but is reducing religious originality to the level of

17

a certain ingenuity in modifying one's religious ideology in the interests of some fundamental social and political interests. This in turn fails to do justice to the individuality and surprisingness of the particular creations of religious innovators. Thus it is not hard to see why theologians have tended to opt for the first, sociologists and historians for the second part of the disjunction. In neither case, however, do the results succeed in providing an account which does justice both to the individuality and originality of particular religious figures, and to their place within a particular historical continuum, as the heirs and creators of tradition.

This discussion may be related to the questions which were raised earlier in connection with Reimarus and Lessing. First, if we are to understand how genuinely innovative changes can be made within a religious tradition, we need a more adequate analysis of how language changes within a given community, in such a way that interestingly new beliefs can be expressed in a language which can still be understood by those to whom it is addressed. Too often it has been assumed that a certain word refers, within a given tradition, to a particular idea and that its meaning is established once that connection has been ascertained. What I shall suggest is, put simply, that we need to distinguish between the core meaning of a particular word or word group and its conventional associations in a particular community which may be modified and altered in such a way that the term takes on quite different meanings, which nevertheless remain intelligible within a particular tradition. That is to say the question, for example, of Jesus' originality in his use of a term like 'kingdom' can be grasped only when we have first seen the range of associations which the term had for his contemporaries, and secondly seen the way in which when Jesus uttered it he reworked its associations in order to say something very different from, for instance, what Zealots said when they used it.

Further, to take up the second set of questions discussed earlier, we need a better understanding of the connection between beliefs and changing political, social, economic, technological realities than is provided either by saying that beliefs are *determined* by certain sociological realities, or by asserting the fundamental *independence* of religious beliefs from their social context. Either of these courses

18

leads to a serious misunderstanding of the religious endeavour. The first reduces religious movements to what are really—or at a deeper level—political or social movements subserving the goal of man's striving for self-preservation; the second leads to the 'privatization' of religion, seeing it as fundamentally a relation between an alone and an Alone. While I do not pretend to be able to offer answers to all these questions, two things may help to provide a more satisfactory working basis. First, talking of a term's 'core-meaning' and its 'conventional associations' will help to explain the links between sentences where it is used to say things about God and sentences about politics, society, and so on, with which it is conventionally associated within a particular community. That is to say we need first to understand the connections which are actually made within a particular community between theology and politics, etc., before we impose on them our own prior understanding of the link.

Secondly, we shall have to be careful to avoid simplistically mechanistic models of causality in explaining the relationship between sociological factors and religious beliefs. Principally we must avoid supposing that there is one cause for every event, whether it affects the development of religious beliefs, the spontaneous pure reason, or some change in the political or social field. Cross-cultural comparisons may indeed suggest helpfully that certain forms of religious belief and movements are associated with certain sociological constellations. This should not deter us from looking to see what is the particular way in which a religious leader or innovator has used such forms, what, that is to say, marks them out as distinctive from other comparable movements and beliefs. I shall develop these theoretical points more fully in the next chapter.

2

Religion and Change

In the last chapter we traced the emergence of certain questions about the nature of religious change and innovation and of the interrelationship between theological beliefs and social and political policies and realities. In this chapter I want to take up the suggestion that progress may be made in answering these problems by offering a rather different account of religious language and of the interrelationship between religous beliefs and events in the history of the religious community.

As we saw, Troeltsch[1] believed that those who studied religions had to choose from the start between two options. Either religion has to be seen as an outpouring of the pure spontaneous reason, and hence true religious change was to be seen as an act of creation of the human spirit on the basis of its own internal necessity: on this view true religious innovations were independent both of the religious tradition from which they sprang and of the social, political, economic and technological circumstances of their times. Or religion was to be seen as the response by 'the formal power which orders positive facts' to changes in its general situation, adapting its traditions to fit and meet the demands and vicissitudes of its particular historical situation in order to enable the tribe, the clan, the nation to survive as best it may. On such a view religious change is largely determined by changes in its world.

Troeltsch was indeed a perceptive commentator on the state of religious studies of his day, and it is possible to see how these two options have in fact controlled subsequent study of religion. As we suggested in the previous chapter it is the theologians who have mostly followed the first, and in particular the social anthropologists the second. What I want to do now is to examine briefly the different ways in which theologians and social anthropologists have consequently dealt with questions of the nature of religious language, and in particular the question of change in religious language and also to look at what, if anything, they have to say about the inter-relation of religious beliefs and sociological factors.

For Dodd expressions such as 'the *malkuth* of God' have certain connotations, e.g. the fact that God reigns.[2] The expression, the *malkuth* of God, to follow out Dodd's discussion of this term, may be used in two main ways in contemporary Judaism: in one sense, relating to God as King over Israel, to 'submit oneself unquestioningly to the Law' is 'to take upon oneself the *malkuth* of heaven'.[3] In 'another sense "the Kingdom of God" is something yet to be re-vealed. In this sense the idea is capable of entering into association with various views of "the good time coming" '[4] either of a temporal and political or of a transcendent character. Although these ways of using the term express very different beliefs, 'in all these forms of belief the underlying idea is that of God's sovereign power becoming manifestly effective in the world of human experience. When it pleases God to "reveal" or to "set up" his kingly rule, then there will be judgement on all the wrong that is in the world, victory over all powers of evil, and for those who have accepted His sovereignty, deliverance and the blessed life in communion with Him.'[5] That is to say, what is characteristic of Jewish first-century ways of speaking of the Kingdom of God is (a) its temporal determination, (b) its association with ideas of, for example, Israel's obedience, a 'good time coming', etc. Thus in analysing Jesus' use of the 'Kingdom of God' Dodd concentrates attention on the temporal determination of Jesus' utterances, arguing that his distinctive use is (a) to affirm that it 'has come', viz. to announce that what was otherwise spoken of as a future event has already occurred; and (b) to assert this in conjunction with the reference to his own ministry in terms which clearly allude to prophecies of the 'good time coming'.[6]

Now this analysis in terms of an 'underlying idea' and its uses and associations is quite helpful. It does allow one to offer an account of the considerable diversity of first-century Jewish use and to show how Jesus' use is both coherent with it and yet distinctive

21

from it. It does moreover allow one to give an account of the richness of meaning of the expression.[7] My main criticism is twofold. Principally, that the analysis is not carried far enough, but singles out two only of the idea's main associations, viz. the *time* of God's exercise of his coming and 'the good time coming' itself. What he does not explore are the other associations of the term relating, for example, to the manner in which God rules, gains victory, executes judgement; to what is expected of his subjects when he comes; to what is the nature of God's power and justice in itself. This is neglected although he is clearly aware of the 'even more profound originality in the new content' (as opposed to that which is formally new) 'given the idea through His revelation of God Himself,'[8] and which Dodd indeed refers to—rather in passing—in his treatment of the parables of the lost sheep, the lost coin and the prodigal.[9] In this way his treatment of the idea remains fairly abstract, something it seems to me that is not notably rectified by trying to translate Jesus' sayings into language about the absolute entering history.

The second point in my criticism may help to explain why Dodd stops short of such further explanations as he does. Dodd's analysis is worked out in terms of an 'underlying idea' and its uses. Too radical or original a use—as in the case of Jesus—is said to make 'room for a new set of ideas'. 'The teaching of Jesus upon the character of God and his attitude to men—His unqualified benevolence and beneficence towards all His creatures, His unlimited forgiveness, His desire to seek and save the lost—leads necessarily to a new view of what it means for God's righteousness to be manifested and for sin to be condemned.'[10] This is right—and yet to talk about this teaching as 'a new set of ideas' *alongside* the idea of the Kingdom is to fail, crucially, to explain what the relationship betwen them is. We need instead to be able to offer some account of how Jesus has reworked the sense of the expression 'the Kingdom of God'. It would, I shall argue, be better to speak of the 'core-meaning' of a term where Dodd speaks of the 'underlying idea' and then to speak of a range of associations such a core-meaning may have at any time, which is subject to change. We can then see that the sense of the expression used in a given sentence may be substantially reworked by varying its associations and that we shall

22

discover the sense of what Jesus is saying only when we have charted these new associations. In this way the term 'core-meaning' indicates that the meaning of the term as such is not restricted to the underlying idea, but that it may receive new associations and be stripped of old ones.

In the light of this, what does Dodd say on the subject of the relation of Jesus' teaching to the political situation of his day? Jesus certainly referred to political events, not least in the form of predictions of the downfall of the Jewish nation at the hands of the Romans; in such judgements we have a dramatic expression of Jesus' perception 'that the historical Jewish community as at present constituted is not serving the advancing purposes of God.'[11] This is again less than wholly informative. And the subsequent explanations in terms of idealist philosophy 'Die Weltgeschichte ist das Weltgericht'[12] again do nothing to elaborate Jesus' meaning. We need to know more about the relation of Jesus' views about the coming judgement on the people of Israel to his views about how to deal with one's enemies, and indeed to his views about the nature of the advancing purposes of God. Instead, however, we have interpretation in the form of translation into idealist philosophy.

Bultmann's treatment of Jesus' sayings in *Jesus and the Word* starts from a very different understanding of language. He is not out to discover the ideas to which words refer but, where Jesus' preaching is concerned, to hear the call and challenge which Jesus' sayings make on those who are moved by the fundamental existential questions of life and death, of the transitoriness of existence, of man's sinfulness in the sight of the all-holy God. Jesus' sayings come out of his own struggle with such questions and offer man an answer in terms of accepting God's judgement, forgiveness and commands.[13] Thus Jesus' teaching about, for example, the near and far God can be distinguished from contemporary Jewish views which 'objectivized' such language. In Jewish apocalyptic, God was thought of as removed from this present evil age, but was shortly to come in judgement to vindicate the righteous. In Jesus' preaching, by contrast, those who accept his call to repentance and obedience are promised the intimacy of a new relationship with the Father, while those who reject it are said to set a barrier between themselves and God.[14] Hence Jesus' preaching of the coming of the Kingdom is construed in terms of the new self-understanding which is mediated to those who hear and accept his call.

The understanding of language is, one might say, instrumental.[15] Jesus' sayings are connected in so far as they are all directed towards effecting a new self-understanding. When we encounter the words of Jesus in history, we do not judge them by philosophical systems with reference to their rational validity; they meet us with a question of how we are to interpret our own existence. In Jesus' words the *viva vox evangelii* brings men to repentance and faith, just as for Luther the central meaning of scripture is to be construed in terms of the way in which it 'promotes Christ' (*Christum treibet*). But while in this sense Bultmann's interpretation of Jesus indicates powerfully and interestingly the *force* of Jesus' theological utterances, it says very little about their *sense*. His sayings about God's coming are construed in terms of the new attitudes they produce in men, not in terms of what they *say* about the course of world-history. Similarly, Jesus' command to love one's enemies is construed in terms of a command to unconditional obedience, challenging radically man's self-will, rather than in terms of an injunction—albeit a broad one—to adopt certain attitudes and modes of behaviour towards one's *enemies*. Hence it is not surprising that Bultmann's account of Jesus' preaching has little to say about its relation to the social and political circumstances of the times. It is too much concerned with the existential realm of '*Jemeinigkeit*'.

These two theological interpretations, though so different in methodology, have however this much in common. They both see Jesus as standing over against his contemporary world in the originality of his teaching, whether in terms of its theological ideas or its theological anthropology, and neither of them offers a satisfactory account either of how Jesus reworked Jewish language, such that we might see more fully what he was actually saying, or of how what he said was related to the social and political realities of his day.

By contrast, social anthropologists may indeed seem to offer more in the way of an explanation of the way religious beliefs are related to the societies in which they are held. Clearly there is here a great diversity of approach and I shall discuss only the work of Mary Douglas which seems to me particularly interesting both in respect of her interpretation of religious language and of the account she offers of the interrelation between religious beliefs and social realities. In her book *Purity and Danger*[16] she relates and analyses a myth told by the Coorgs of Southern India, a group within the Hindu caste system, living in an isolated community in the mountains. The myth is as follows:

> A Goddess in every trial of strength or cunning defeated her two brothers. Since future precedence depended on the outcome of these contests, they decided to defeat her by a ruse. She was tricked into taking out of her mouth the betel that she was chewing to see if it was redder than theirs and into popping it back in again. Once she had realized she had eaten something which had once been in her own mouth and was therefore defiled by saliva, though she wept and bewailed she accepted the full justice of her downfall. The mistake cancelled all her previous victories, and her brothers' eternal precedence over her was established as of right.[17]

Professor Douglas sees the point of this story as being a double one, relating, that is, both to the Coorgs' position within the Hindu caste system and to their geographical position as a mountain people. In the first place the Coorgs stand in a hierarchical system, where status is conceived in terms of purity and impurity, the lowest being the most impure. From the point of view of any individual within the system, the system is 'structured upwards'. Those above him are more pure. 'All the positions below him, be they ever so intricately distinguished in relation to one another, are to him polluting'. Barriers must then be erected against what lies below. 'The sad wit of pollution as it comments on bodily functions symbolizes descent in the caste system by contact with faeces, blood and corpses.'[18]

Professor Douglas argues further that the story refers symbolically to the geographical situation of the Coorgs.

Living in their mountain fastness they were also an isolated community, having only occasional and controllable contact with the world around. For them the model of exits and entrances of the human body is a doubly apt symbolic focus of fears for their minority standing in the larger society. Here I am suggesting that when rituals express anxiety about the body's orifices, the sociological counterpart of this anxiety is a care to protect the political and cultural unity of a minority group.[19]

Now whether such a claim could be made good in every case may perhaps be allowed to pass. Certainly in the present case the analysis is attractive. It seems hard to think that the purpose of the story is simply to provide information about the past history of the Coorgs' deities for its own sake. Equally, any interpretation must do justice to the significance which is given in the story to the incident in the trial which is clearly concerned with saliva re-entering the body. A social explanation does indeed here seem very plausible. The body is an obvious symbol of the community and hence when one finds a minority mountain community treating the body in the ritual life 'as if it were a beleaguered town, every ingress and exit guarded for spies and traitors'[20] it seems reasonable to suppose that this does indeed give expression to and reinforce their views about their society and its exposure to danger from without. In this context the particular significance of the incident with saliva is seen as follows: 'Anything issuing from the body is never to be re-admitted, but strictly avoided. The most dangerous pollution is for anything which has once emerged gaining re-entry.'[21]

Professor Douglas thus construes the meaning of the myth and of purity rituals in terms of (a) their literal meaning and (b) their symbolic meaning where the body stands as an analogue or model or image of the society itself. Now clearly this is attractive, partly because it offers some way of making sense of otherwise strange and apparently useless practices and myths, partly because it offers a way of connecting beliefs about goddesses—or regulations about purification—with attitudes towards the external and internal boundaries of a society. The language of the myth is symbolic in the sense that it is a code language which really refers to social structures. Moreover such myths and practices may exercise a powerful control over people's social attitudes without their being conscious of the code-character which they possess.

However a number of criticisms can be made. Most importantly, the sharp distinction which Mary Douglas makes between the literal meaning of the myth and its 'sociological counterpart' which has to be read off its symbolism breaks down when we look at the actual account of the story given by the ethnographer. The story in fact contains more or less explicit references to loss of caste, to customs which are associated with the Coorgs' patterns of social behaviour, and to purity regulations and terms. The literal theological and the symbolic sociological levels of meaning seem to be intermingled. That is to say the sharp distinction between the literal and the symbolic levels of meaning may lead one to overlook the fact that explicitly theological sentences may be conventionally linked to sentences descriptive of social relations in such a way that an understanding of the former requires a knowledge of how they are linked by convention to the latter. If this is so then the sharp distinction between literal, explicit and symbolic, implicit hidden meanings needs careful scrutiny and in any case needs to be argued against alternative accounts in terms of the sentence links within a given language. We should not assume that meanings are hidden just because they are not expressed in a given sentence, if the sentence is understood within a given community to be linked with others which do have that meaning. What Mary Douglas's analysis does is to make us consider seriously the question of the kind of link that exists between, for example, stories about gods and social attitudes and beliefs.

Two further points. Like Bultmann, Mary Douglas draws attention to and, as we have seen, offers interesting explanations of, the emotional force of such 'symbolic' utterances. Such myths, because they are linked with the group's sense of its danger, and with certain beliefs about how the group can withstand such danger (whether or not the nature of the link is such as Mary Douglas suggests) clearly arouse powerful emotive responses of allegiance, fear, aggression if challenged, etc., and this accounts in part at least for the power of religious symbols. But we need not restrict the source of the emotive force of such utterances to their links with the beliefs

27

about the well-being of society. Unless we want to say, as indeed Mary Douglas's talk of two levels strongly suggests we should, that theological utterances are really sociological utterances, then we must also allow that a substantial measure of their force, and their ability to evoke powerful emotions of loyalty and obedience, fear and hope, or joy, lies in their association with gods and goddesses who are held to be objects worthy of such responses.

This leads on to the second point which concerns the relation between religious beliefs about gods and goddesses and the social, political, geographical situation of the group. There is a clear strain of determinism in Mary Douglas's writings, to the effect that religious beliefs are formulated under pressure of certain sociological forces, for example, the isolated and threatened position of the Coorgs in South India, and therefore represent ways of enforcing certain social and political policies appropriate to the position of the group. With purity regulations this may be in terms of their function in regulating and reinforcing certain boundaries within society; or it may be in terms of a more general expressive function whereby they symbolize the dangers of alien forces outside the society in terms of dirt, spittle, excrement, anomalous beasts, etc. This is a suggestion which we shall take up later (Chapter 6). Where, however, Mary Douglas goes well beyond what she has shown is in suggesting that there is a *necessary* connection between certain types of situation and certain types of social policy and their attendant religious beliefs. Indeed it seems hard to see how one could establish such a proposition empirically. In one instance in particular, when she asserts: 'It would be impossible for the leaders of an occupied but still resisting nation to adopt an effervescent form of religion',[22] there is, as I shall hope to show, powerful evidence to the contrary. For while she is right to assert that religious beliefs do often represent responses to particular social and political situations, this is quite different from saying that they are simply determined by those situations. The misunderstanding here lies, I believe, in supposing that we must find one main cause for any significant change rather than seeing such changes as being the product of a number of contributory causes. This will be considered below, but before that let me return to the main theme of our

28

discussion so far, the analysis of religious language and of changing meanings within a given natural language.

What I have been trying to suggest is that none of the accounts of religious language we have looked at so far does justice to the way in which sentences of quite diverse kinds are *linked* together in a given language, such that the meaning of a particular sentence uttered in that language has to be spelt out in terms of the other sentences it implies. Such criticisms are suggested by views of language which see it as an articulated structure and I want now to give a brief account of how such a view can be built into a theory of interpretation which can then be set to work. In fact, because of its complexity we shall have to work with a rather simplified form of the theory, though we shall occasionally fall back on the more complex model. In what follows I am greatly indebted to Alan Millar of Stirling University[23] for notes, discussions and detailed comments on my various drafts.

Let us start by saying that what we are concerned with is the interpretation of people's *utterances*. We may know *what someone uttered*, but we may fail to grasp *what he says*. We may, that is to say, hear him utter a sentence in a natural language with which we are familiar, using vocabulary and grammatical structures with which we are familiar, and yet fail to understand. The central task of interpretation is to make the transition from knowledge of what is uttered to knowledge of what is said.

Before proceeding to describe this process further it is necessary to offer some account of terms and distinctions used in the theory. First, we may distinguish sentences and utterances. An utterance is a particular event consisting of either an act of speech or an act of writing. Not all utterances are linguistic, unless you count a yell or a scream as linguistic. We are concerned only with utterances which are obviously linguistic, that is, which involve the use of recognizable linguistic expressions in some natural language. Within that class of utterances we are interested in those which involve the use of whole sentences.

Whereas an utterance is a concrete particular event, sentences are abstract types which can be employed by different people, and by the same people at different times. My utterance now of 'My

29

goodness' is a different utterance from your utterance now of 'My goodness' though the same sentence is employed by us both.

We may then proceed to make two further distinctions which are fundamentally important for keeping separate aspects of our problem which are easily confused. Let us include in the *meaning of an utterance* both the *sense* which the speaker intends to convey and any effects which the speaker intends his utterance to have on his intended audience. (Where a speaker directs an utterance towards himself he may be identified with his intended audience.) The term 'force' may be used to cover all intended effects of an utterance upon an intended audience. Examples of such effects include the audience's coming to believe something or to feel something or to do something. The actual effects of an utterance upon an audience may not be those intended. The speaker may be mistaken about what the effects of his utterances will be, or he may have an audience which is not his intended audience and this might result in a difference between intended effects and actual effects.

The central task of interpretation as applied to texts is not normally or, at least, not primarily, to determine the force of utterances but rather to determine *what they say*. What an utterance says cannot be straightforwardly identified with what we referred to above as its sense, though very often the two coincide. Whereas the sense of an utterance is what the speaker intends to convey by its means, what the utterance says is the sense which its constituent expressions actually have in the context of their use. It is not difficult to find examples of utterances in which what is said is not the sense of the sentence used. Saying 'Pass the salt' when one means 'Pass the pepper' may be a slip of the tongue or may be due to an inadequate grasp of the language. In either case what is said is not what the speaker intends and is thus not the sense of the utterance. Another type of case is where a speaker knowingly employs a sentence having a sense quite different from that which he intends to convey. For example, by saying in an exasperated tone of voice 'That was a great help' in response to some obviously unhelpful act, the sense one conveys is that the act was no help at all. Here what one does say is what one intends to say but that is not identical with the sense which one intends to convey.

30

Unless there is evidence to the contrary it is reasonable to assume that the sense of an utterance is what it says. In interpreting texts for which there is little independent background information one often has no other option. Let us focus now on what is said by an utterance. As we noted above what an utterance says is the sense which its constituent expressions have in the context of their use. A difficulty arises here which is both theoretically and practically important. It concerns the relation between what is said and what we shall call the standard or conventional sense of a sentence. The point of this distinction is this. While in many cases what I say is no more and no less than the standard conventional sense of a sentence as uttered in a particular context, there may be important occasions on which I want to use language in a slightly or even substantially different way from that in which it is ordinarily used. The poet and the wit provide striking examples of this use: the metaphorical use of sentences, where it has not already become clichéd falls into this kind of category; the religious and political reformer may employ language which is familiar and which yet in the sentences he utters says something new which challenges the old conventional sense of such statements. An understanding of this distinction may then provide an important key to the way in which traditions can be reworked.

Let us start with the standard conventional sense of a sentence as uttered in some context. This depends on (i) conventions governing the sense of the expressions which the sentence contains and (ii) the context in which the sentence is uttered. The first point is that in any given community at any given time particular expressions have a number of agreed, conventional associations. The term 'lady' is associated variously with gentility, 'good' breeding and upbringing, membership of the aristocracy, etc. The point is that within a given community these associations are agreed and that if you wish to communicate within that community you must observe or at least relate what you say to these conventions. If an utterance is made in conformity to the relevant conventions then what is said by its means is identical with the conventional sense of the sentence in the given context of use. The second points relates to the sentences containing indexical expressions, for example, 'I', 'you', 'here', 'now', 'then'. The sense of 'I am bald' as uttered by you is not the same as the sense of the same sentence as uttered by me. In cases like this the sense of the sentence as uttered in a context is determined by the conventions governing the sense of the expressions contained in the sentence together with the values of the parameters which constitute the context.

What is said may or may not correspond with this standard conventional sense of a sentence. In most cases it will, but there are cases where other aspects of the context in which an utterance figures may show that what is said is not directly determined by the sense which standard conventions in conjunction with particular values for the parameters mentioned above assign to the sentence as uttered. That is to say, there are cases in which some of the standard conventions are broken; in which some of the conventional associations of a term are, as it were, cancelled, or other associations suggested. The aspects of the context which show that such changes have occurred and which indicate the nature of the changes may be linguistic, i.e. other sentences uttered by the speaker, or they may be provided by the events, actions and physical circumstances in which the sentence is uttered. We shall discuss this further below.

With these preliminary distinctions in mind we may now return to the question of how we move in interpretation from knowledge of what was uttered to knowledge of what was said. What we have to know is not only (1) what conventions govern the sense of expressions contained in sentences uttered in the linguistic community of which the speaker or writer is a member (together with those contextual factors—relating to indexical expressions—which we shall from now on ignore) but also (ii) how the speaker or writer stands with respect to those conventions.

Let us consider these points in turn. We have already suggested that terms in a given natural language have a number of associations. We can say indeed that the sense of a term is determined by its location within a network of conventional associations with other terms and with sensory experience. So far, so good. We shall now offer a further analysis of such conventional associations which we must note, although in practice we shall make rather limited use of it. The *conventions* which determine the conventional associations of terms used within a given language (*semantically relevant conventions*) *relate in the first place not to terms but to sentences.* Basically they tell you that if you accept such and such a sentence in this language, you must also accept sentences x, y and z (or at least some of them). If you accept 'Fred is idle', you must also accept 'Fred is lazy', 'Fred is not a good worker', etc. By 'accept' in this context is not meant that you must affirm 'Fred is idle', but that you *would* affirm it if the occasion arose. Thus conventions determine sentence-links within a given natural language. They also link sentences to certain kinds of experience. If you accept 'There is a dog in that room' or 'There is no justice in that society' you expect to have certain kinds of experience if you go into that room, visit that society. Thus what was previously discussed in terms of a network of associated terms and experiences can now be discussed as a network of linked sentences and experiences. The importance of this will become apparent if we consider the practical problem of determining what conventions are in fact being used in any given utterance. If we wish to determine what particular conventions govern the expressions used in a particular text, then we must observe, or make plausible conjectures about, the uniformities of acceptance and rejection which exist in the linguistic community of which the speaker is a member. Shorn of refinements, *conventional* uniformities are those shared uniformities which each member of the linguistic community conforms to because he believes everyone else does. The types of conventional uniformity which are centrally relevant to the conventional sense of a sentence S are those which determine what the acceptance of S commits one to and those which commit one to the rejection of S. One should not underestimate the theoretical and practical difficulties which arise here. It may not be easy to determine whether a link between two sentences used by some speaker or writer is truly conventional or whether it does not rather depend on some particular belief that he has. A truly conventional link would be one which the utterer would expect all other members of his linguistic community, though not necessarily all other speakers of his natural language, to acknowledge irrespective of differences in background beliefs. Moreover a conventional link relative to one linguistic community may be a belief-mediated link relative to an-

33

other. Suppose that among Platonist theologians there is a conventional link between '*** is perfect' and '*** is unchanging' while in the wider community of English speakers, including non-Platonist theologians, no such link is acknowledged. In the wider community accepting 'God is perfect' is not taken to commit one to accepting 'God is unchanging'; the belief that whatever is perfect is unchanging is taken to be a substantive and debatable belief. As a rough guide one should posit conventions only to account for those sentence to sentence links which cannot be explained as mediated by beliefs for which some rationale would be thought appropriate.

As we noted earlier, in order to know what is being said by an utterance we must know how the speaker stands with regard to the existing conventions governing the expressions he uses. To do this we need to say rather more about how conventions may be challenged or reworked, as well as how we may recognize that this is occurring.

Let us stick here to the more simple talk of networks of conventional associations with other terms and take a fairly topical example to illustrate the challenge to conventional uses of terms. Movements like the Black Consciousness Movement in South Africa are faced with a problem of what terms to use in order to speak about members of the 'non-European', 'non-White' South African community, whose self-consciousness, self-esteem and self-confidence they wish to raise. The difficulty arises simply from the fact that all the available terms have conventional associations which are in one way or another negative and humiliating: 'black', 'kaffir', 'negro', 'bantu'. What they have done is to choose the term 'black', which has an acceptable *core meaning* referring to skin pigmentation and then to delete certain of its conventional associations such as laziness, cheekiness, servanthood, ugliness, by affirming and acting out their contraries. Thus 'black is beautiful' as a slogan clearly challenges one of the conventional associations of 'black', replacing it by its contrary. But equally the relaxed, self-confident and humorous conduct of Steve Biko at the trial of the nine activists of the Black People's Convention and the South African Students Organization provided a living challenge to the associations with which the term is linked by the majority of the white South African population at the same time as suggesting others. Similarly modes of dress, hairstyles, etc., which emphasize blackness and other physical characteristics rework the term's associations.

Evidence that a speaker or writer is not using terms in their standard conventional sense may be of two kinds, as it were external and internal. Externally, he may signal this by his self-confident and challenging tone of voice, or he may expressly state that what he is saying is new: by announcing a movement with a new name, by laying claims to a revelation, vision or some other source of knowledge. Internal evidence may be provided by an actual breach of the conventions, either by associating a term with other terms which are not part of the accepted network or by uttering sentences containing the term in conjunction with actions or in situations which produce sensory experiences other than those which would conventionally be associated with the term. Thus in order to interpret utterances which challenge the standard conventional sense of sentences we have first to establish what the existing conventions are; we have then to look for evidence of the speaker's or writer's stance in relation to these conventions for which there may be both external and internal evidence. In practice the main emphasis of any inquiry will tend to be on the internal evidence. Even if we know that a speaker claims to be, for example, the recipient of a new revelation, it is only his actual use of terms which will enable us to determine *which* conventions he is challenging and this will also tell us in what way he is reworking them.

Finally, we return briefly to the distinction between the sense of what is said and the force of an utterance. The point is that what is said may be said for different reasons. You may say, for example, that 'Johnny is Mummy's darling' either with the intention of comforting or of teasing and humiliating. In either case you may intend to stir emotions in the hearer. What is of particular interest in our context is the emotional response which can be achieved by the modification of the conventions which govern certain key religious terms. It is evident that religious utterances, i.e. those which contain key religious terms, have a rich range of meaning in respect of their force. They are intended to comfort, to uplift, to chasten, to edify, to strike men with awe, to inspire, to give hope. In this respect they

35

may be spoken of as having a certain affective charge in the sense that they are in people's memories associated with the invocation and production of powerful emotions.

Moreover, the fact that such terms refer to God and man in relationship to God means that the conventional associations of such terms condition the central beliefs of the community. If, for example, it is a convention in a community that to accept 'x is just' means that you also accept 'x is not slow to punish the wicked', then you cannot assert God's justice without also accepting that he is not slow to punish the wicked, unless, that is, you challenge and change the conventions relating to the term 'justice'.

It follows, I think, from this that the affective force of utterances in which key religious terms are being used in a manner contrary to their standard conventional sense is likely to be considerable for two reasons. First, because in using such a term at all, the speaker is using a term which has a strong affective charge. Secondly, because the challenge to accepted notions about God and man may itself awaken feelings of fear, liberation, excitement, hope and anxiety.

We might summarize as follows. When someone utters a sentence what he says is understood when we know what other sentences he would accept or reject if occasion arose. In any community there will be conventions determining acceptance or rejection of certain sentences consequent on the acceptance of any particular sentence. In order to know what a person is saying when he utters a particular sentence we have to know not only what the conventions are, but to what extent he accepts them.

We can now say something about the way such an account of language helps us to understand, first, changes in religion and, secondly, the relation between religious beliefs and changes in the political, social, economic and technological circumstances of a particular society.

The first point should by now be fairly clear. Someone who wishes to enunciate new truths in a particular society may have to change some of the conventions which govern which further sentences you accept if you, for example, accept 'the Kingdom of God has come'. If there was, for instance, a convention such that if you accepted 'the Kingdom of God has come' you would also have to accept 'God has acted to destroy his enemies' then if you wanted to affirm a belief that God acts through loving his enemies at the same time as wanting to use kingdom-sentences, you would have to change the conventions. Put more simply, if you wanted to use the term Kingdom and to talk about God's forgiveness of his enemies, you would have to change the conventional associations of the term kingdom. You might of course choose not to use the term at all, but that presupposes that you could find more suitable ones. If he is to communicate at all, the religious innovator clearly has to take some terms from his own language and in his choice he may be guided not only by their suitability, but also by their affective value, the extent to which they are associated with the community's hopes and aspirations. The originality of the religious innovator thus lies not least in his ability to forge new terms, retaining their core-meaning, deleting some associations and creating new ones. As we have seen, this links the religious innovator with others, poets, wits, political reformers who use language creatively.

Secondly, we must say something about how such an analysis helps us to understand the relation between religious beliefs and changes in the circumstances of a particular society.

We can start by noting that it follows from this account of language that strictly theological beliefs may have social and political implications, which are perfectly well recognized within that society. Thus for example, for the Zealots to accept the sentence 'God alone is King' meant accepting others like 'God's subjects should not pay taxes to Caesar', 'should engage on a holy war to overthrow foreign rulers'. All of this may simply be part of what is said by uttering the sentence 'God is King'.

Again we must notice that accepting certain sentences means having certain expectations about the kind of experience you might have if certain conditions were fulfilled. This is obvious, for example, in the case of predictions. To accept 'There are some of you standing here who will not taste death till you see the Kingdom of God come with power', means that you expect to enjoy certain experiences within the lifetime of the group. But it also applies to descriptive statements such as 'The Kingdom of God has come', which would

37

lead people to expect some signs of the overcoming of evil, oppression, the power of Satan.

I want now to look at one or two quite well documented types of situation which lead to religious changes and to suggest the kinds of linguistic moves which can be made in response. This will help to indicate the diversity of response possible; we shall conclude with some observations on the question of how far such religious changes are simply determined by changes in the circumstances of the group.

Let us take first situations where beliefs held by a community are clearly 'disconfirmed' by events, more specifically by the non-occurrence of certain events.

If we are to understand what happens, such beliefs need to be seen first as related to other beliefs. Thus, if a first-century Jew uttered the sentence 'God is just . . .', he would also accept a range of sentences such as 'God will punish the wicked', 'God will reward the just'. If moreover he also believed that God's just rule over the world would be established by a great assize within his lifetime, he would expect within his lifetime to *see* the wicked punished, the righteous rewarded. Equally there would be other chains of sentences which would specify the nature of these rewards, etc.

Now suppose that there is a specific belief expressed in the sentence 'God will visit the earth in the days of x', and that the days of x come and go without any noticeable change in the estate of the righteous or the wicked. In these circumstances a number of moves are possible. One may in the extreme case reject the sentence 'God is righteous' along with its implications 'God will visit the earth . . .', etc. Or one may simply abandon one's belief that he will visit the earth in the *days of x* and substitute some other calculation. In these cases the conventions are upheld, but some or all beliefs rejected.

A rather different kind of strategy, however, would be to modify some of the conventions, so that, for example to accept 'God is just' will no longer mean that one also accepts 'men will see—at some time—the righteous rewarded and the wicked punished'. Such moves were made earlier, for instance, when the belief in God's present distribution of rewards and punishments was contradicted by the prospering of the wealthy Hellenists in the third century B.C., but there is no reason why they should not be reintroduced after a period of apocalyptic expectation and its disconfirmation.

Such deletion of some of the conventional implications of sentences like 'God is just' may well go hand-in-hand with the introduction of new sentences which are linked with the implications to give rather different networks of implied sentences. Thus Qoheleth introduces the notion of 'times' and links 'There is a time for . . .' with sentences about God's justice. Similarly Jesus may, in the light of John's beheading, have abandoned the belief that God's justice will be demonstrated at the imminent judgement of John's 'stronger one' when those who repent will be vindicated. He may not, however, therefore have rejected the link between 'God is just' and sentences like 'there will be some imminent resolution of the plight of the righteous', only *'repentance* will lead *directly* to vindication by the "stronger one" '. We shall suggest he may also have believed that those who accepted the Kingdom will be called to some kind of struggle against evil and that it is only on their conduct in that struggle that their ultimate vindication would depend. In expressing such beliefs Jesus used some sentences which were taken from the old system of John, but introduced new ones to produce a new network of linked sentences. The point I wish to emphasize is that it is not only the retained sentence but also the new sentences which in consequence take on a new sense. In searching for sentences in which to express his new beliefs Jesus was almost bound to take those which have conventional implications which he did not accept. Thus just as *what is said* by Jesus in sentences which are retained from John is different from what was said in them by John, so too what is said by Jesus in the Kingdom sentences is different from the standard conventional sense of such sentences in perhaps the Zealot or Scribal communities. Simplifying, we may say that some of the conventional associations of the terms which Jesus retained, as well as of those which he introduced from other quarters were deleted and others added, so that the terms now gained a new sense in the new network of association.

Other changes occur not because a particular belief itself is challenged, but because changes in the political, social, economic structures of a society mean that terms used in certain religious sentences

39

no longer have the same associations. Thus, as Monica Wilson has suggested[24], while there may be a similarity of symbol in the same language family, different economies lead to modifications in the symbolism. The symbolism of the Mpondo based on cattle varies from that of the Nyakyusa, based on bananas. This may not mean that any far-reaching changes in religious belief have occurred, rather that because of changes in the conventional association of certain terms, changes have to be made in religious practices and utterances in order to affirm the same beliefs as before. One might suggest in passing that, if a society changes from an almost exclusively male leadership to one where there is equal opportunity for women and men, then institutions which continue with an all-male leadership will most likely end up by asserting very different beliefs about authority and power from those they have traditionally entertained. Some evidence for this is to be found in the importance given to the maleness of Christ—even of God—in some of the arguments against the ordination of women.

Change of this general kind, i.e. in response to a change in the meaning of certain central terms, occurs within Christianity when Palestinian communities move out into the Greek cities where, for example, the term 'king' has very different associations from that which it had in Galilee for the Zealots. The centrality of terms like 'righteousness' and 'Lord' in Paul's theology represents, I think it can be shown, not a substantial change in belief over against Jesus, but the kind of substitution of terms which is necessary where changing circumstances lead to changes in the associations of terms.

Lastly, we should also note changes in religious beliefs which are related to the onset of circumstances which make it difficult to uphold traditional norms of behaviour. In a community where righteousness is associated with obeying the Law, paying tithes, avoiding contact with dead animals, etc., the advent of conditions of land-tenure which make it difficult to earn a living at all may impose severe strain on those who wish to uphold such traditional norms. That is to say, changes in a person's or a group's economic and social status and position, for the better or for the worse, may make for difficulties in holding to inherited norms. Where these are thus challenged, people may wish to rework the traditional associations of the term 'righteousness', thereby modifying their norms, rather than abandon the search for righteousness altogether, though that too is a quite possible response. Criminality, the attempt to reinforce traditional norms as well as the prophetic challenge and radicalization of such norms are all possible responses to such a situation. While the first two, largely at least, retain the traditional associations of 'righteousness', the prophetic strategy seeks to redefine the notion, again by deleting some associations and replacing them with others, while retaining the core-meaning of the term 'righteous'.

The discussion so far should, I think, indicate the very considerable diversity of relationship that may exist between the religious beliefs of a group and events and changes in its history. There is nothing in this which suggests that there is a necessary connection between certain changes in a group's situation and changes in its belief system. There is, of course, not an infinite range of possibilities of change; no group can simply jump out of its skin, and abandon all the religious terms that it has previously used. But within the kinds of moves we have suggested that are connected with different types of situation, there is room both for different types of response as well as for very considerable diversity of instantiation within a given type. Thus there seems little ground for believing that changes in the situation of a religious group are the sole cause for changes in its religious beliefs. Such changes are undoubtedly often important contributory causes of changes in belief or in the mode of expression of religious belief, but the strength of beliefs of a particular community and the originality and inspiration of particular religious leaders and figures also stand in a causal relationship to the outcome of any such conjunction and must be given their place in any account which is offered of such changes.

I have given a fairly full account of this theory of interpretation in order to indicate its strength. In what follows, however, in view of the range of material to be covered I shall follow the rather more simplified account of the theory which I have indicated in the course of this exposition. That is to say, I shall principally be concerned to discover the conventional associations of given terms, and to determine what is said in any given utterance in the light of how

41

the speaker or writer stands in relation to these conventional associations. In particular, where Jesus is concerned, we shall look at how he may take over a term like 'kingdom', retaining its core-meaning, deleting some of its conventional associations, and substituting others. As well as considering what is said by any utterance of Jesus, we shall also consider the meaning of such an utterance in terms of its emotional and affective force, and in terms of the kind of response it represents to the political, economic and social situation of Palestine in which it is uttered. We shall be interested too to see to what extent changes in the Jewish tradition can be analysed in terms of changes in convention or changes in belief. Obviously this will not preclude us from discussing the relation between different sentences which Jesus uttered and in which he expressed his beliefs about God, man and the world. But we shall make only occasional use of the notion of the conventional implication of sentences, which, though it is central to the general thesis, would require a far more detailed analysis than space or the present state of the inquiry would allow. What is offered then is a preliminary survey which, it is hoped, may lead to more detailed studies of the networks of sentences in which terms like 'purity', 'kingdom', etc., occur in the various communities of first-century Judaism.

In conclusion to this chapter let me try and suggest how such an analysis of religious utterances and their relation to the changing circumstances of a particular community may help to resolve the dilemma to which Troeltsch pointed in his disjunction. According to that account one could either see religions as free spontaneous products of the human spirit or as forced, determined reactions to changes in the situation of the group. The danger of pursuing the first account of religions is that one arrives at an account of religious development which is quite unrelated to changes in the situation of the group; the danger of the second is that it may lead to too simple a correlation between certain types of social, political and economic situation and certain types of religious response. 'Millenarian' movements may be defined, that is to say, in terms of the social conditions of the group, viz. as religions of the oppressed, in such a way that due account is not taken of the different nature of the responses to such general situations. What, it is to be hoped, the proposed analysis offers is a way of analysing the religious responses to different types of situation which does justice both to the inter-action between the religious group and its particular circumstances and also to the particular content and nature of that response. This, first, because the proposed theory of interpretation recognizes that *what is said* depends in part on the context in which a saying is uttered; secondly, because it distinguishes between *what is said* and the *meaning* of an utterance, in such a way that one is free to consider both the cognitive content and the social and political intention and force of a particular utterance.

3

The Study of the Synoptic Tradition: Sources, Methods and Criteria

Theoretical questions about the interpretation of religious utterances may have their particular fascination and difficulty, but we encounter an apparently quite different set of problems when we attempt to answer historical questions about who said what, and when and where. For many, any attempt to understand Jesus' teaching simply founders on the impossibility of knowing what material in the synoptic tradition should be attributed to him, what to his Jewish and Greek contemporaries, what to the early Christian communities. Confidence in such matters is as much a function of one's assessment of the past performance and results of scholars working in this field as of any confidence one may have in the possibility of resolving outstanding difficulties. In sifting and ordering the synoptic tradition in the light of what is known of other contemporary religious movements, no one starts *de novo* but builds where he feels there is already a firm foundation. Nevertheless, precisely because what we are sifting and ordering is the deposit of an intricate historical religious development, theoretical questions of how religious language works and changes are clearly relevant and at certain points may enable us to see farther.

Let us look first at the period of inquiry from Reimarus[1] to the end of the nineteenth century.[2] The first attempts to take up the search for the authentic teaching of Jesus were concerned with an examination of the sources, in particular with the Gospels. Lessing in his 'New Hypotheses Concerning the Gospels'[3] posited a Gospel of the Nazarenes behind the synoptic Gospels; Griesbach, Wilke and Weisse proposed further answers to the problem of the similarities between the first three Gospels, not so much in terms of their independent relations to another common source, but in terms of the literary interdependence of the three. While the debate is still pursued in some quarters, it seems to me unlikely that any significantly different view will gain wide acceptance from that set out clearly at the end of the nineteenth century by Paul Wernle,[4] namely that Matthew and Luke both used Mark and a collection of sayings, Q, as well as material of their own. Thus it came to be widely held that Mark and Q were the earliest records of Jesus' life and teaching and that they therefore (!) could be used with confidence as a basis for the life of Jesus. Mark provided the basic outline of Jesus' life, while Matthew and Luke had preserved the teaching of Q as well as a number of extra sayings. Critical scholars held that the Fourth Gospel by contrast was much later, and dependent on the synoptic Gospels for most of its historical material. The Johannine discourses with their high christological language were held to be creations of the later Church. However, while the so-called 'two document theory' has continued to command support[5], the conclusions which scholars drew from it about the reliability of Mark and Q came to be questioned, partly because of the difficulties scholars encountered in trying to give a picture of Jesus' life and teaching on that basis; partly because of the development of new literary critical methods.

The difficulties scholars encountered sprang, one may say with a certain amount of hindsight, from the diversity of the material which was contained in Mark and Q. Not only do they contain legal and ethical sayings, but also wisdom sayings and sayings in the prophetic-apocalyptic mould. The narrative material contains miracle stories about Jesus' teaching and stories about his encounters with opponents, as well as the baptism, passion and resurrection narratives. It was as scholars began to discover the closeness of some of this material to other first-century material that the problems emerged.

Two works may serve to illustrate the problems encountered. J. Weiss's *Jesus' Proclamation of the Kingdom of God* brought the results of research into Jewish apocalyptic literature to bear on the synoptic sayings. What he showed was how far this removed the language of the Kingdom sayings from the largely Kantian interpretation which they had been given by Ritschl and others. The Kingdom of God was not a task given to men by Jesus in his teaching, to be realized through man's 'self-activity' in historical communities or churches.[6] It was the catastrophic act of God's breaking in on this world to establish his rule by putting an end to the old order and establishing by his activity a new world.[7]

This in itself was not sufficient reason for questioning the value of Mark and Q as *sources* for a life of Jesus, only for abandoning Ritschl's account of the Kingdom sayings. But the fact was that Ritschl's account of other aspects of Jesus' teaching, the legal and wisdom sayings, still appeared to many to be satisfactory. Hence Weiss's work appeared to point to discrepancies between various aspects of Jesus' teaching as recorded in the synoptic Gospels. How could Jesus both proclaim the end of all men's works and efforts in 'this evil generation' *and* exhort men to works of justice and charity? A gulf appeared between the teaching of the Q material in the Sermon on the Mount and the Markan summary of Jesus' preaching: 'Repent and believe the Gospel' (Mark 1:15) coupled with the eschatological emphasis of Mark 13.

At the same time, as we have just seen, different problems were being raised by scholars working in the field of Hellenism. To what extent were the Gospels, and within them especially the passion narratives, the product of a Christianity which had assumed the form of a Hellenistic mystery religion on its emergence into the Hellenistic world?[8] Were the Passion narratives cult-dramas? Were the Gospels dominated by a belief in Jesus as Lord analogous to some of the Hellenistic cult figures—and therefore to be treated as anything but straightforward historical narratives? These questions were suggested notably by Bousset's *Kyrios Christos*. The picture he drew was of a Palestinian Christianity centred on a belief in a Son of Man who would shortly return and a Hellenistic Christianity which worshipped the Lord *present* in the cult. This suggested strongly that there was a far-reaching diversity of dogma within the Christian community *before* the composition of the Gospels. This as Bultmann, taking his lead from Bousset, saw clearly[9] meant that one had to distinguish between various strands of tradition within the Gospels. Indeed his picture, with a certain inevitable circularity, depended on making such a distinction, though it could also find support in the Pauline Epistles and the Johannine literature. Similarly Wrede pointed to dogmatic motifs in Mark[10] which would have to be stripped away before one could find bedrock on which to build a life of Jesus. He did not simply suggest, as is often said, that therefore we could know nothing about Jesus.

In sum, the work of the first period of inquiry produced a fairly solid view of the literary relationships of the synoptic Gospels but raised deeply disquieting questions about the diversity of the traditions and communities which lay behind those documents. Thus the task of discovering what Jesus actually taught and did became more complex. Because of the new view of the nature of the documents it became part of a wider enterprise, namely that of discovering how Jesus contributed to the developments in first-century Judaism which led to the emergence of both Palestinian Christian communities with strong eschatological expectations and of a Hellenistic Christianity with perhaps quite different christological beliefs. Clearly the first task was to look for methods which could assist one in the task of discerning and ordering different layers of the tradition.

Form criticism[11] is based on a simple insight that all acts of verbal communication, stories, sayings, hymns, confessions etc., have their *form* and that these forms are both culturally and sociologically determined. Hence an analysis of the form of a unit of a particular tradition is helpful in establishing both its cultural and its sociological setting. Some forms may be written forms, e.g. gospels and epistles; others originally oral forms, e.g. prophetic and legal sayings, controversy stories, paradigms. Some forms may be found in a relatively wide range of cultures and settings, e.g. wisdom sayings; others may be fairly strictly limited to a particular culture,[12] e.g. Jewish legal controversy stories. Analysis of the form will not tell one where and on what specific occasion[13] a saying was uttered; it may tell one in what *kind* of situation and in which cultural milieu it was shaped and handed on.

What this means in practice where one is dealing with literary documents which draw on oral tradition such as the Gospels is this.

First, before one can analyse the form of the units of tradition one must of course work back to the form in which they existed before they were written down. We can see clearly how Matthew and Luke edited Mark and we can judge with some confidence that they have proceeded similarly with Q. On this basis we can hypothesize that Mark has handled his material similarly, creating simple links or seams between units, treating his material with fundamental respect, but making small changes which may give it a characteristically Markan note. It was principally the work of K. L. Schmidt which cut away the Markan framework from the tradition. In so doing he showed that a great deal of the detail relevant to the course of Jesus' life was redactional and thus of very little historical worth.

Once one has got back to the units of tradition one can then proceed to classify them according to their form, for example, whether it is in the form of narrative or of sayings or collections of sayings, or of some combination of the two. Further classification will be according to the general nature of a saying's subject matter,[14] its logical form, e.g. principles, questions, definitions, etc., its rhetorical character, parables, metaphors, discourses. Narratives may be subdivided according to their complexity, consideration being given to the number of characters, the sequence of the action, the subdivision into scenes; and again according to the general character of the subject matter, miracles, call stories, controversies, etc.[15]

Such work is a necessary preliminary to any attempt at assessing the authenticity of sayings in the synoptic tradition, i.e. whether they were originally uttered by Jesus. It may help in various ways. If when the forms are analysed we find material whose form clearly belongs to a Palestinian cultural milieu, then there is a presumption that they are early and may be close to the sources of the tradition; if we can find material which belongs to the cultural milieu outside Palestine,[16] then we shall have to regard it with very considerable caution. In fact the classification of the synoptic tradition showed that there was a substantial body of sayings attributed to Jesus which were cast in forms taken from the Jewish apocalyptic-prophetic, wisdom and legal traditions. Such sayings will probably have been preserved in the Palestinian Church and the presumption was then that Jesus had used all these forms.

Secondly, Bultmann[17] believed that it was possible to discern certain regularities in the way in which units of a given *form* were developed and modified in the course of tradition. Wisdom sayings may be elaborated, details may be added to stories, scenes may be created out of introductory statements, indirect speech turned to direct speech, etc. If these modifications do follow certain observable regularities, then it is possible to make reasonable conjectures about the earliest form of a particular saying or story, and also to discern some of the theological tendencies which formed the tradition and which may therefore also have been responsible for the creation and addition of material to it. This in turn may enable one to get nearer to the source of the tradition, 'to the centre, which holds the secret of its historical power'.[18]

Such was the general strategy which Bultmann brought to the task of analysing the synoptic tradition and attempting to discover which were the genuine sayings of Jesus.[19]

It is, I think, important to bear this general strategy in mind when considering the judgements which Bultmann actually makes about the authenticity of sayings within the synoptic tradition. Sometimes he is presented as simply having set up a number of fairly rigid *criteria*[20] by which to judge the authenticity (i.e. the originality to Jesus) of a particular saying. This is misleading in so far as it abstracts the judgements about the authenticity of a saying from the general process of constructing the history of the synoptic tradition; moreover Bultmann himself disclaims having any such hard and fast criteria. What he does say is this: 'Though one may admit the fact that for no single word of Jesus is it possible to produce positive evidence of its authenticity, still one may point to a whole series of words found in the oldest stratum of tradition which do give us a consistent representation of the historical message of Jesus'.[21] It is true that he operates with certain fairly rigid tests for rejecting sayings as inauthentic, for example because their christological content indicates them to be creations of the early Church; and that he regards the fact that the saying is Jewish in form but distinct in content from known contemporary Jewish utterances as a strong indication of its authenticity. Nevertheless, the process whereby he arrives at his list of sayings which give a consistent representation is more detailed and differentiated than the simple talk of 'criteria' would suggest. Thus one needs to look at the detail of his argument if one is to judge the success or otherwise of his general strategy. Because it is the keystone of his argument, we shall look at his treatment of the prophetic-apocalyptic sayings.

The form of the sayings places them, so Bultmann argues,[22] fairly clearly within the Palestinian Church, which with its high eschatological expectation will have attached particular importance to such sayings, and whose prophets equally may themselves have uttered sayings of this kind. Thus the problem here is twofold: to discern both what in the tradition is distinctive from contemporary Judaism and also what is unlikely to have been formed in the eschatologically orientated Palestinian Church. To some commentators[23] this has seemed an impossible task. Assuming that the Church's eschatology was distinctive from that of contemporary Judaism, will not such an inquiry automatically rule out all Jesus' sayings, or all but a few which the early Church regarded as unimportant? By accentuating that which is different in Jesus' teaching from other contemporary Jewish teaching and from the teaching of his followers, we clearly run the risk of emphasizing elements which were peripheral to both and hence making the task of explaining the continuities between the two well-nigh impossible. Let us see how Bultmann proceeds.[24]

He starts with an analysis of the individual sayings in the tradition which attempts not only to establish the earliest forms of particular sayings, but also to discern the theological tendencies which come to expression in the modifications which were made. Such work is, of course, open to criticism at every point, but it must be questioned *in detail*. Bultmann's subsequent judgements about the history of the tradition and the originality of certain sayings to Jesus are based on it and not on some general preconceived notion of what the Church's eschatology was like.

Bultmann believed that a number of observations could be made about the tradition of the prophetic-apocalyptic sayings. First, the Church took over and modified certain Jewish apocalyptic prophecies (*Weissagungen*), notably the text underlying Mark 13:5–27. By contrast, sayings like Luke 17:21, 23f., with their rejection of apocalyptic calculations, are sufficiently different from the typical warnings and prophecies of the end that it is unlikely that they stem from Jesus' Jewish contemporaries. Similarly, but less confidently, Bultmann believed that there were sayings more prophetic than apocalyptic in character which may nevertheless be of Jewish origin, e.g. Matthew 24:37–41. Sayings, however, like Luke 6:20f parallels, while as general prophecies they are close to the last chapters of Ethiopic Enoch, have, at least in the tradition, a reference to the present which suggests that they are not taken over from Jewish tradition.

Even so the authenticity (as sayings of Jesus) of those sayings which Bultmann retains is not yet established. Bultmann believed that an examination of Mark 13 showed how the Christian community had incorporated into a Jewish text references to the person of Christ and to the present situation of the Church, viz. to persecutions, etc. The same tendencies can be seen at work elsewhere. A reference to Jesus' person is, for example, incorporated into the picture of the final judgement (Matt. 25:31–46), and into the interpretation of the sign of Jonah (Matt. 12:40). Similarly, Luke has corrected and altered Mark's Christian apocalypse in the light of contemporary events and concerns. Further, it is likely that the beatitudes (Luke 6:22f parallel), in which persecuted disciples are praised, are a creation of the community itself. Prophetic sayings uttered by members of the Christian community were not so sharply distinguished from those of Jesus. Bultmann concludes:

> Thus it is essential in the light of this discussion to ask whether even those units which there is no *prima facie* reason to question, are not in fact of Christian origin. The less there is any reference to Jesus' person and to the history and interests of the Christian community, the more a saying manifests a characteristically individual spirit, the more negative our answer will be. This is true of the units already mentioned which give expression to a heightened eschatological consciousness with a feeling both of joy and of the seriousness of the decision with which men are confronted.[25]

In sum, Bultmann does not believe that he has hard and fast

criteria for distinguishing authentic sayings of Jesus. Rather, he has certain aids to help him establish the course and development of the tradition which runs from Jesus to the Christian communities who produced the synoptic tradition. Bultmann's assumption is that these communities were both Palestinian and Hellenistic and that, in creating the synoptic tradition, they not only drew on early traditions about Jesus and genuine sayings of his, but that they also drew on contemporary Jewish and Hellenistic material as well as creating sayings and stories of their own. Form-criticism is of assistance in mapping this complex history, first, in that a classification by forms enables one to distinguish, so Bultmann argues, those units which are Palestinian and those which are Hellenistic, thus enabling one to determine which kind of Christian community may first have brought them into the tradition. Secondly, analysis of the history of units of a particular form may provide one with guidelines for distinguishing the original form of a unit from its subsequent modifications. Thirdly, examination of modifications made to units of tradition during their history may give one a key to the theological tendencies operating within the Christian communities and so give one indications as to what material may be the product of the Christian communities themselves. Fourthly, given this picture of the development of the tradition which has to be carefully built up it may then be possible to discern within the earlier strata of the tradition a group of sayings which show a consistently distinctive character, i.e. which are sufficiently different from what we know of contemporary Judaism, to explain the subsequent divergence of Christianity from other forms of Judaism as well as being of such a character as to render intelligible the subsequent developments and reactions of the Christian community itself. It is as if one were to attempt to pick out the works of a particular painter from a collection of broadly contemporary pictures, knowing something generally about the different developments in the art of that time, and something about the interrelations of schools of artists. What one would look for would be shared characteristics among a group of pictures which were sufficiently distinct from the characteristics of other paintings to suggest that they came from one man, but not so distinct that one could not trace influences from this

52

group of paintings to others of the same time. Clearly the more original a painter, the easier it will be to pick out his work in this way.

Thus, with Jesus' sayings one is looking for a group of sayings sufficiently distinct either in form or content from other contemporary religious thought to account for the importance attributed to him in the religious developments of the time, but not so distinctive as to separate him entirely from such developments. To talk thus of looking for a group of sayings is, I think, a useful corrective to speaking of two separate 'criteria', viz. of dissimilarity and coherence, for judging the authenticity of any given saying. It is not simply a matter of finding individual sayings which are beyond doubt authentic and moving out from these to those which are closest to them. What one is looking for is a *group* of sayings sufficiently distinctive that, although one cannot be sure of the authenticity of any one of them, one can say with some confidence that, taken as a group they present characteristic features of Jesus' teaching. One can then use this group as a basis for assessing sayings about whose authenticity one is less confident.

We can now return to the criticism we noticed earlier, viz. that this method of proceeding distinguishes so sharply between Jesus' teaching and the views of contemporary Judaism on the one hand and of the early Christian communities on the other that it makes it impossible to give any account of the continuity between them. Clearly this is not Bultmann's intention. His general strategy, we have argued, is to distinguish a group of sayings within the synoptic tradition which is sufficiently remarkable both over against contemporary Judaism and over against what one can perceive of the theological tendencies of the Church as to explain the substantial changes which occurred in first-century Judaism and which led to the growth of the Church. It is in these terms that one should understand the distinctiveness which is being looked for.

Nevertheless there are difficulties. In practice Bultmann distinguishes Jesus' eschatological sayings from those of contemporary Judaism in terms of their content: Jewish apocalyptic speculated about the end, while Jesus proclaimed the imminence of the Kingdom as a joyous event which confronted men with a momentous decision. It may well appear that thus set out the ideas expressed are so different as to have little if anything in common, an impression strengthened by Bultmann's own book, *Jesus and the Word*.[26] The problem with Bultmann's position is not, I think, that he wants to look for what is distinctive in Jesus' teaching but that he does not give an adequate account of the way in which language changes in a religious tradition such that new beliefs can be expressed in a way which is still intelligible to members of that tradition. In default of such an account it may well appear that what is distinctive or dissimilar must by definition have nothing in common with that from which it is distinct. Such objections can however be met if it is possible to give an adequate account of how sayings which are, in respect of their vocabulary, very similar to other sayings found in contemporary Judaism may nevertheless be given a quite distinctive sense by being linked to other sentences very different from those with which they were conventionally linked; if, simplifying, we can show how the conventional associations of certain terms have been reworked by their use in certain contexts and in conjunction with other terms with which they were not conventionally associated.

Two points are noteworthy. First this provides, I think, not a wholly new set of data for assessing the distinctiveness of certain sayings in the synoptic tradition over against sayings in contemporary Judaism; rather it enables one to develop and see more clearly the nature of the distinctive content of, for example, those apocalyptic sayings which Bultmann had already fairly correctly distinguished as distinctive on grounds of their heightened sense of eschatology. Secondly, it confirms Bultmann's instinct that what we are looking for is a *group* of sayings. It is, that is to say, only when we have seen how the various sayings of Jesus are linked together that we can be confident in the authenticity of any of them.

The form-critics' work led them to a number of conclusions relating to the historical-critical study of the life and teaching of Jesus. While one can hardly say that they have been as widely received as were the earlier results of source-criticism, some of them have been increasingly accepted even in relatively conservative circles; in any case they represent a major stage in the development of the discipline, so that any subsequent work must take account of them. First, form-criticism showed the basic untrustworthiness of the Markan framework as evidence for the course of Jesus' life.[27] This view has been if anything strengthened by the subsequent work of redaction critics. Secondly, they concluded that the references to Jesus' person in the synoptic sayings were in a very large measure the creation of the Church and that therefore we had no evidence on which to construct theories of Jesus' messianic self-consciousness. They did, however, believe that Jesus' movement was generally messianic in character and that it was because of the Romans' recognition of this fact that Jesus was crucified, i.e. was executed as a political offender. This has undoubtedly, as regards the statement about knowledge of Jesus' self-consciousness, been the most controversial of the form-critics' claims and we shall discuss it further in Chapter 8. Thirdly, they classified most of the narratives in the Gospels as Hellenistic in form and consequently late. Hence they believed that it was difficult to draw much historically valid info᾽ mation from them. Only in the case of the paradigms or apophthegms were we dealing with Jewish forms. Here opinion about their historical reliability was divided. Dibelius believed that the narrative element was early; Bultmann saw it as having been created to provide a suitable setting for the concluding saying. Even so he was prepared to allow that the situation so constructed might reflect accurately typical situations in Jesus' ministry. This we shall consider in Chapters 5 and 8. Lastly, and most importantly, they believed that one could identify a significant body of sayings, prophetic-apocalyptic, legal-ethical and wisdom sayings which had their origins in or reflected accurately Jesus' teaching. What this meant in the context of the debate which had been initiated by Weiss's work on the Kingdom sayings was that any account which was offered of the meaning of Jesus' teaching would have to do justice to all three aspects;[28] and that therefore it was not permissible, as in their different ways Weiss, Schweitzer, Wrede and Harnack had done, to subordinate one to the other.

Such was the contribution of this generation of scholars to the study of the synoptic tradition. It was almost exclusively concerned with the literary critical study of the Gospels. To the questions which had been raised by the History of Religions school about the relation of Palestinian Christianity to the churches outside Palestine, about Jesus' and early Christianity's debt to Judaism and Hellenism, Bultmann provided answers which were little more than faithful elaborations of Bousset's original thesis, buttressed by Lidzbarski's edition of the Mandaean writings.[29] Influenced by Barth's attack on the History of Religions school's method of exegesis,[30] scholars in this period turned to other forms of explanation and tended in consequence to neglect these issues.

It remains to say something briefly about developments in the generation of scholarship after Bultmann's major work.[31] The major contribution to the study of the synoptic tradition has been not so much in the development of completely new methods of study, but in the refinement and development of the form-critics' methods and inquiries. Thus redaction criticism[32] has developed the work of scholars like Wrede, Wellhausen and K. L. Schmidt on the theological motifs and editorial contributions of the evangelists and by giving greater attention to the evangelists' own voices has shown more clearly their contribution to the development of the tradition. Some practitioners of the art have suggested that it is the kind of work which *can* be done on the Gospels, as opposed to the attempts of the form-critics to get back behind them and to reconstruct the teaching of Jesus.[33] This seems to me unduly optimistic about the results of redaction criticism because of the closeness of the evangelists to their tradition, just as it is unnecessarily sceptical about the work of the form-critics. Above all, such a view fails to realize that, particularly—but not only—where Mark is concerned, form-criticism and redaction criticism are complementary disciplines. Our understanding of how the evangelist has combined and modified the units of tradition which came to him in oral form marches together with our understanding of the way in which such units were modified and developed in the tradition. Redaction critic and form-critic are both contributing to an understanding of the history of the synoptic tradition and are as such dependent on each other's labours.

What the development of redaction criticism means for our purposes is that we may approach the synoptic tradition with a more

56

informed eye, more able, that is, to spot the work of the evangelists in modifying or adding to the tradition. It means almost certainly a loss, as we see, for example, how some sayings fit so well into the situation and message of Matthew, that we must question their originality to Jesus. But equally it is gain in that it enables us to chart more clearly the development of the tradition and to place certain theological tendencies in the history of early Christianity.

Similarly Dibelius's and more espcially Bultmann's work in plotting the history of the synoptic tradition has been developed by 'traditio-historical' criticism. Here one may think of the work of S. Schulz.[34] This work proceeds on the basis of form-critical analyses of the development of individual units of tradition. Dibelius and Bultmann believed that such analyses enabled them to point to later theological tendencies which moulded the tradition.[35] Bultmann in particular emphasized that this led one to make substantive judgements[36] about the authenticity of a saying, for example. Schulz attempts to extend this kind of judgement by attributing sayings and their developments to different communities within the primitive Church. To this end he applies a number of tests to the material: linguistic (e.g. semitisms, use of the LXX); formal (use of apophthegms); those based on the occurrence of certain motifs (e.g. preexistent wisdom) or on content (the delay of the parousia, the nonapocalyptic use of the Son of Man). By this means he believes he can distinguish two groups of congregations which formed and preserved the Q tradition, a Palestinian Jewish Christian group located on the Syrian border and a later group which is Hellenistic Jewish Christian and located in Syria itself.[37] As against Dibelius's caution in disclaiming knowledge of the date of Q and the chronology of its development[38] Schulz's precision in locating the communities in time and space is surprising, but without firm foundation. As we shall see below, quite different constructions of the development and spread of different kinds of Jewish Christian groups are possible and indeed plausible. When one takes into account that the Q sayings, also according to Schulz, had an editor[39] one can see how difficult the task is of plotting accurately the different theological positions represented by the communities who formed and preserved the Q tradition. Nevertheless, if one is thus forced to be rather cautious about Schulz's detailed reconstruction, his work does at least show up some of the theological diversity of the Q sayings and alerts us to two rather different kinds of theological systems which are embraced by the material found in the Q tradition. What in particular the work not only of Schulz, but also of Lührmann and Hoffmann, has suggested strongly is that at the heart of the Q tradition there is a group of sayings of an enthusiastic prophetic kind, proclaiming the radical ethic of non-violence and the inbreaking of God's Kingdom. Whether this group of sayings was, as Schulz believes, then subsequently developed by a later community which added further material of a more 'Hellenistic' kind, or whether this material was from the start preserved by Hellenistic Jewish Christians is a question which it is difficult to decide simply on internal evidence alone. Any decision on this question will obviously reflect closely a scholar's views on the general question of the development of Hellenistic Christianity, i.e. of the way developing Christianity was related to the various religious movements of the time.

If questions of this latter kind had tended to be rather neglected in the period of the thirties and forties, subsequent developments have done much to revive interest. For Bultmann, the synoptic tradition took its rise in Jesus, whose teaching was Jewish. The earliest Christian communities were characterized by him as Palestinian: they were distinctively Christian in so far as they proclaimed the risen Jesus and expected the coming of the Son of Man; but they were Jewish in the sense that their language and mythology were still derived from first-century Judaism, in particular from apocalyptic. From here Christianity moved out beyond Palestine into the Hellenistic world and became Hellenistic Christianity with a different missionary propaganda, a different cult and a quite different attitude to the Law. Bultmann clearly related the various forms which were represented in the synoptic tradition to this picture of the development of Christianity and on this basis charted the development of the synoptic tradition.

A number of important developments have occurred both to sharpen and to question this picture of the growth of Christianity from Palestinian to Hellenistic Christianity. In the first place study of contemporary Judaism has made great advances, partly as a result of the finds at Qumran, partly because of the recent growth of Jewish studies, not least since the creation of the state of Israel. The discoveries at Qumran have substantially enlarged our knowledge of Jewish renewal movements in the second Temple period and offer far more extensive and more manageable evidence for other Jewish beliefs contemporary to Jesus than is available for, say, the Zealots, Pharisees and Sadducees. At the same time this evidence for the beliefs of one Jewish group in the first century A.D. has given at least certain markers for the study of other contemporary groups. Equally Jewish historical studies in general have been much more firmly grounded on historical-critical principles than was formerly the case, perhaps not least because they now have a much more independent base from which to operate. A number of important contributions have been made to the study of contemporary Jewish society and politics as well as religion by Israeli scholars.[40] The effect of these developments is to give the historian a much greater possibility of discerning the distinctive contribution of Jesus to Jewish renewal movements of the first century A.D.

At the same time there has also been a reappraisal, notably by Bickermann[41] and Hengel[42] of the interrelation between Judaism and Hellenism. They have argued that the sharp geographical distinction between Palestinian and Hellenistic Judaism was fundamentally misleading. Palestine had on the contrary been under Hellenistic rule and influence since the time of Alexander. In consequence the Judaism of first-century Palestine can be understood only in terms of a long history of interaction between Hellenism and Judaism, such that even in the Jewish renewal movements there was a good deal of assmilation of Hellenistic forms of organization, modes of argument and theological ideas. Equally there was more contact and traffic between Diaspora Jews and Jerusalem,[43] and more Greek spoken in Palestine than had previously been recognized.

This view, which has been widely received,[44] has a number of consequences. It first leads us to see the extent to which Judaism of the first century represents a response, or a series of responses, to an economically, technologically and politically more powerful culture. Jesus and Christianity, Pharisaism and Rabbinic Judaism, the Zealots, Qumran and the Sadducees all represent different responses to this situation with very different degrees of success and permanence. Secondly, it means that one has to revise one's overall picture of the development of Christianity. Hengel has recently suggested[45] that Christianity had very early on, perhaps almost from the very start, consisted of two different groups: an Aramaic-speaking Jewish Christian congregation and a Greek-speaking Hellenistic Jewish Christian congregation (Acts 6).[46] The Aramaic-speaking congregation centred on the Twelve remained in Jerusalem after the Greek-speaking congregation with its leadership of seven had been dispersed northwards towards Syria. The latter was an enthusiastic church, critical of certain points of the Law, ready to embark on Gentile mission, whereas the Aramaic-speaking Jerusalem congregation was more conservative in its attitude to Law and saw its mission as (primarily?) to Israel. This suggests that Hellenistic Christianity was not, as Bousset had argued, the form which Christianity had to assume when it went out into the Hellenistic world, but rather one of the earliest forms of Christianity stemming from Jerusalem, preserving the more radical teaching of Jesus and arguably more receptive to it than the Jerusalem community itself. If this view holds good then it would also suggest that Schulz's view of the two different Q communities would have to be abandoned in favour of a view which identifies the Q community as Hellenistic Jewish Christian from the outset, preserving and modifying the enthusiastic-prophetic Q material in a Hellenistic mould. This would of course then strengthen the probability that in the core sayings of Q we do indeed have authentic sayings of Jesus[47] which come close to the heart of his message.

In conclusion, what such a survey shows is first that we may be reasonably confident that we do have a group of apocalyptic-prophetic, legal and wisdom sayings which can be attributed to Jesus but that we need to look at the reliability of the narrative material in more detail if we want to place any great reliance on it. Secondly, we see that, when it comes to understanding the course of the development of Christianity out of first-century Jewish sectarianism into the various Christian communities in Jerusalem, Galilee, Syria and out into Asia Minor, there is a great deal of work that needs redoing, principally because of the new accounts of the nature of the relation of first-century Jewish sectarianism to Hellenism which have been offered by scholars like Martin Hengel. Here the theoretical proposals which we made in the previous chapter may be of use both in offering accounts of developments and modifications within a tradition and in understanding the interrelationship between Judaism and the political, social, economic, technological and cultural forces which are referred to as Hellenism. Clearly the task of describing this whole development is a massive one. We shall be concerned only with Jesus' transformation of first-century Judaism in response to the particular conditions of his time. We shall want to see both how Jesus modifies the conventional associations of certain key terms in first-century Judaism, while rejecting others altogether, and how his teaching constituted the basis for a very different response to Hellenism from those of other contemporary Jewish groups.

4

Developments in Judaism to the
Time of Jesus

In this chapter I want to do three things. First, to give a sketch of the political, economic and cultural factors bearing on Judaism in the period of the second Temple. Then, to show what kinds of changes occurred in the Jewish tradition during this period, i.e. which conventions were modified and were the subject of controversy, which were accepted apparently without question. Finally, I shall give a somewhat more detailed account of the political, economic and cultural factors which obtained in Palestine, and in particular in Galilee, at the time of Jesus. Thus what is offered is very much a selective survey of aspects of Judaism in the second Temple period, not a systematic account of its development. What we have selected are those aspects which will provide the nearer context for our further discussion of how Jesus modified and developed the tradition he received. In what follows we shall be drawing heavily on the recent work on the interrelation between Judaism and Hellenism and on the social and political history of first-century Palestine which we referred to at the end of the last chapter.

I

For more than three hundred years before the birth of Jesus Judaism had been influenced by Hellenism. With Alexander's victory over Darius III in 333 Palestine came under Hellenistic rule, first, after Alexander's death in 323 under the Ptolemies in Egypt, later from the end of the third century under the Seleucids in Syria. Even though after the Maccabean revolt the Jews established their own monarchy, the Hasmoneans, they still paid homage to Hellenism, while the Hasmoneans' successors, the Herods, owed their throne to the Romans and gradually lost their independence to their temporal overlords, who in their turn had enthusiastically and powerfully embraced Hellenism.

What then was Hellenism?[1] Clearly it was sufficiently long-lived to manifest considerable diversity, but certain general characteristics may be discerned which gave it its extraordinary resilience in the Mediterranean world. The Hellenism first brought by Alexander's armies and officials was a system which embraced many aspects of life: military, technological, political, economic, social and cultural. Its military[2] and technological aspects would be those which would first have impinged on Jews living in Palestine. Trade,[3] carried largely by Phoenicians, would have introduced manufactured goods such as pottery, papyrus, glass and linen. In due course, under Ptolemaic management, Palestine would come to play an important part in the economy of the Ptolemaic empire, exporting slaves, wheat, oil and perfume and receiving its share of goods in return, largely for distribution among the wealthier Jews and Ptolemaic officials.[4]

Undoubtedly the sheer weight and power of Alexander's armies will have made the first really deep impression on Palestinian Jews and this lasting impression is reflected in some of the apocalyptic writings, as in Daniel 7:7 and Jeremiah 27:16 (LXX). Some Jews entered the Greek armies as mercenaries and through them something of Greek language and culture was introduced to the Jews.

With Hellenistic military and technological skills came also new forms of government. Under the Ptolemies a system of government was introduced centred on the king, the country being conceived for the most part as his estate (*oikos*) governed by a centralized bureaucracy.[5] The king's land was farmed by free tenants (also by military settlers and high officials) under the strict supervision of royal officials. Taxes were farmed out, again under strict supervision, and brought in a substantial income. Even temple-lands were under strict state control. The consequence of this system was the accumulation of great wealth by the Ptolemies and equally the real oppression and exploitation of the lower levels of society.[6] Nevertheless it was necessary for the Ptolemies' survival in their struggle against the Seleucids with their much larger lands and population to exploit their own territories to the full.

As well as those areas which came thus under the direct rule of the king's household, there were others which were allowed a measure of independence in self-government[7] and administration. Most notable were the cities which, although not enjoying the full independence of the Greek city states, were responsible for their administration and the collection of taxes. Many such cities existed along the coastal seaboard of Palestine. Equally, certain national groupings (*ethnē*) enjoyed a measure of independence.

In Palestine the Ptolemies appear to have operated a similar mixed system of government, ruling in part through the Jewish aristocracy, recruiting such men as Tobias and his family[8] to collect taxes and administer the lands. Jerusalem was treated as a temple-state under royal control. The high priest was nominally the head of the Jewish *ethnos* and the Temple. Hengel conjectures that he would have been assisted by a 'special Jewish temple official, authorized by the foreign régime ... responsible for the finance of Judea and the temple', and working along with other Ptolemaic officials.[9] Bickermann thinks that these powers were vested wholly in the high priest.[10] At the same time the high priest's influence was checked by the development of the 'Gerousia',[11] a body made up of the heads of larger families. In this way the aristocracy were given a share in the wealth and authority of the state and were open to Hellenistic influence.

Hellenism was not only a political and economic force; it was also a cultural force of great power.[12] Its chief medium was the *koinē* which became widespread in Palestine in this period, and is evidenced not only in documents and inscriptions but in the large number of Greek names and of double names, both Hebrew (or Aramaic) and Greek. Greek culture was centred on the notion of *paideia* (education). Theoretically at least it was possible for all men, not simply those born Greeks, to become Hellenes. In consequence schools became the gate to the upper ranks of society: the elementary school, followed by the gymnasium. Emphasis was placed on physical and military training, on music and then thirdly on the study of literature, primarily Homer. The gymnasia had an established position in the life of the city, though they were private foundations. They played an important part in local festivals, and encouraged a cult of heroes and the worship of the king or emperor. Pupils retained contact with their schools, membership of which was thus almost a *sine qua non* of membership of the privileged élite. They were, that is, conservative institutions, training and fitting students for a particular established place and role in society to which particular privileges were attached. They were the means of assuring that the Hellenistic minority did not become assimilated to its barbarian society and they were for some the means of entry into the privileged ranks. Such schools were gradually introduced to Palestine in the third century B.C., culminating in the establishment of a gymnasium in Jerusalem in 175 B.C. at the time of the Hellenistic Reform.

Hellenism as it confronted the Jews in Palestine, both in Jerusalem and Judaea and in areas where Hellenistic influence was greater, like Galilee, was thus a force which bore on many aspects of Jewish life. In political terms they became part of an empire which demanded a very considerable degree of *Gleichschaltung* into the royal administrative, fiscal and economic system. It was not simply that they lost their independence, but that in the process important institutions and offices were incorporated into a quite foreign system and subjected to outside control and taxation. This led to a conflict of legal systems, to the oppression of the poor and the suborning of the Jewish aristocracy, and consequently undermined the programme of national reconstruction which the Aaronides[13] had carried through successfully after the Exile. The dangers, however, were not always acute. The majority of people could, if they desired, continue to practise the Law, and the Temple cult could proceed provided it made suitable contributions to the royal treasury. Where the danger was greatest in the first instance was in the pressures put upon the Jewish upper classes to conform to Hellenism and thus to play down or to abolish the specifically Jewish character of the institutions which they controlled. On the other hand as the far-reaching changes in administrative, fiscal and economic arrangements began to take effect they must have borne heavily on the peasant and agricultural classes who formed the bulk of the population and we have clear evidence of this in the numerous uprisings of the period of Roman domination.[14] Doubtless the pressures will have varied considerably from time to time, as did the incidence of unrest. Overall it is probably fair to say that the Jews' experience of Hellenism was of an encounter with a vastly superior economic, technological and political power which offered undreamt-of possibilities to a few and posed a serious threat to the self-esteem of many and their ability to pursue their traditional ways of life.[15]

As we have said, the pressures will have varied considerably and with them the kind of responses. During the period of Ptolemaic rule the impact of Hellenism seems to have been far less oppressive than under the Seleucids. Under the rule of the latter one can see the two basic reactions of Jews to Hellenism most clearly characterized: on the one hand the Jewish aristocracy and ruling priests who were friendly to the Reform and wished to introduce Hellenistic institutions into Jerusalem and abandon the traditional Temple cult; on the other the—lower order?—priests, the family of the Maccabees, the Hasidim, and a strong popular following, located in the rural areas which formed the majority of the country, who were determined to renew Judaism, to turn back from all accommodation to Hellenism and to pledge themselves to strict observance of the Law. These turned to military revolt and a planned restoration of the Jewish kingdom. But as well as these forms of response, there were others which attempted to prosecute Jewish traditions while accommodating in some manner, consciously or otherwise, to the Hellenistic environment. The development of a class of sages and of Jewish schools[16] and synagogues[17] with which the Pharisees were closely associated was undoubtedly one way of reinforcing Jewish knowledge and observation of the Law, but equally, as Hengel has pointed out, both in its institutions and modes of exegesis, it borrowed quite heavily from Hellenism. Similarly the Hasmonean monarchy established by the Maccabean revolt developed its own form of Hellenistic Judaism.[18] Of course alongside these groups which made positive responses to Hellenism, there would be the broad mass of people who remained relatively inactive except in times of extreme pressure which lead to revolt. Thus responses to Hellenism over the period were many and varied and we can assume that even within groups of considerable homogeneity, such as the Qumran community, there was a measure of variation from one period to another.

II

The purpose of this chapter is not, of course, to attempt a detailed history of the period. Rather, having now seen something of the different factors which bore on Judaism at this time and noticed the different kinds of response represented by various groups, I want to look next at the Jewish linguistic conventions which held during this period as they can be found in the major literary traditions, the wisdom and apocalyptic literatures. The importance of these 'writings' is precisely that, because of their *literary* character, they present linguistic usages which had a degree of authority and acceptance within the communities which read and preserved them. Clearly of course attempts will have been made to modify such conventions after their writing and some of these attempts were subsequently successful in the sense that they were committed to writing within particular communities: the Dead Sea Scrolls, the Gospels, the Mishnah. For the present however it is the ruling linguistic conventions of the period that we shall consider.

Before looking at the wisdom and apocalyptic literature we must say something briefly about the major authoritative literary corpus of the second Temple period, namely the Pentateuch.[19] The singular achievement of the editors of the Pentateuch was to have created a system of divine laws centred on the worship of the Temple and administered by a hereditary priesthood, the Aaronides. In so doing they set very firm limits on the prophets and subordinated Israel, not to the living word of Yahweh, spoken through his prophets, but to the codified Law given once to his servant Moses and now administered by a central authority, the High Priests and the Great Council. Because of this orientation towards the high priesthood and the Temple, great importance attaches within the Pentateuch to the priestly regulations about purity, which serve both to regulate the conduct of the worship of the Temple and also to remind the people of Israel of their separation from the Gentiles and their distinctive constitution as an holy people.[20] This constitution is, of course, based on God's election of his people, his faithfulness to them and the covenant he made with them; it is conditional on their obedience to his Laws. What is significant now is that within the Pentateuch obedience to God's laws becomes conventionally associated, not only with faithfulness to the covenant on Sinai, but also with separating oneself from the Gentiles, with maintaining the *purity* of Israel, above all of its worship. These conventional associations hold within a system of power and the administration of power which gives the chief responsibility for the maintenance of the covenant to the high priests who both interpret the Law and control the Temple worship, and which sees the Temple as the central place of communion between God and his people. Indeed only if one understands the centrality of the priests within this system can one understand the concern of subsequent Jewish groups with purity and priestly symbolism (e.g. Qumran and the Pharisees) or with the actual control of the High Priest's office (the Hasmoneans).

This system is based on certain assumptions about the nature of God's power and the manner of his dealings with his people which are reflected in the conventional associations of certain key terms. God is a God of holiness, justice and mercy. These terms combine the priestly and prophetic emphases on God's power with the more generally Jewish consciousness of election. In the institutional context of the second Temple period there can be little doubt that the priestly emphasis on holiness had the pre-eminence. The central notion is of a God whose holiness is such that no impure thing can exist in his sight but will be consumed by his sheer presence (Exod. 19). Only those who are at the centre of a system of religious purity can approach him and then only after a series of elaborate preparations to make sure that they are free from all taint of that which is foreign to the nation which God has chosen out for himself.[21] Thus by convention God's holiness is associated with his separation of clean from unclean, with his bringing Israel out from Egypt and driving out the nations from the land and giving it to Israel. It means that he has dealings only with that which is pure, whole, perfect; that he will destroy all that is not.

Such a God is, however, not arbitrary. The prophetic emphasis on God's justice is given its place within this priestly system, not, as in Hosea, as a principle potentially opposed to the priestly cult (Hos. 6:6) but as one which speaks of his *orderliness* in creation, in his dealings with his people and with the nations. God has made a covenant with his people and those who obey he will protect and reward, just as he will destroy and punish those who offend. This notion of God's justice finds its fullest exposition in the historical books which attempt to give an account of Israel's misfortunes and occasional triumphs in terms of the obedience and disobedience of its kings to God's Law.[22] Thus conventionally God's justice is associated with his punishing and rewarding his *people* for their obedience and disobedience, a process which occurs in terms of the material and political well-being of the people.

The Judaism of the Pentateuch which gave particular expression to these basic assumptions about God's holiness and justice came under pressure during the period of Hellenistic influence and rule in two main ways. First, as we have said, the chief threat of Hellenism was that it suborned the religious leaders of the Jews, notably the priests and the aristocracy. If the guardians and administrators of the Law are being corrupted, then it is necessary to set up alternative systems of interpreting and administering the Law. Hence the development of the sages, of the schools and synagogues[23] and communities like that at Qumran, which make particular claims to have received traditions or revelations which authorize them to interpret the Law. Secondly, because the Temple cult was in the hands of those who compromised and mixed with the alien rulers, control of the sacral institutions had to be wrested from their hands.[24] At the same time groups like the Pharisees and Essenes began, consciously or unconsciously, to develop alternative sanctuaries surrounded by protective purity regulations, whether in the *ḥaburah*, the home, or the worship of the community at Qumran. Such changes in the institutional structure would lead to changes

69

in the conventional associations of key terms like holiness and righteousness. Equally some of the major associations of these terms, particularly those relating to the conceptions of rewards and punishments associated with God's righteousness were challenged by the beliefs Jews came to hold on the basis of their experience of Hellenism. The misfortunes of the devout non-Hellenized Jews in this period, as well as the erosion of Israel's independence led men to doubt whether God would indeed reward those who were faithful to him with material blessings. Jews clearly believed that those who were unfaithful to the Law would at least in this life prosper.[25] Hence again the conventional associations of God's righteousness had to be reworked. Some at least of the major changes of this time are documented in the wisdom and apocalyptic literature.

The question which principally concerned the writers of the wisdom literature was that of God's justice in his dealings with men. As Hengel has shown, while there is wide diversity in the way in which writers as distinct as Qoheleth, Ben-Sira and Baruch answer this question, there is this much in common, that they all incorporate Hellenistic motifs into their work. For our purposes we can on the basis of Hengel's findings suggest various ways in which the conventions about God's justice were modified.

Qoheleth[26] moves furthest away from the affirmation of God's providential governance of the world through rewards and punishments by denying that man can perceive any rationale to the way pleasure, prosperity, success are apportioned in this world.[27] While still affirming the righteousness of God in his dealings with men[28] he discards associated beliefs that God deals with men in this world in terms of punishments and rewards, as well as beliefs that God in his dealings with men distinguishes significantly between Israel and the nations in virtue of the covenant.[29] Rather the notion of God's righteousness is now reduced to its core-meaning of God's ordering of the world, and is interpreted in terms of a doctrine of fate, of divinely appointed 'times', of which however man is ignorant.[30] In a great deal of this, as Hengel has shown, Qoheleth is affirming beliefs which may also be found in Hellenistic 'New Comedy' and in the epitaphs of the time.[31] That such beliefs became conventionally associated with the notion of God's righteousness is shown, not only by the authoritative position of Qoheleth within Judaism, but also by the occurrence of similar beliefs in other forms of wisdom literature as well as in apocalyptic Judaism and the literature of Qumran.[32]

By contrast with these very substantial modifications, we find in Ben-Sira and Baruch a much more traditional working out of the notion of God's righteousness. For Ben-Sira 'all wisdom is the fear of the Lord and in all wisdom is included the performance of the Law'.[33] Equally he reaffirms the doctrine of the divine apportionment of rewards and punishments, particularly as relating to God's dealings with Jews in the past. He praises the fathers of the Jews[34] and their deeds and admonishes the rulers to rule with justice: 'May he give you a wise heart to judge his people with righteousness'.[35] It is perhaps not unduly harsh to say that Ben-Sira is a fairly typical reactionary, reaffirming past beliefs and glories at a time when they are in fact being seriously challenged, freely issuing criticism and advice to the Jewish aristocracy, whilst failing to grasp the political realities which were undermining the kind of Judaism he espoused.

Even so Ben-Sira introduces certain elements which are new, and bear interesting resemblances to similar features in Hellenism. The very fact that he gives his name[36] is itself an innovation and indicates a shift from the central—official—interpretation of the tradition to its exposition by the practised sage. More interestingly Ben-Sira develops a doctrine of the divine purpose in creation, affirming that all things have their purpose in the divine order, whether to reward or to punish, so that 'all these things are good to the godly, just as they turn into evils for sinners'.[37] This clearly moves along the same lines as Qoheleth in associating God's righteousness with his ordering of the world; but the idea is now given an interesting twist by being further associated with the doctrine of divine rewards and punishments, so that the purpose of everything is now determined by reference to God's exercise of his justice thus conceived. This becomes the more remarkable when one recalls that for Ben-Sira the lines between the good and the wicked were drawn sharply in terms of obeying the Law, thus putting the Gentiles comprehensively into the camp of the wicked: 'the nations will incur his wrath'.[38] Thus the combination of Jewish particularism, which

71

makes observance of the Mosaic covenant the touchstone of God's apportionment of punishments and rewards, with the universalistic doctrine of God's ordering of creation leads to an intensification of Jewish particularism. Observance of the Law is the pivot around which world history turns. In line with this Ben-Sira introduces the Wisdom myth to affirm the cosmic significance of the Law[39] and speaks of God in universalistic terms as *hakkol*, the 'all'.[40]

Thus in Ben-Sira the traditional (pentateuchal) conventional associations of the term 'God's righteousness' are preserved, despite the challenge to them presented by the actual conditions of the Jews. Not only are they reaffirmed, they are underlined and re-emphasized by the addition to them of the doctrine of God's purposes in creation—analogous to that developed by Qoheleth. In this way the point is made that obedience to the Law is not only the key to Israel's fate but to the fate of all the nations.

One further move in this tradition needs to be noticed, for which some evidence is found in Baruch. In Baruch there is a sharpening of the particularism which we noticed in Ben-Sira. Wisdom is hidden to the foreign rulers, Canaanites, the Arab traders and giants of primeval times, and is revealed only to Israel in the form of the Law.[41] All attempts to discover 'traces' of wisdom in foreign peoples are to be rejected, as is any attempt to communicate the Law to those outside.[42] Along with this greater exclusivism goes a greater stress on the observation of the Law within Israel. Law is to be applied to *all* aspects of everyday life.[43] Thus Baruch, which emphasizes the purity regulations, argues that their application should be extended from the Temple to everyday life. It is plausible to see here the origins of Pharisaism and later Rabbinic Judaism.

The Mosaic Law—given to the Jews—is thus affirmed as the source of all wisdom, by contrast with all other philosophies and creeds (such as Hellenism); but at the same time a fundamental change is made in the understanding of Torah. It is no longer, as in the earlier part of the second Temple period, a system for regulating an (autonomous) Temple State. It has become, or is on the way to becoming, a *modus vivendi* for Jews anywhere, because its application is to the everyday life in the home and the ḥaburah. The exclusivism which had previously associated doing the Law with not doing as the nations do was nationalistic; it had contrasted the way things were done in Judaea with the way they were done elsewhere. From now on the contrast would be with the way one's Gentile (or non-observant Jewish) *neighbours* did things. Hence the importance of centring the regulations of the Law on the local unit, the home and the ḥaburah, etc., and of fencing these off from contamination by purity regulations. Thus the purity regulations become not only a reminder to the Israelites of God's election and separation of them from the nations,[44] they now become, as they are applied to the home and everyday life, a means of preserving that separation in a situation where the land has been extensively infiltrated by the nations.

Such developments however already lie on the other side of a major divide in the history of Judaism in the second Temple period. The optimistic, if reactionary, reaffirmation of the tradition by Ben-Sira sounded a rallying call to Jews. But the events of the Hellenistic Reform and of Antiochus Epiphanes' desecration of the Temple would test Ben-Sira's doctrine of history, would find it wanting, and produce in the apocalyptic writings a very different picture.[45] The experiences and resultant beliefs of this crisis would leave their marks on the whole of the subsequent period, so that even if in the calmer intervals Jews would again contemplate less radical refor-mulations of the tradition, the apocalyptic visions were from now on a part of the armoury of Judaism which could be drawn on in times of crisis. More even than that, they permanently modified the doctrine of rewards and punishments by affirming that these would only finally be reconciled in a future state.

Apocalyptic writings like Daniel and the earlier parts of Enoch changed the tradition which we have been contemplating at a num-ber of significant points. Whereas Ben-Sira saw God's rule in history as being exercised through material and political rewards and pun-ishments in this life, the apocalyptic writers increasingly looked forward to a future time of reckoning when the present sufferings of the righteous would be vindicated. At the same time they believed in the resurrection of the dead,[46] a belief which Ben-Sira had per-haps explicitly rejected.[47] The manner in which changes in the tradition are effected here is interesting. The basic conventional associations of the term 'God's justice' do not change. God is still held to order the world in accordance with his Law, still punishes the wicked and rewards the righteous. God's justice is still closely related to his holiness, in that those whom he vindicates must be purified before they are finally vindicated.[48] Equally God's rule is exercised over his people, the saints, whose everlasting kingdom he will firmly establish.[49] The writer, that is, still associates God's governance of the world with the establishment and maintenance of a particular Jewish state. Where Daniel and Enoch differ radically from Ben-Sira is in their belief, forced on them by the bitter experience of the desecration and the persecution of the devout Jews under Antiochus Epiphanes, that *at the present time* Israel's suffering cannot be understood exclusively as God's punishment.

In consequence Daniel and Enoch have to work out a quite different view of God's control over history. The belief we encountered in Qoheleth that God orders the world according to certain times or periods reappears in interestingly different form. The history of the world is divided into different ages which represent a progressive decline in Israel's fortunes until the point when God will intervene through some saviour figure to re-establish his kingdom. These ages are portrayed in visions by means of vivid symbols representing power and destruction—metals,[50] and beasts,[51] false shepherds[52]—and by these means a dualistic element is introduced into the understanding of history. The forces which hold sway over Israel at present are forces of evil and destruction which God tolerates for a time, but which will eventually be destroyed. Meanwhile the saints must endure and be purified so that they will eventually inherit the kingdom.[53] This historical perspective opens out on to a vision of the final joys of the saints in the kingdom and the exquisite and eternal sufferings of the wicked.[54] Similar treatment of the themes of the ordained times and future hoped-for visitation of the righteous and the wicked are to be found, as we shall see more fully,[55] in the Qumran writings and were doubtless also entertained by the Pharisees.

What has happened here can perhaps best be brought out by a comparison with Ben-Sira. For that writer God's justice is manifested in his giving of the Law to Israel, his present rewarding of those in Israel who obey that Law and his punishment of the disobedient and the nations. God's *gubernatio* thus conceived is moreover related to his ordering of creation, for all things are related to the purposes of God's justice.

What changes in Daniel is first and foremost that rewards and punishments are no longer thought of as being distributed *now* but at a future date. This future is moreover related to an overall picture of God's *ordering* of world history into different epochs, such that the kingdom of the saints will be established only after a long period of testing and suffering. These changes in the details of beliefs about God's righteousness in turn open the way for the development of further beliefs (a) about the nature of the present age and the powers which rule it, and their relation to God's overall sovereignty, (b) about God's intervention through some saviour-figure, (c) about the nature of the future *kingdom* and the extent to which those who have died will be involved in it through some kind of resurrection. Many different beliefs were in fact expressed in relation to these topics and it is hard to know which of them may in any given community have become conventionally associated with the term the 'righteousness of God'. Certainly this will have included in many cases references to the overthrowing of the powers, to the coming of a saviour-figure, to the resurrection of the dead, to the establishment of God's kingdom. The precise way in which such beliefs were formulated will doubtless have varied substantially. What I want to stress at this point is the fundamental nature of the change which occurred in the understanding of God's righteousness, even though this is effected, not by deleting a large number of its associations and substituting others, but by making a fairly minor adjustment in the beliefs about when punishments and rewards will be apportioned. That this is nevertheless a fundamental change in understanding can be seen if one considers that it effectively means the abandonment of the belief that the present political constitution of Israel is a divinely established theocracy and the substitution for it of a hope for some future restoration.

Such far-reaching changes require due authentication. The Pentateuch rested on the authority of the divine revelation given on Sinai. In the apocalyptic literature knowledge of God's ways and dealings with men is given through arcane revelations about God's mysteries, whether through dreams and interpretation of dreams as in Daniel[56] or through visions and celestial journeys as throughout Enoch. Two things seem to be happening here. First, control of the means of redemption is being wrested from the priestly groups in Jerusalem who control power according to the Pentateuchal system as alternative sources of power and authority are suggested. Secondly, the stress on the esoteric nature of the revelation represents an important shift away from the Wisdom tradition with its search for a rational understanding which could be formulated in terms of maxims and proverbs. God's dealings with men (so earlier Qoheleth) cannot be comprehended by men's efforts alone, not even by Greek philosophy and learning. The mystery of God's ways can be grasped only if God chooses to reveal it to men. Such a belief in the mysterious character of the knowledge of God, here in the Jewish context applied to his righteousness, is widespread in the Hellenistic counter-cultures of the time[57] and was an important feature of Jewish sectarianism in the rest of the period.

In summary: during this period certain basic conventional associations of the terms 'holiness' and 'righteousness' are sustained throughout. It is part of the meaning of these terms as applied to God that he will destroy all that is impure; that he orders the world according to his Law; that he punishes those who disobey his Law and rewards his people when they obey. The corruption of the Jerusalem leadership, the oppression and suffering of the poorer classes, the disastrous events of the Hellenistic Reform, however, led men to challenge some of the beliefs expressed in these terms. If the priests are unfaithful to the Law then it cannot be that God has entrusted the administration and the interpretation of the Law solely to them. If the just suffer, and the faithless prosper then punishments and rewards must either be hard to discern or else they must be given at a future date. If God allows his sanctuary to be desecrated then the nations can no longer be seen simply as his agents in punishing Israel, but as forces of evil and destruction which presently hold sway in the world. If that is so, then Israel must wait till God puts an end to this age and establishes his rule.

To his seers and prophets he has revealed his mysterious purposes for mankind.

Schematic as this is it provides, I think, the framework into which the subsequent developments of second Temple sectarian Judaism can be fitted: Pharisaism, Zealotism, Essenism and Jesus. In what follows, rather than attempting a comprehensive history of this development we shall work back from Jesus, trying to discover what particular conventions he is working with and how he has modified them in order to express new beliefs. Thus we shall consider Jewish sectarianism only piecemeal as it is brought into view by an examination of the tradition Jesus used. There are doubtless dangers in such an approach. It might be said that we shall view the development of the tradition from too narrow a standpoint, thus running the risk of obscuring the complexity of the tradition. We must leave the reader to judge the results of our inquiry. Moreover, it is only fair to point out that our evidence for the development of Jewish sectarianism is of very different kinds. The evidence for Qumran is very much more reliable than either the fairly scant and polemical references we have to the Zealots or the much later Mishnaic and Talmudic sources on which we have to rely for knowledge of the Pharisees. The evidence for Jesus' teaching has indeed its own particular problems, but they are not I think crippling. In all, I think, there is a reasonably strong case for saying that a reconstruction of the tradition working back from Jesus and taking cross-bearings on other contemporary developments may in itself make a useful contribution to our knowledge of first-century Judaism.

III

It remains, as a preliminary to that undertaking, to give some account of the social, economic, political and cultural conditions obtaining in Palestine and in particular in Galilee in the time of Jesus.

Politically, Palestine underwent very considerable changes in the period from 63 B.C., when it came under Roman rule, to the Jewish

Revolt.[58] After an initial period under Pompey, when the Hellenistic cities were given back their independence and the authority of the high priests and ethnarchs was substantially reduced, clever use by the ethnarch in Jerusalem of the changing fortunes of the Roman civil war eventually led to Herod's installation in 40 B.C. as king over the Jewish territories, albeit an area from which he had first to drive out the Parthians. Thus Herod owed his throne to a combination of Roman favour—he was quick to make his suit to Octavian after the latter's victory at Actium—and his own resolution and ruthlessness in establishing and maintaining control over his subjects.

As Theissen has observed,[59] Roman policy during this period wavered disconcertingly for the Jews between direct and indirect rule. After Herod's death (4 B.C.) his kingdom was subdivided and gradually brought under Roman rule. After Archelaeus' deposition (6 A.D.) Judaea, Samaria and Idumea came under the direct rule of a Roman governor whose residence was in Caesarea. By contrast Herod Antipas enjoyed a long reign in Galilee (4 B.C.—39 A.D.) eventually being deposed by Caligula whose suspicion and displeasure he aroused by asking to be made king. From 44 A.D. all Palestine was under the direct rule of Roman governors. It is fairly clear that the periods of indirect rule were tolerated by the Romans only so long as their puppet rulers were successful in imposing order on their subjects and in reassuring the Romans of their loyalty. Those Herods who succeeded, notably Herod I and Herod Antipas, did so by a mixture of military skill, ruthlessness in dealing with opponents and attempts to conciliate their mixed populations of Jews and Hellenizers. Herod I built not only Hellenistic cities but also enlarged and rebuilt the Temple. Nevertheless neither his Hellenism nor his ruthlessness endeared him to his people. Antipas appears to have been less conciliatory to Jewish feeling and to have caused offence to Jewish sensibilities by building his residence, Tiberias, on the site of a former cemetery.[60] On the other hand, by contrast to his brother Philip, he refrained from having his own image on his coins, out of respect for Jewish feeling.[61] However his ambitious building programmes[62] as well as his extravagant international diplomacy put heavy financial burdens on his subjects.[63]

The Herods' replacement of the Hasmonean dynasty represented a major change in political rankings in Palestine which was bitterly resented by the Jews, as is witnessed by their support for the Hasmoneans in the period before Herod's gaining power.[64] This resentment of the Herods was frequently expressed in uprisings during Herod I's reign, and came out most sharply in the violent uprisings after Herod's death and the massacre of Jews in the Temple by Archelaus.[65] In Galilee the opposition was led by a powerful figure, Judas the Galilean, whose family continued to oppose Roman rule, direct or indirect. By contrast the revolt in Peraea was led by Simon, one of Herod's slaves, while another prominent figure was a shepherd, named Athronges. Thus opposition was drawn from all ranks of society.[66]

Under Herod I Palestine was administered after the Ptolemaic model.[67] Some areas were designated *poleis* with a certain independence of their own, while the major part of the territory constituted the King's *chora* (country estate) and was administered through a system of *mereis* (provinces) subdivided in toparchies. All officials, down to the village scribes,[68] were appointed by the king. Taxes[69] were levied in part as direct taxes on agricultural produce, in part indirectly on sales and purchases. The main burden of these taxes fell on the Jewish peasantry. Part of these monies was paid to the Roman State, part went to finance Herod's elaborate programme of building and diplomacy. Revenue from taxes is reckoned at a thousand talents under Herod I, a sum which, impressive though it is, was exceeded under Agrippa I. After the deposition of Archelaus, Judaea, Idumea and Samaria were governed as a Roman province and taxation was based on Quirinius's census of A.D.6.[70] This formed the basis for a poll-tax, but taxes were also levied on agricultural produce. According to Josephus,[71] the Romans did not use tax-farmers but collected taxes through the local officials. There is some evidence[72] that the burden of taxes was greater under direct Roman rule than under the Herods.

Thus one may characterize the period of Roman rule as one in which there was a steady increase in foreign intervention in and control over government in Palestine. The Herods were clearly seen to be vassals of the Romans, dependent for their position on Roman favour and power. Rome moreover aggravated the unstable state of Jewish society by its frequent changes in the mode of government. Direct rule brought with it heavier taxes, more inflexibly administered. The Herods remained an unpopular dynasty, though they managed to gain the sympathy of some of the old ruling class,[73] and to create new members, partly through the importation of Jews from the Diaspora.[74] Galilee, which was fierce in its opposition to the Herods, particularly after the death of Herod I, appears to have remained fairly quiet during Herod Antipas's reign. The main evidence for unrest of any kind in Herod Antipas's territories is provided by the popular messianic movements of John the Baptist and Jesus.

The political changes which Palestine underwent in the period of Roman rule bore heavily on all classes, but most heavily on the peasantry. The same is largely true of the economic conditions of the time. Palestine was a largely agricultural[75] community, producing a range of crops, wheat, barley, olives, rice, vegetables, flax, balsam, dates, figs, etc. There was a flourishing trade based on agricultural produce. Balsam was in considerable demand and was grown around the Jordan valley, particularly in the Jericho and Dead Sea area. Animal husbandry and fishing were of considerable importance, even if the latter may not have yielded large catches. There was a certain amount of home industry,[76] notably weaving. Pottery and glass were produced where suitable materials were to hand. Other products included silk, leather and stone goods, ropes, baskets. The largest concentration of industry was in Jerusalem, much of which was designed to cater for the needs of the Temple. The difficulties of the agricultural population and the division of the country into town and country[77] were both productive of social tension and unrest.

Apart from the coastal strips which in the first century A.D. were largely in Greek hands, the country was not easy to farm. The mountainous territory in Galilee required strip lynchet farming or terracing as well as the construction of small dams to stop the top soil being carried away by the mountain streams. Climatic conditions, winter rains and long dry summers made water conservation imperative and meant a serious danger from drought if the rains failed. Thus while it was quite possible to gain a living by hard work, the farmer's livelihood would depend on conditions of land-tenure, of marketing and on the weather.

In this respect Applebaum has argued that the pressure on arable land was intense throughout the period as a result of the movement of Jews from the Hellenistic coastal cities by Pompey after 63 B.C.[78] Whether or not that alone is a sufficient explanation of the difficulties of farmers during this period, the archaeological evidence from Galilee[79] shows a pattern of small enclosed fields which supports his general contention that pressure on land was considerable.

Equally the settlement patterns and conditions of land-tenure[80] will not have eased the burden on small tenant farmers. The precise picture is not clear. Archaeological evidence shows the existence of estates with a central villa or settlement (*'ir*) and dependent villages (*'ayaroth* or *kerayoth*). Literary sources indicate that Herod I increased his estates considerably and that these were subsequently sold off, presumably to the wealthier Jews.[81] Similarly the increase in exports of foodstuffs during this period argues for the growth of large estates producing a surplus, rather than the persistence of an economy based on small subsistence farms.[82] Conditions of tenancy varied. The tenant paid either a fixed percentage of his harvest (a half or a third), or a fixed amount in money or in produce. Evidence from the Gospels[83] suggests that this situation could lead to very considerable enmity between tenants and landlords. In a bad year the tenant might not be able to get a sufficient price for his produce—after tax—to pay the rent, particularly if the larger farmers controlled the market prices,[84] and might thus be forced to take on substantial loans. His debt might grow to such an extent that he and his family would be sold into slavery[85]. Further evidence of the prevalence of debt is provided by Hillel's introduction of the *prosbul*,[86] a device for circumventing the cancellation of debts every seventh year, and later by the destruction of the debt records in Jerusalem during the Jewish Revolt.[87]

As well as landowners and tenant farmers there were also day-labourers and slaves who would compete with the tenants for work on the larger estates or in fishing or other forms of labour in the

81

settlements. Matthew 20:3–7 indicates that unemployment was by no means unknown.

It is a matter for some debate whether the contrast between life in the country and the towns was a serious cause of dissension and rivalry. Large towns were relatively few in Palestine; Jerusalem, Caesarea, Gaza and Ascalon, Tiberias in Galilee. Of these Jerusalem was a major centre of commerce. The large towns were controlled by councils governed by the local aristocracy, in most cases large landowners. If there was rivalry between town and country this may have been less because the towns were identified as centres of commerce and industry than because they were identified with the ruling group who fixed the market prices and were composed in part of large landowners loyal to the Herods and the Romans.[88]

The effect of these political and economic conditions on Jewish society at the time of Jesus is not easy to gauge. On the one hand we have to bear in mind the relative political quiet of the period;[89] on the other the incidence of radical religious movements of a prophetic kind like those of John the Baptist and Jesus.[90] The political instability caused by the creation of a new aristocracy by the Herods, as well as by the frequency of constitutional change, was obviously considerable and meant that there was not only a substantial degree of popular support for revolutionary movements at times of crisis, but also no lack of leadership.[91] Economic pressure, resulting from heavy taxes and rents, from shortage of employment, etc., coupled with shortage of land and the demands of the terrain will have affected the main mass of the Jewish peasantry more immediately and continually. Families could be faced at almost any time with disaster—loss of land tenancies and ultimately with slavery—as a result of poor harvests or adverse market conditions.

Theissen has argued that we can go further and claims on the basis of evidence of social uprootedness in the period that there existed a state of social 'anomie'.[92] He instances emigration, brigandage and vagrancy as general manifestations of social uprootedness which have their more specifically religious counterparts[93] in Qumran (rebuilt at the turn of the century), the Zealots (who were however less active at this period) and certain prophetic movements. Theissen's thesis is admittedly difficult to substantiate as it depends on being able to show that the incidence of social uprootedness was higher than normal and this kind of quantification is not possible. Nevertheless evidence which can be produced for changes in social status affecting most levels of society[94] does lend support to his general thesis. When one takes into account the long process of erosion of Jewish norms during the period of Hellenism, it is clear that there was a deep crisis in the Judaism of the period. Many Jews found they were no longer able to conform to the norms which were set in their society and were forced to adopt forms of deviant, anomic behaviour. Such phenomena are often the signs of an approaching change in the general norms of society.

Lastly, before turning to the way in which Jesus responded to this situation of social disruption and pressure, we shall offer some remarks on the patterns of religious organization of the period and attempt to assess the relative vigour and character of Jewish traditions in first-century Galilee.

The most obvious fact about Judaism in the first decades of the first century A.D. is that it was divided into parties of varying degrees of cohesiveness and internal organization, who regarded each other with varying degrees of hostility. Sadducees, Pharisees, Essenes and Zealots promoted very different forms of Judaism. If the Sadducees[95] were an essentially conservative party, attempting to preserve the purity of the Temple worship at the cost of a substantial measure of political compromise, then the other groups sought a renewal of Judaism, either by an intensification of observance of the Law linked to certain eschatological expectations, or by direct military action. In their various ways all these groups struggled for control of the means of redemption centred on the Temple. The Sadducees attempted to maintain their position of control by diplomacy and compromise; the Zealots, somewhat after the model of Judas Maccabeus, sought to purge the Holy City of foreign domination.[96] The strategy of the Essenes and Pharisees was more subtle. The Essenes declared the present Temple cult impure, but expected the restoration of true worship at the appointed time. Meanwhile they themselves lived out the life of a priestly community, observing and developing regulations concerning ritual purity, seeing their own worship as analogous to the worship of the Temple.[97] Similarly Pharisees who belonged to the *ḥaburoth*[98] set up communities which applied the laws regulating the priests' consumption of sacred food to their own eating of secular food and thus created a sacred realm of fidelity to the Law.[99]

As well as such groupings we also encounter, particularly in the literature of the Sages, a group referred to as the *'am ha-aretz*. This group of Jews was distinguished, in the eyes of the Sages at least, by their less than scrupulous observance of the laws concerning tithing and purity.[100] In view of what we have just said about secular taxes and rents, tithes, which were levied on agricultural produce, must have fallen particularly heavily on tenant-farmers, as opposed to urban traders and craftsmen. Moreover the regulations about tithes were difficult and contradictory and involved the bringing of the tithe to Jerusalem, which clearly imposed an extra burden on those living at a distance, not least the Galilean. But while it is clearly thus not wrong to suppose that the *'am ha-aretz* contained many and mostly peasants, it would be mistaken to see it as being composed completely of such. Many of the references to the *'am ha-aretz* concern matters of ritual purity and there is less reason[101] to suppose that this, as opposed to tithing, bore more heavily on farmers than others, though corpse impurity may have had its particular problems for them.[102] The fact too that the *ḥaburoth* clearly separated themselves from other non-*ḥaberim* wherever they were, in town or country, suggests that the *'am ha-aretz* were to be found everywhere. Nor are they to be thought of as wholly unfaithful to the Law. We know only of their reputation in respect of tithes and purity; in other respects they may have been relatively faithful. True, their loyalty may have been greater to the popular festivals,[103] to pilgrimages and sabbath observance and their knowledge of the Law may not have been very detailed on some of the more intricate and confused points.[104]

Against this very general background we may be able to say something about the state of religious culture in Galilee. Galilee had been forcibly Judaized by the Hasmoneans and its subsequent loyalty to the Hasmoneans in the struggle with Herod suggests that at least for substantial elements of the population this had been accepted and had resulted in a basic loyalty to Judaism as presented by the Hasmoneans.[105] On the other hand we must be careful about the conclusions we draw from this. While there can be little doubt about the basic Jewishness of its population,[106] this does not mean that we can therefore identify it with any particular variety of sectarian Judaism of the time. What we may do is to treat with considerable caution views which present Galilean Judaism as a subject of general scorn and disapprobation by the more orthodox Judaeans.[107] There is evidence from the Gospels,[108] and the Rabbinic writings and Josephus[109] for the existence of schools, synagogues and Pharisees in Galilee in the second Temple period and for its contibution and receptiveness to developments in Judaism in the period of Jabneh.[110] But alongside that, for the mass of the people, particularly the tenant-farmers, the Pharisaic *halakhoth* about tithing and purity will have been burdensome and they may well have opted for less strict and complicated forms of Judaism.

This view is supported by such evidence as we have about religious groups specifically associated with Galilee: the Zealots, Jesus, the prophets,[111] and the 'men of deed'.[112] None of these movements is characterized by a particular concern with purity.[113] They tend to gather around inspired leaders and seek to enlist God's power and support either by military action or by prayer and prophetic action. This may provide some clues as to the general character of Galilean Judaism of the first century B.C. and A.D. Popular Judaism[114] of the period, we may well suppose, will have given prominence to the heroes of the Jewish—and Hasmonean—past: Moses, Phinehas, Elijah, David, Judas Maccabeus.[115] With such figures there will probably have been associated the hope for some future saviour of the people, who like David would come to liberate and vindicate his people. Such Judaism was broadly—often indeed fiercely—faithful to the traditions of popular religious observance and the customs enshrined in the Law but the complexity of the latter as well as their inaccessibility to many[116] may have meant that there was considerable selectivity with regard to which regulations were observed. Moreover there is evidence for readiness to adapt the traditions where necessary. The Maccabees abandoned their practice of not fighting on the sabbath when threatened with extinction;[117] Ḥanina ben Dosa regarded the finer points of the purity regulations as of small consequence.[118] None of this should be taken as evidence of disregard for Jewish tradition *as such*, but only as an indication of the rather different views which popular Judaism may have had of what was of central importance in the tradition from the more scholastic and learned scribes. This is in a sense to do no more than to recognize the often considerable differences that exist between the beliefs which are actually held by adherents of a particular religion, and those promulgated by its official teachers and institutions. But it is probably also true to say that these differences were somewhat magnified by the distance between Galilee and the principal centre of Judaism in Jerusalem.

Again, it should be stressed that figures like Judas, Jesus, Ḥanina and the prophets give us only clues as to the general character of popular Judaism of the time. They all represent different responses to the situation, and cannot in themselves be equated with popular first-century Judaism. But they do provide us with the possibility of making some general inferences about the beliefs of those to whom they addressed themselves and this seems to indicate again that the religious traditions of the Galilean Jews were, if strongly held, nevertheless fairly simple and unsophisticated. Jesus, for all his originality and freshness of thought, does not work with a very complicated classification system.

What we shall consider in the remainder of this book is how Jesus, in response to the particular pressures of his time, *reworked* and *renewed* the religious traditions which he inherited. To that end we shall have to follow such leads as we can find in his teaching as to which terms he took over and which he rejected, and we shall be guided by what we have already seen of the major conventions operating in Judaism in the second Temple period. What I hope this final section of the present chapter has shown is both something of the social and economic pressures on Judaism at the time, which call for more radical religious responses to the general breakdown of established norms *and* something of the relatively impoverished state of the religious traditions which Jesus inherited, however strongly they were held.

5

Jesus' Preaching of the Kingdom

At the heart of Jesus' ministry and preaching lie his sayings[1] about
the Kingdom and repentance.[2] Such a message sets him clearly in
the ranks of those who sought a renewal and restoration of Judaism.

If that is clear at first sight, little else is. In the first place, we
shall have to relate Jesus' sayings to the particular traditions and
conditions of first-century Galilee which, as we have seen, were by
no means typical of Palestinian Judaism as a whole. Secondly, while
Jesus' preaching of the Kingdom bore some of the traits of Jewish
apocalyptic language of the previous two hundred years, Jesus'
followers nevertheless ultimately broke away from Judaism and
established a quite separate religion. There is then a presumption
that, while there may be continuity between Jesus' teaching and
Jewish apocalyptic, there is also significant discontinuity. Thirdly,
Jesus, apparently at least, preached the imminent coming of the
Kingdom and of the Son of Man, yet these events failed to materialize. It might then seem that whether or not Jesus' preaching of
the Kingdom was central to his message in his eyes, it was not the
really distinctive and enduring gift which he gave to mankind. In
what follows I shall attempt to argue both that it was central and
distinctive, and that in Jesus' reworking of the conventional associations of the notion of the Kingdom is to be found a radicalization
and transformation of first-century Judaism such that his followers,
if they were to be faithful to him, could in the end not but break
out on their own.

Let us start by examining the synoptic evidence. A form-critical
analysis of the relevant material in the synoptic Gospels[3] reveals
that Jesus is recorded as having uttered sayings of all the known

87

prophetic types. One type, namely accounts of visions or auditions, is represented by only a single example: Luke 10:18: 'I saw Satan fall like lightning from heaven', but that should not necessarily lead us to be sceptical of its authenticity. These sayings are classified by Bultmann under four heads as follows. I give some examples for ease of reference.

(1) Preaching of salvation

Luke 10:23f. Blessed are the eyes which see what you see. For I tell you that many prophets and kings desired to see what you see, and did not see it, and to hear what you hear, and did not hear it.

Luke 6:20–23. Blessed are you poor, for yours is the Kingdom of God. Blessed are you that hunger now, for you shall be satisfied. Blessed are you that weep now, for you shall laugh . . .

Matt. 11:5–6. The blind receive their sight and the lame walk, lepers are cleansed and the deaf hear, and the dead are raised up, and the poor have the good news preached to them. And blessed is he who takes no offence at me.

Mark 10:29f. Truly, I say to you, there is no one who has left house or brothers . . . who will not receive a hundred-fold now in this time, houses and brothers and sisters and mothers and children and lands, with persecutions, and in the age to come eternal life.

(2) Woes and threats

Luke 6:24–26. Woe to you that are rich . . . full . . . that laugh now . . . when all men speak well of you.

Matt. 10:32f. So everyone who acknowledges me before men, I also will acknowledge before my father who is in heaven; but whoever denies me before men, I will also deny before my father who is in heaven.

Matt. 11:21–24. Woes on Galilean towns, etc.

(3) Warnings and exhortations

Mark 1:15. The time is fulfilled, and the Kingdom of God is at hand; repent, and believe in the gospel.

Luke 12:35–38. The master who comes in the night.

Matt. 24:43–44. The parable of the thief. Matt. 24:45–51. The parable of the faithful and unfaithful servant.

Matt. 25:1–13. The parable of the ten virgins.

Luke 12:47–48. The servant who knew his master's will, but did not make ready or act according to his will, shall receive a severe beating. But he who did not know, and did what deserved a beating, shall receive a light beating.

Luke 21:34–36. But take heed to yourselves lest your hearts be weighed down with dissipation and drunkenness and cares of this life, and that day come upon you suddenly like a snare. . .

(4) Apocalyptic predictions

Mark 13:2; 14:58; Matt. 26:61. The destruction of the Temple.

Mark 9:1. There are some standing here who will not taste death before they see the Kingdom of God come with power.

Luke 17:20f. The Kingdom of God is not coming with signs to be observed; nor will they say, 'Lo, here it is!' or 'There', for behold, the Kingdom of God is in the midst of you.

Luke 17:23–24. And they will say to you, 'Lo, there!' or 'Lo, here!' Do not go, do not follow them. For as the lightning flashes and lights up the sky from one side to the other, so will the Son of Man be in his day.

Mark 13:5–27. The synoptic apocalypse.

Mark 13:28–29. The parable of the fig-tree.

Mark 13:30. This generation will not pass away before all these things take place.

Matt. 25:31–46. The sheep and the goats.

Matt. 7:15. Beware of false prophets, who come to you in sheep's clothing but inwardly are ravenous wolves.

Mark 9:12–13. Elijah does come first to restore all things; and how is it written of the Son of Man, that he should suffer many things and be treated with contempt? But I tell you that Elijah has come, and they did to him whatever they pleased, as it is written of him.

As well as these sayings which are prophetic and apocalyptic in form we shall have to consider other sayings of Jesus: wisdom logia, 'I' sayings and other parables,[4] by means of which he expounded his message of the Kingdom. In the first place let us concentrate on the types of sayings listed above.

Even a fairly cursory glance at these sayings shows the very substantial diversity of type and content. The contrast is perhaps sharpest and most obvious between the first and fourth groups. In the first group the majority of sayings show Jesus announcing salvation as a present reality; in the fourth he predicts its coming in the future. Closer examination, however, shows that the tension between present and future runs through the groups. The Lucan beatitudes in group 1 have a clear future reference, just as the sayings in the fourth group which attack apocalyptic speculation about the coming of the Kingdom, emphasize its present—or imminent—reality; so especially Luke 17:20f., 23f. Again sayings in the second and third groups seem to have a general orientation to the future, while their point is to call people to a present attitude of watchfulness and repentance. But even here there is emphasis on the mighty works which have been done, as in Matthew 11:21, which demands the total reorientation of men's hearts. Thus some tension between the present and future orientation of Jesus' prophetic apocalyptic sayings seems to be generally characteristic of them. The tension, however, may be differently expressed. On the one hand the present reality of Jesus' words and works may indicate the coming of the Kingdom which will embrace the future as well as the present. On the other there may be a very strong divergence between sayings which look to a future son of man figure coming on clouds to judge men and those which are much more closely orientated to Jesus and his works and sayings and the Kingdom which he proclaims. *Prima facie* it seems likely that if there were indeed such tensions in Jesus' preaching they may well have been distorted into outright contradictions by different groups in the early Christian community. This at least seems more plausible than to suppose that the outright contradictions, such as there are, go back to a single source in Jesus.

Contradictions of this kind may, I believe, be found between those sayings such as Luke 17:20, 23f., which reject the demand for signs of the coming of the Kingdom, and those which offer a detailed scenario of the end, such as are found in Mark 13:5–27. The fact moreover that the sayings in Mark 13:5–27 are more typical of Jewish apocalyptic revelations of supernatural mysteries than of the rest of the sayings attributed to Jesus in the synoptic tradition leads one further to suppose that it is these sayings which have been subsequently introduced into the tradition,[5] rather than the sayings like Luke 17:20. Similarly the son of man saying which is found in the Markan apocalypse, Mark 13:26f., is linked with doctrines about election and with references to the signs which precede it in a way that makes it more than likely to be a later introduction.

However, even if we exclude Mark 13:5–27 and other similar material from the corpus of Jesus' own prophetic apocalyptic sayings, we are still left with the problem of reconciling future and present eschatology within his preaching. Numerically the weight of the sayings is on the side of the future, and this is notably so in those sayings which are predictive or which are designed to urge people to rep⌐⌐t and to await its coming in the second and third groups. Nevertheless the first group of sayings remains and is powerfully supported by other sayings and parables which have a similar reference to the present.[6] Such sayings are moreover very distinctive within a first-century Jewish context, and indeed arguably constitute some of the most distinctive material attributed to Jesus in the synoptic tradition. Hence I propose to start with them in order to discover to what extent the conventional associations which the notion of the Kingdom carried in first-century Judaism are here being remoulded by Jesus. Perhaps then we shall be able later to assess the authenticity of other prophetic-apocalyptic sayings of a more specifically predictive kind.

In general terms kingship is a notion whose core meaning in the ancient world was power, sovereignty, supremacy, right. The king rules in power over his subjects. He does so by divine right; he is duly appointed, anointed, enthroned and acclaimed.[7] He rules, or should rule, according to divine law and justice.[8] The king is thus not simply a figure of strength and power, as is the lion or horse, but of cosmic power: he is the one through whom divine power and justice are channelled. His power then is not naked, amoral power, but the holy power of justice and mercy. The idea of kingship occurs in a wide range of instances within the Old Testament tradition.[9] Used of God it occurs in the ancient myth of the divine king who yearly renews the creation after its winter death. In the cult the people pray to God to come and reign and renew the earth.[10] But equally in Israel God's reign is seen in his guidance of Israel, his 'mighty acts' by which he has preserved and rescued his people in the past and will continue to do so in the future. Thus to speak of the Kingdom of God is to speak of God's power over creation and over the nations; it is to speak of that power which holds the destiny of all men in his hands and on which Israel's hopes are centred.[11]

More specifically, the idea of the Kingdom of God is related to the actual institution of the kingship in Israel, as it features in Israel's historical tradition. It is of course true that kingship was not unequivocally welcomed in Israel. It was a foreign innovation whose institution could be seen as an act of disloyalty to Yahweh.[12] But a more powerful tradition represented in the Psalms and the historical books sees the king as God's agent, the concrete representation of the divine will and power: 'Give the King thy judgements, O Lord.'[13] Moreover in Israel's history the reign of David is looked on as an ideal age and hence serves as a focus for future hopes. David becomes the figure of a future, anointed deliverer who will save Israel from her enemies and institute a reign of peace and justice.[14] Such hopes become increasingly transcendental in times of great national distress: Daniel in his vision[15] looks for a heavenly figure who will come to restore God's kingdom when earthly efforts can be of no avail. And if the efforts of the Maccabees shortly proved him wrong, the image of a heavenly redeemer figure remained in the tradition to provide hope and comfort to subsequent generations of Jews in their oppression.

Daniel interestingly shows two aspects of the development of the conventions relating to the use of kingship in Judaism. The first is that in Daniel kingship is also closely associated with the institutions of oppression of the Jewish people: so that here the Kingdom of *God* is contrasted with the kings and kingdoms of the earth.[16] The second, which can be seen clearly from Daniel 7, is that the notion of God's Kingdom is associated with the notion of judgement, in particular with the *destruction* of the wicked.[17] The notion of kingship and judgement were of course widely associated. Equally justice was conceived widely in terms of punishments and rewards, with 'destroying all the wicked in the land'.[18] What is striking here is the prominence given to the notion of God's avenging, destroying justice, which is portrayed in terms of the flames of fire which constitute his throne.[19] This is clearly related to the writer's apprehension of Israel's condition as a people oppressed by evil rulers who must be destroyed. There is here not so much a change in the associations of the term 'kingship' as an emphasis thrown on to the vindictive and destructive aspects of judgement.

All this is to do no more than to indicate some of the conventional associations of kingship language prior to the first century A.D. For a more detailed consideration of these associations let us turn to movements contemporary with Jesus.

Of these the closest, geographically, to Jesus is the Zealot movement which has its origin in Judas the Galilean.[20] The immediate cause of the uprising under Judas is the census by Cyrenius.[21] The grounds for this revolt, given by Josephus, are that to submit to the census would be to accept slavery; and that God would help the Jews only if they actively worked and fought for their freedom.[22] Judas is further reported to have rebuked his people for paying taxes to the Romans and for recognizing mortals as rulers as well as God.[23]

Judas's military response to the Romans is based on certain clearly held dogmas, central to which is the belief that God alone is King.[24] The implications of this belief for Judas were also clear: one must refuse obedience to the Romans specifically in the matter of taxes, and one must take active steps to overthrow them, secure in the belief that God was stronger than they.

Now the belief that God alone was King is nothing particularly new or original to Judas the Galilean. It can be found in a considerable range of inter-testamental texts frequently used in address to God in prayer.[25] Its widespread first-century A.D. usage suggests that it goes back beyond Judas. What is significant about Judas is that he clearly accepted a number of implications as following from this which were not previously accepted. He insisted (a) that obedience to the only King meant not giving obedience to others; (b) that obedience to the only King entailed the duty of freeing oneself, if necessary by violent means, from others. One may reasonably conjecture that the belief which governs such implications is one which asserts that 'king' means one who requires *active* obedience from his subjects in all important fields of life, obedience which may certainly entail military service. Moreover the requirement of military service is clearly linked with the belief that God is a God of battles who will overthrow and destroy his enemies. This gives a rather different twist to the notion of God's avenging justice which we saw in Daniel 7 linked with the idea of the heavenly assize. It is then justified to see here a shift in the tradition from a view of God's kingly power which believes that he will act at the end of time to judge and destroy his enemies to one which believes he is now calling men to deliver themselves from tyranny—in which cause he will provide decisive support. It is thus difficult to know to what extent God's kingdom was conceived of as a present or future reality. Certainly Judas does not appear to have believed that the world had temporarily been given over to Satan, before God finally established his rule. He *may* have seen the census as the point of apocalyptic testing prior to the full establishment of God's authority over the Romans. Certainly his insistence on co-operation with God as a necessary condition of God's active intervention presupposes that God will indeed act, and presumably act finally.[26]

The Zealots provide the geographically nearest example of the use of kingship language to Jesus. We should also note some points about the use of such language in Jewish prayers of the time, for here we can see something of the Pharisaic use of the term. Hengel has given examples of the widespread use of this term in the literature of the time.[27] What for our purpose is significant is the linking of the notion of the Kingdom of God in the later Rabbinic tradition with the daily recitation of the Shema. Here the monotheism of the

Shema is linked with a whole system of religious observance and practice in which notions of purity and avoidance of pollution play a central part. 'To take the yoke of the Kingdom upon oneself' is to submit oneself to the purifying discipline of Rabbinic practice, to live out a life carefully fenced off from alien influence.[28] Thus the affirmation of God's sole kingship implies not military revolt but the submission of one's whole life to the regulations of the Torah, notably to its ritual prescriptions.[29] It means severing oneself from all that is *outside* the realm of God's rule, viz. from all those who do not 'take the yoke upon themselves'. Such severance does not entail military action but probably the expectation that God will ultimately destroy his enemies. Equally where taking the yoke of the Kingdom upon oneself is associated with the necessity of daily set prayers and of following a complex set of ritual prescriptions we may reasonably conjecture that the God who is addressed as King in such prayers is conceived of as a God of holiness and purity such that he will not tolerate the presence of that which is ungodly, impure, polluted.

The Kingdom language is also to be found in another interesting modification which again has a long history. In the War Rule, preserved in the Qumran Library, the notion of God's rule (*malkuth*) is found in relation to another similar pair of terms: the dominion (*memshalah*) of Satan and the dominion of the Community.[30] To be a member of the *memshalah* of the community meant both that one expected to vanquish the hosts of Satan and that one must prepare oneself by strict spiritual discipline for the coming struggle. Again purity regulations play an important part in this understanding of the dominion notably in the preparation for the struggle. Such traditions which, according to Becker, go back to a period earlier than Qumran, were clearly taken up by the community. In the community rule the notion of a final apocalyptic struggle gains less attention, though it is still clearly present, interestingly linked to the notion of two Messiahs: a priestly and a kingly one.[31] But the emphasis is now more strongly on the discipline of the community in which purity again plays an important part. There is nothing in itself remarkable about this: the document is expressly about the ordering of the community's life. Nevertheless it may well be that it represents also a general shift of attention from the apocalyptic expectation of the final battle to the community's struggle to keep itself pure from external influence. This does not amount to a major change in the associations of the term dominion from the War Rule. There and in the Community Rule dominion is associated both with the military destruction of one's enemies and with preserving the purity of the community and its worship. The difference between the two is one of emphasis.

It is interesting to contrast the Pharisees and the Essenes at this point. If it is true that they both have their origin in the Hasidic movement then I think one can see how they have both preserved important conventions governing the use of Kingdom language, conventions linking God's sovereignty over all earthly powers with his holiness and purity and with his refusal to tolerate that which is evil and impure. As between the Pharisees and Essenes there may have been differences about the implications of kingship-sentences with respect to the manner of God's asserting his rule over all the earth; Qumran may have been more open to the notion that it would involve active struggle on the part of the community. There certainly do seem to have been considerable divergences of opinion about the implications of such sentences in virtue of the conventions concerning God's purity.[32] For Qumran it meant withdrawal into the desert; for the Pharisees the law was given to the people to guide them in their daily life. The Pharisees, that is, believed that holiness was possible under the existing conditions of foreign rule, by virtue of some kind of inner immigration; something which both the Zealots and Qumran denied.

Lastly a word must be said about John the Baptist in this context even if he probably did not use the term 'Kingdom of God.' John preached repentance and baptism for the forgiveness of sins in the face of the coming judgement of God.[33] We shall consider John's teaching in more detail in relation to Jesus' teaching about the End, but here one feature is of major importance. For all the groups which we have been considering what distinguished those whom God would ultimately vindicate from those whom he would destroy was obedience to Torah, even if emphasis was laid on different aspects of Torah and different hermeneutical principles for its interpretation were advanced. In John the Baptist, as far as we can see, we find a twofold attack on Jewish particularism: an attack directed against Jewish reliance on descent from Abraham[34] and a diminution of the importance of Torah as a criterion for judgement and the adoption of what can be described as a natural ethic, applicable to the situation of Roman soldiers as well as to Jews in all walks of life.[35] That is to say in John there is a major shift in the fundamental assumptions about power and value. God is no longer a God who will have dealings only with his chosen, whose circumcision is a sign of the covenant between them; nor a God who will have dealings only with the pure. He is a God who will reward works of fundamental humanity and justice and equally punish those who neglect them. This break which John made with an emphasis on the ritual prescriptions of Torah is important for understanding Jesus' use of Kingdom language, particularly in view of the known contact between Jesus and John.

One might characterize these various usages of kingship language at the time of Jesus by saying that the term is either associated, as in Qumran or the Pharisees, with an intensification of Torah obedience and a strong emphasis on ritual purity or else that there is a relative indifference to detailed observance of the Law coupled with a fierce rejection of claims to sovereignty by foreign powers, strong loyalty to certain Jewish institutions and the demand for total commitment to a plan of action for national liberation and renewal as in the Zealots. In this respect the Zealot movement of Judas the Galilean may be referred to as 'radically theocratic',[36] by which is meant a movement which rejects any foreign intrusion into the running of Israel's sacred institutions and which therefore sees the involvement of the Herodians and the high-priestly class in Jerusalem with the Roman government as deeply subversive of Jewish freedom and independence. By contrast the Pharisees and Essenes are much more concerned with the establishment of a sacred realm which guarantees them access to God and hence religious protection and power. For them salvation ultimately lies with God's destruction of the wicked, the impure; meanwhile it is to be found in separation from the impure, in fencing oneself off from all contamination from external forces.

97

All of this can be related to the situation of social anomie which, as we saw in Chapter 4, obtained in first-century Palestine and which may have been particularly acutely felt in Galilee. Under such conditions there is likely to occur either an intensification or else a radicalization of norms.[37] That is to say, either existing norms are reinforced by an insistence on their detailed application, or else there is a tendency to emphasize only certain selected—even new—norms, while discarding many of the traditional norms which have become impossible to observe. The situation that we find in Jesus' lifetime is one where patterns of response to anomie which intensify the norms, like those of the Pharisees and Essenes, seem to predominate. Here we see the development of systems of legal interpretation which reinforce Torah by specifying its application to the Jews' changing circumstances and by supplementing Torah where it has no rulings to offer. On the other side are responses like those of the Zealots and John the Baptist and Jesus which concentrate on certain basic demands, abandoning the attempt to construct a complex set of regulations for every situation. Such responses to the situation in Galilee are theocratic in the sense discussed above and also radically innovative in that they break with existing norms and mores, thus making possible the introduction of new norms and codes of behaviour which take shape around certain fundamental assumptions about power. These are expressed in the demands of the charismatic-prophetic leader[38] to follow him and to obey God, whose will is expressed in certain radical commands: variously, to wage war on the Romans, to love one's enemies.

It is not my intention to offer *explanations* for the particular nature of Jesus' radical response to the situation of Judaism in first-century Galilee: his emphasis on God's love and forgiveness. The broad analysis of social factors pertaining at the time does not allow more than the kind of classification which we have just offered.[39] At most one might venture the suggestion that the conditions of severe economic hardship must have made the Pharisaic response to anomie with its emphasis on tithing and its restrictions on farmers difficult for many Galilean peasants to follow. Hence more radical alternatives, which broke sharply with the existing norms,[40] which were opposed to foreign domination and mores and which proposed new alternative norms, were likely to have been a more lively option in Galilee. To say anything more would be not simply deterministic but incomplete explanation. What I want to do is to show *how* in the light of certain beliefs which Jesus clearly held—viz. that God was a God of forgiveness and mercy who willed that men should love their enemies and forgive each other—he set about transforming the traditions of his day and the apprehensions of God, man and the world which they enshrined.

The fundamental problem in giving such an account is to show both continuity and change. As Professor Dahl has it, we have to show the distinctiveness of Jesus' teaching at the same time as doing justice to 'historical considerations of synchronic similarity and diachronic continuity'.[41] Or to put it in different terms, we have to show how Jesus communicated and expressed new beliefs and views in a language many of whose terms had strong conventional associations contrary to the beliefs he held. In part, we shall argue, he did this by deleting some of the associations of a particular term, e.g. kingdom, retaining its core-meaning and bringing it into association with other ideas and terms; in part, by rejecting outright the use of certain terms, e.g. purity. There are also cases where he uses a term in such a way that very little of its original sense remains, e.g. rewards.

This is our basic task. The question why Jesus believed so strongly in the mercy and forgiveness of God when many contemporaries held such widely differing views cannot, obviously, be answered solely in terms of social factors when it is already admitted that others under similar circumstances held different views. We can point to Jesus' association with John as having perhaps influenced his beliefs in respect of certain aspects of the Law and the End. Some have even suggested that Jesus' espousal of 'pacifist' as opposed to 'militaristic' values is not unconnected with the defeat of the Zealot risings and the relative stability of Antipas' rule which made military and political solutions to the problems of anomie fundamentally unrealistic.[42] But this does not explain why Jesus took this particular path, nor the reasons for his elaboration of it in the particular way that he did. The most one can say is that the calamities which befell the Jews at Sepphoris and the firm control

99

which Antipas exercised over Galilee may well have led Jesus to the conclusion that *if* God was to vindicate his people, to establish his rule, it would not be through military struggle, just as his awareness of the burdens which bore upon the Jewish people may well have led him to look for alternative solutions and accounts of God's action. However, his conviction that God was indeed in process of establishing his rule, and the manner in which he conceived and experienced 'the Kingdom' are things for which we can offer no such explanation.

As we have said our basic task is to show *how* Jesus communicated and expressed his new beliefs and views about God, man and the world in terms which could be understood by his contemporaries.[43] Putting it simply, Jesus had to use terms which were understood by his contemporaries or they could not have understood him at all; but he had to use them differently, if he was to say something new. As we have seen he chose to utter new truths in terms of the 'Kingdom', a term which had strongly nationalistic as well as— variously—militaristic and ritualistic associations. I would contend that he could use such a term, despite its conventional associations, because its core-meaning, God establishing his rule over men, is something which could, if stripped of its existing associations, be used to talk about God's dealing with Jews *and* Gentiles in quite new ways. By contrast the term 'purity' was so firmly defined in terms of separation, that it is hard to see how in the context it could have been reworked, even if in other periods and communities it could be to some extent associated with moral purity, and so stripped of some of its—for Jesus—more unusable associations. In this sense Jesus' choice is, as we have suggested in Chapter 2,[44] interestingly analogous to that of Black Consciousness leaders who had to choose from among the terms available to them to refer to Black–White relations.

What I want to argue is that Jesus changed the conventional associations of the Kingdom term, first, by the *context* in which he chose to utter it. In this he succeeded in deleting its militaristic and ritual associations and bringing it into association with notions of forgiveness and healing, of joy and service. These new associations were then, secondly, further developed in the parables and thirdly given more explicit form in his teaching about the Law and about providence and history. In this chapter we shall concentrate principally on the context of his kingdom sayings, making some reference to the further elaboration of the new associations in the parables.

By 'context' I do not mean the precise historical circumstances of any given utterance, something which it would anyway be difficult to ascertain, but rather the setting of such utterances in the general context of certain actions which are typical of Jesus' activity during his life. The point I have in mind can again be illustrated by reference to the rise of Black Consciousness and Black Power. The reworking of the term 'black' was achieved by the use of certain basic slogans, such as 'Black is beautiful', in the context of certain kinds of actions and manners. Thus Afro-hairstyles and styles of dress—all-white suits—which emphasized black physical characteristics, as well as styles of speech and behaviour—relaxed and humorous self-confidence in dealings with whites by contrast with submissiveness or 'cheekiness', certain acts of defiance—all served to delete the negative associations and replace them with those which asserted the worth and distinctive value of blacks. In a similar way certain types of actions performed by Jesus, his sharing meals with tax collectors and sinners, his healings and exorcisms, his call to discipleship, served to delete some of the conventional associations of the term 'kingdom' and replace them with others.

A problem arises here. How sure can we be that we know what were the typical actions of Jesus in this sense? As we have already seen[45] Dibelius and Bultmann disagree on the trustworthiness of the paradigms or apophthegms which constitute a good deal of our evidence for Jesus' actions. Dibelius believes that they represent the earliest kind of stories about Jesus which would subserve the interests of Christian preaching, viz. 'to win men and further to convince and confirm those whom they had won'.[46] Such stories were in short 'edifying', not neutral accounts, but told to make a point about Jesus and probably to lead to further reflection and teaching. They were sermon material. Dibelius regards such stories as substantially reliable. 'The nearer a narrative stands to the sermon, the less it is questionable, or likely to have been changed by romantic, legendary or literary influences.'[47] Indeed he concludes that they are so un-marked by such influences that one can only place them in the first decade after Jesus' death, when eyewitnesses of the events were still alive. If eyewitnesses could check and correct, then that is a guar-antee for the 'relative reliability' of the paradigms.[48]

Bultmann's analytic approach to the subject leads him to quite different results. For him the stories are to be classified as apophth-egms—stories which lead up to a saying of Jesus. Sometimes such stories have been created to provide a suitable setting for an isolated saying as, for example, Mark 2:15–17 where the point of the saying is only loosely related to the situation.[49] In other cases, the saying was from the beginning handed on with its setting as with the healing of the paralytic (Mark 2:1–11) where the saying has been added to an original miracle story to justify the Church's forgiveness of sins by reference to its healings; or the greatest commandment (Mark 12:28–34), where however Bultmann offers no equivalent explanation for its genesis. Bultmann then argues that, if the settings of such sayings as Mark 2:17 are manifestly 'ideal settings', then this is also true of other settings which are less obviously creations, because of the detail they contain. He concedes that it is more than probable that Jesus performed actions of the kind described, but the point is that the settings were composed for the sayings which were to be used for polemical and apologetic purposes, i.e. that they were not historical accounts created out of an interest in the events themselves. Hence, while he does not wish to deny that tradition may have made use of historical memory e.g. 'about his (sc. Jesus') intercourse with the tax-gatherers',[50] he does urge caution against taking the whole class of stories as basically reliable narratives.[51]

It is in a sense perhaps enough for our purposes to note that on either view it is granted that certain actions were typical of Jesus. One might even turn the point and say that the fact that Jesus' consorting with tax-collectors was regarded as typical of Jesus' behaviour by the early Church is more significant than the fact that he, on one or two occasions, ate with them. However justice de-mands that one takes some stance on the issue itself here. Briefly: while Bultmann's analysis of the apophthegmata seems to give a more adequate classification of the material and to show their relatedness to other contemporary forms, I fail to see why he should conclude from the fact that in some cases ideal settings have been constructed for originally isolated sayings, that therefore the settings in all cases are similarly 'ideal'. For example, if the saying about the greatest commandment should go back to Jesus, then it seems more than likely that it was preserved in the form of an apophthegm. But if so, then there can surely be no reason to suppose that those who preserved accurately the saying constructed an ideal setting for it when an actual one was available. Hence we may agree that the emphasis is indeed on the saying; that in some cases typical settings have been constructed for originally isolated sayings; and still affirm against Bultmann that there are other apophthegms where the setting was preserved accurately with the saying. With these preliminaries let us now turn to a consideration of Jesus' use of Kingdom language.

Jesus announced the coming of the Kingdom in the context of his ministry to the sick, to the possessed, the poor, the outcast and the oppressed. This context was seen, at the latest by the earliest Church, as eschatological. That is to say, the events of Jesus' ministry corresponded to those which were expected to occur in the final age. The pericope which records the Baptist's question to Jesus and Jesus' answer[52] makes this clear; just as it makes clear the difference between John's expectation of a coming 'stronger' one who would judge men, purifying the just and destroying the wicked with fire, and the actual character of Jesus' teaching and healing work. The Isaianic prophecies,[53] which are alluded to, show the conformity between Jesus' work and eschatological expectations of a type rather different from John's. Thus we can already say from a consideration of the setting of Jesus' proclamation of the Kingdom in his ministry as a whole that, while he retains the core-meaning of the term, viz. that the coming Kingdom of God means that God will establish his rule over his people thus fulfilling their deepest hopes, he modifies this in so far as such rule is now said to be established through the healing of the sick and the preaching to the poor. This already indicates a distinct modification of the traditional association of the term with the destruction of God's enemies. Equally of course the fact that such healing is already occurring in

103

Jesus' ministry implies clearly that in some important sense God's power and spirit are already at work, are already available to men, rather than being an object solely of their expectation.

A closer examination of Jesus' typical actions allows us to form a somewhat clearer picture of how Jesus achieved this modification in the use of Kingdom language. First, Jesus' healings and exorcisms. Illness, especially mental illness, was understood in first-century Palestine in terms of demonic possession. That Jesus shared this understanding is indicated fairly clearly by the Beelzebub controversy.[54] Jesus' cures and exorcisms are a sign of the divine power overcoming Satan and his forces in the world: 'If I by the finger of God cast out demons, the Kingdom of God has come upon you.' In this Jesus' actions bring him close to contemporary figures like Honi the Circle-Drawer and Hanina ben Dosa[55] who found in prayer the source of divine power which enabled them to perform similar deeds. The linking of such deeds specifically with the coming of the Kingdom can be contrasted with the more aggressive and militaristic associations of the term in the Qumran literature which we examined. Thus, whereas in the War Rule and the Community Rule the rule of Satan would be overcome only in the battle between his armies and the armies of the covenant, here Satan is overcome by the power of God flowing out of those who pray.[56] Moreover with such prayer, if we can press the analogy with Hanina ben Dosa at this point, what is important is not the regular observance of daily times of prayer as in Rabbinic Judaism, but rather the quality of the prayer which unites the charismatic with God. Such prayer, that is to say, is conceived of as a direct experience of the power of God, and such experience has its visible correlate in the healing of the sick and the possessed. Moreover Jesus' teaching on prayer links the prayer for the coming of the Kingdom to the address to God as Father as well as to the petition for forgiveness;[57] here the basic beliefs which now govern Jesus' understanding of the coming of the Kingdom of God become apparent. God is not a God of battles, a warrior destroying his enemies, but a Father who forgives and commands his children to forgive. This will be developed in Jesus' more explicit teaching about God's will and nature.

Jesus' proclamation of the coming of the Kingdom occurs also in the context of his fellowship meals with his followers and with tax-collectors and sinners. Meals have played an important part in the history of Israel. The cultic meal was seen as a means of partaking in the power of God and sharing in communion with him.[58] Often this was celebrated in the form of a communal sacrifice[59] for which the participants must be sanctified beforehand. The participants then became brothers, not only of each other, but of Yahweh. Such occasions were occasions of celebration and joy. In the post-exilic period such sacrifices largely disappear; the sin and guilt offerings of the priests gain prominence, although these too tend to assume the character of a common table-fellowship with Yahweh. By Jesus' time the principal meal was the Passover meal which celebrated Israel's deliverance and Yahweh's faithfulness. At the same time[60] the meal becomes a common symbol for the eschatological salvation.[61] The distinctiveness of Jesus' fellowship meals[62] can be brought out in three ways. In the first place they appear to have been relatively spontaneous. That is to say they were not tied either to particular cultic times as was Passover, nor were they, as in Qumran, part of a strictly ordered pattern of communal life. This is significant for an understanding of the spontaneous, unscripted nature of the eruption of the divine power in Jesus' ministry. But the very fact that meals were seen to form a part of his ministry[63] sheds light on his preaching. Here the contrast with John the Baptist is again illuminating. The Baptist is properly contrasted as an ascetic figure with the charismatic nature of Jesus' appearance.[64] John comes dressed in camel's hair and eating locusts and wild honey, while Jesus is a 'glutton and a drunkard',[65] whose followers cannot fast so long as he is with them. This represents a powerful emphasis on the present reality of salvation, on the enjoyment of life and fulfilment now. Thirdly, Jesus' meals were open to those who were morally and ritually impure, to those who posed a serious threat to the survival of Judaism. The tradition records this as being a particular offence to the Pharisees[66] and this would certainly be consonant with their concern to set ritual and actual boundaries between themselves and those who accommodated with Hellenism and the occupying powers. Equally Jesus' meals stand in stark contrast to the meals of the Qumran community, which were open to members of the community only after an initial period of testing and purification and which thus bear much closer resemblance to the earlier communal sacrifices.[67] Equally the Qumran meals were strictly ordered in accordance with the hierarchical structure of the community and with regulations governing the purity of food and vessels.

Thus Jesus' announcement of the coming of the Kingdom of God in the context of his spontaneous, festive meals with the poor and the outcasts suggests that a number of conventional associations of the term 'kingdom' were being deleted. Most evidently the associations relating to the purity and holiness of God and to his avenging judgement were clearly called in question by Jesus' tolerating the presence of sinners and tax-collectors at such Kingdom meals. Jesus' understanding of God must be quite different from that of the Pharisees and of Qumran or of the Zealots if the Kingdom of God is proclaimed in such a context, as indeed is indicated by the parables of the lost sheep, the lost coin and the prodigal. Moreover the celebration of such meals while Israel is still under foreign rule with the, albeit indirect, agents of such foreign rule, challenges the sharp disjunction which Zealots made between the Kingdom of God and the kingdom of Caesar, which was no kingdom at all. God's Kingdom is not established only where other rulers have been overthrown; rather God's power erupts in the midst of oppression, forgiving and healing, and wherever that power is, there is cause for rejoicing. The world is not, that is to say, given over to Satan, or to Caesar, until God will restore his rule over it by destroying the alien rulers. On the contrary, God is already present in this 'evil age', overcoming it by his mercy.

One other aspect of the general context of Jesus' proclamation may be noticed. Jesus proclaims the coming of the Kingdom at the same time as he invites—some at least—to join him as his disciples in a vagrant ministry of healing, preaching and exorcism. As Hengel has shown[68] Jesus' call to men to follow him, to leave all that they have, even to leave the dead to bury their dead, has a number of interesting parallels with apocalyptic Zealot circles. The inspired Zealot leaders also called on men to follow them and to leave security and possessions in order to engage in a holy war against

106

their enemies. Jesus' discipleship sayings calling on men to share his own vagrant mendicant existence also stressed the radical break with security and possessions and with cherished customs and beliefs that is necessary if men are to follow him. Discipleship is not a thing to be lightly undertaken but rather a task which must be weighed up carefully before one embarks on it. In this Jesus clearly modifies the Zealot convention which conceives active obedience to God in the face of foreign rule as entailing military resistance. For him the 'holy war'[69] to which men are called is to be waged not with military might but with the power of love and prayer: 'Love your enemies and pray for those who persecute you, so that you may be sons of your Father who is in heaven'.[70] These sayings serve strongly to emphasize that Jesus' call to share in the fellowship of the eschatological community is not simply an invitation to some kind of paradisal, if illusory, conventicle, but to a missionary eschatological community.

At this point we may begin to appreciate something of the force of Jesus' preaching. Jesus proclaims the coming of the Kingdom of God as a present reality, as the reality of God's forgiveness and mercy in a world of oppression and enmity. The Kingdom of God is something which for Jews represents all their deepest aspirations and longings for deliverance from foreign domination and oppression, for renewal, peace, joy, justice. To announce the coming of the Kingdom is to awaken hopes of a Kingdom of peace and justice and a paradise of love and joy and communion beyond all trouble and tribulation. Such hopes in the tradition had been directed however in particular directions. They were channelled into resistance to foreign infiltration and control and into hopes of the eventual destruction of one's enemies, hopes which could flare into active resistance. Such hopes are nationalistic and exclusivist. They are based on a vision of God as a God who will destroy all that is opposed to him and who will reward those who separate themselves and are purified and refined by remaining faithful through tribulation. John the Baptist breaks out of the nationalistic Jewish frame of such thought, while still clinging to a notion of God's destructive power in judgement. Jesus, however, announces the Kingdom in the context of a preaching ministry which is marked by healing and exorcism and by fellowship meals with his followers among whom are numbered the outcasts and collaborators, and by his call to men to follow him. In this way a term which has a high affective charge for first-century Jews by virtue of its association with the community's hopes is taken over by Jesus in his very different account of God's action. Again, precisely because Jesus' use of the term is so strikingly different, we may assume that it could lead to deep resistance on the part of those who saw in Jesus' views a dire threat to the hopes the term so powerfully evoked.

But if it is fairly easy to see why Jesus' teaching should have provoked strong resistance, it is perhaps less immediately clear why he should have found a measure of popular support. This can best be understood in the light of the situation which, we suggested at the end of the last chapter, obtained in first-century Galilee. The people to whom Jesus preached are those on whom the burdens of taxation, rent, climate and terrain fell heavily and who therefore found it difficult to meet their basic human, family needs, not to mention the requirements of their own group's agreed values and practices. Some doubtless struggled along as best they could, some abandoned any attempt to uphold the group values, others became petty officials in the service of the Herods. As we shall see Jesus' message to such people is not that they should redouble their efforts to obey the law, but rather to call them to a radical ethic of love and forgiveness. This is related in his Kingdom sayings and the parables to a message to the weary and downtrodden of God's forgiveness and mercy which enlarges and transforms their experience of poverty and loss.

The dominant note of such a proclamation and ministry is joy and confidence and this is expressed clearly in the way in which, in his parables and sayings, as well as in his own actions, Jesus exploits the imagery and symbolism of meals and feasting,[71] of new wine,[72] and specifically of the eschatological messianic banquet.[73] But such joy is not the joy of the untroubled, of the insouciant. On the contrary those who are invited to share in the Kingdom are the oppressed people of Galilee. They are the devout Jews, but also the collaborators and the sinners. What is happening here is a deep remoulding of the consciousness and experience of Israel. The Jews' experience of oppression, of loss, of deprivation of rights and of their religious heritage, of the long struggle to uphold their traditions, of economic worry and hardship, all this is caught up and *enlarged*. Those who are invited to the meal are the poor: but the poor number among themselves not only the oppressed minority of devout Jews, but the tax-collectors and the prostitutes, as well as the peasant-serfs whose work and economic position gave them little chance or encouragement to fulfil the Law and who were despised by the devout. Just as John had enlarged men's apprehension of justice and good, inviting them to see all men standing as equals before God's coming judgement, so too Jesus enlarges their apprehension of men's poverty and loss, inviting them to see themselves as the poor, the mourning, those who hunger and thirst after righteousness, the weary and the heavy laden, the prodigal and the lost, as beset by dark powers, and as burdened by overwhelming demands (the heavy yoke of the Law!), as broken, sick, in need of healing and comfort.[74] All this, one may note, in stark contrast with the self-understanding of the Pharisees as it is portrayed in the story of the publican and Pharisee at prayer.[75]

Yet again, such enlargement of men's consciousness is not simply an accusation, a condemnation of men. It is the basis of a new consciousness which is forged as images of men's oppression and deprivation, of their poverty, mourning, thirst, hunger, lostness, possession, sickness are brought into relation with images of acceptance, of fellowship, of renewal of fellowship and communion, of forgiveness. Jesus' invitation to the outcasts to share tables with him is an enormously powerful gesture of acceptance and graciousness. Again this is echoed and brought out in the parables and sayings: the prodigal son being feasted on his return, the lost sheep borne off in the arms of the shepherd, the woman's sense of release from anxiety and worry when she finds her coin: images which give full expression to this new sense of forgiveness and grace. Moreover men's apprehension of themselves as poor is further transformed in that not only do they know themselves both lost and found, both condemned and forgiven, both cast out and received back into the fold, but that they are also now called to be co-workers with God in his work of forgiveness. The poor, the weak and the outcast are to be God's agents in his work of overcoming darkness and enmity by the power of his light and forgiveness.

God then is a God whose power and rule over men are exercised through his mercy and forgiveness. No matter how far men have fallen into darkness—and Jesus clearly recognizes distinctions—God's invitation goes out to them to join in the fellowship meal of the sons of God. His mercy and grace is found in this invitation, in his acts of healing and exorcism, and those who accept his invitation and who share in the feast rejoice in the confidence that here they have found the very source of true power in the world, that which can withstand and overcome all darkness, the power of God which can heal and transform.

And just as God calls men through Jesus to his love-feast, so he calls them to follow Jesus in his mission to mankind. Here the experience of love and forgiveness received leads into a consciousness of the task which men are to take up, a task entered upon not without deliberation, but in the confidence that they are empowered to do so by the mercy and forgiveness they have received.

Jesus' use of the Kingship language represents, we have argued, a deep challenge to conventions which had previously governed its use in the Jewish tradition, and in consequence affected—or was designed to affect—the hopes and aspirations of Jews' consciousness of their oppression, and of their fears of external and internal changes. In the power of God's mercy and forgiveness lies new wine, which can heal the broken and overcome all evil, not by withdrawing from it or destroying it but by embracing and transforming it. Such a vision has far-reaching social implications. It opens up the vista of a new religio-social world, based not on tightly structured internal and external boundaries but on an internal dynamic and discipline (as we shall see) rooted in God's forgiving and accepting love. The constraints and compulsion in this new society are to be based not on barriers against external pressures or curbs and restraints on internal group rivalries and instability, but on the power of merciful love which creates, sustains and commissions its members: 'Love knows no compulsion save that which comes from itself.'[76]

Whether such a society can be achieved or must always remain a dream only partly realized is something to which the history of the Church provides at least one part of the answer. Clearly the multiplicity of forms of church order and structure shows the extent to which Jesus' preaching of the Kingdom remained—and remains—a powerful remoulding of certain vital religio-social apprehensions, rather than a construction of a specific and detailed religio-social world. But equally the history of the Christian Church, with its enormous vigour and ability to reform and construct social worlds which in some way incorporate this fundamental vision, demonstrates the power which Jesus' reworking of the Jewish tradition has had in sustaining, criticizing and constructing the attitudes and societies by which and in which men live.

As well as having social and ethical implications Jesus' preaching of the Kingdom also has a range of more theoretical or speculative implications relating to the nature of God and his governance of history and associated in the Judaism of his time with questions of God's just rule over history, his distribution of punishments and rewards. In the next chapter we shall look first however at how Jesus himself drew out the social and ethical implications of his preaching of the Kingdom before proceeding to a consideration of his more speculative theism.

6

Jesus and the Law of Purity

If Jesus substantially modified the conventional associations of the notion of Kingship in the Judaism of his time, then we should expect this to have consequences in relation to his use of other terms of theological importance. In this chapter I want to examine the way Jesus spoke about the Law. In particular, I want to focus attention on Jesus' sayings about cultic matters, about purity and defilement, because it is here that there are obvious discrepancies between the sayings in the synoptic tradition and those of Jesus' contemporaries. Here if anywhere one might feel on firm ground in attributing to Jesus views radically different from those of his contemporaries. If we can relate this to what we have argued about what he said in the Kingdom sayings we might have gone some way to understanding the nature of the change which he wrought.

However, just because the views attributed to Jesus in, for example, Mark 7:15 are so radically different from the views of most at least of his contemporaries their originality to him has come under suspicion. Some scholars would find it easier to see here the work of a subsequent generation of Jewish Christians as it breaks away from Judaism. Thus the need for critical sifting is great and what we gain on the swings of outright contradiction we may to some extent lose on the critical roundabouts.

Within the Jewish reform and renewal movements of the Second Temple period Torah had essentially a dual function. On the one hand strict observation of the Law emphasized Jewish distinctiveness from Hellenism; here laws concerning the sabbath, circumcision and purity, such as were given prominence by the priestly writers, were of particular importance. On the other hand, the Law

112

was at the very heart of the Jewish tradition and it was from a rediscovery of the Law that Jews might hope to draw strength and vitality for renewal. For the priestly tradition correct observance of the Law ensured the vitality of Jewish worship. It meant, in effect, the assurance that Yahweh was present in power in the cult. For others who drew more on the prophetic tradition the renewal of the Law meant placing a greater emphasis on the weightier matters of the Law, justice, mercy, praise and thanksgiving. In practice, these two strands are interwoven both in the biblical tradition and in the various movements of the post-biblical period of Judaism. In this chapter we shall focus specifically on the question of purity,[1] as it provides an important indicator of the way in which particular groups in ancient Judaism attempted to assert and maintain their distinctive identity in a hostile world. We may say then that the *meaning* of purity sentences in many cases will be related to such socio-political intentions. We shall however principally be interested in discerning *what is said* by sentences which contain the term 'purity'. To discover this about any known saying we shall have to know first the conventions which governed such sentences. Again in order to simplify the analysis we shall principally concentrate on the conventional associations of terms. In particular we shall want to determine the associations of terms like God's justice, holiness and mercy with others such as the Law, purity, the Gentiles and Israel. We shall further have to ask how any given saying or text may stand in relation to these conventions and to this end we shall have to examine the particular context in which it is uttered.

It is fairly clearly established that the idea of purity has its origin in the priestly caste of Israel.[2] It formed an important part of the programme of restoration after the Exile as is evidenced both by Ezekiel and by the priestly writings, especially Numbers and Leviticus, which contain the large majority of references.[3] The reform after the return from the Exile centred on the Jerusalem Temple and the purity regulations were formulated specifically, though not exclusively, with reference to participation in and the correct observation of Temple worship.[4] In particular such regulations were concerned to distinguish Israel's worship from that of foreign—idolatrous—cults. Renewal of this context meant a return to the traditions of Israel, specifically with regard to the Law and Temple worship; it also meant separation from those who were not dedicated to this programme.

Clearly a detailed analysis of the use of purity language in this long tradition is out of the question here. What we can say is that the notion of purity is fairly obviously related to the notions of the Law and of God's justice, holiness and mercy, and that there are fairly obvious links between such notions and notions about God's dealings with the Gentiles and Israel. Let us start by sketching out some of these networks of associated terms, before looking in more detail at the way they were used in first-century Judaism. The basic associations of the Law with God's justice, holiness and mercy can be fairly simply stated. God's justice is associated with his punishment of the wicked and his rewarding of the righteous, and equally wickedness and righteousness are further defined in terms of disobedience and obedience to the Law. Thus the Gentiles who transgressed the Law were punished by being cast out of the land, while Israel's faithfulness was rewarded by the gift of the land. God's holiness is associated with his avoidance and destruction of all that is impure, imperfect, and his purifying of all whom he chooses for himself. Thus only the pure, notably those specially chosen from among Israel, may approach him in worship, while the Gentiles must be kept from him. God's mercy is associated with his election of Israel, with the covenant and the revelation to Israel of the Law. Thus, if Israel obeys the Law, God will continue to watch over and care for it. The Gentiles are *eo ipso* outside God's covenant and the Law has not been revealed to them. At best they may come to the light through the good offices of Israel.

The question now is: how does the notion of purity, as employed in purity regulations, fit into this network of associated terms? It may be helpful in this respect to look at a particular text (Lev. 20:22–26)

> You shall therefore keep all my statutes and all my ordinances, and do them; that the land where I am bringing you to dwell may not vomit you out. And you shall not walk in the customs of the nation which I am casting out before you; for they did all

these things, and therefore I abhorred them. But I have said to you, 'You shall inherit their land, and I will give it to you to possess, a land flowing with milk and honey.' I am the LORD your God, who have separated you from the peoples. You shall therefore make a distinction between the clean beast and the unclean, and between the unclean bird and the clean; you shall not make yourselves abominable by beast or by bird or by anything with which the ground teems, which I have set apart for you to hold unclean. You shall be holy to me; for I the LORD am holy, and have separated you from the peoples, that you should be mine.

This is clearly a difficult passage but one might analyse it into the following lines of argument:

(a) Israel is to keep all Yahweh's statutes and not to do as the Gentiles did. If Israel does this it will inherit and possess the land; if not, like the Gentiles, they will be cast out. Thus *doing the Law* is associated here with *not doing as the Gentiles do*, and the consequences of doing the Law are contrasted with the consequences of doing as the Gentiles do. One may argue whether this association of 'doing the Law' with 'not doing as the Gentiles do' became conventional, such that it became for a Jew part of what is said by saying, for example, 'he does the Law'. I think, in view of the constant repetition of this theme in the tradition, that it is likely that in time it did, though this may well not be the case here in view of the way such statements are justified and argued for.

The other important point to notice is that the Gentiles' customs are said to be abhorrent to Yahweh. Here the same verb is used as is used later in the passage in the sentence: 'You shall not make yourselves *abominable* by beast . . .' (v.25). Yahweh's abhorrence of the Gentiles' customs, the Land's vomiting them out, are powerful images expressive of the utter incompatibility between God's nature, his holiness and the deeds of the Gentiles.

There follow two rather different lines of thought which specifically relate observation of purity regulations to Israel's election by Yahweh and to Yahweh's holiness.

(b) asserts that Yahweh has separated Israel from the peoples and that they shall therefore make a distinction between clean and unclean beasts.

(c) asserts that they shall not make themselves abominable by eating teeming animals because Yahweh has set such animals apart as unclean; whereas Israel is holy to him for he has separated it from the peoples.

The first of these sentences suggests strongly that purity regulations are seen as signifying the division between Jew and Gentile which Yahweh makes. What is being said is that observation of such regulations serves *as a reminder* of the distinction which has given them the land and on whose upholding Israel's life and relation to Yahweh depend. The second sentence forbids eating birds and beasts which teem because God has clearly distinguished them, not from the clean birds and beasts, but from the Jews. This suggests that a connection is being made here between beasts and birds which creep and the nations which do not live according to the Law. Here I find persuasive Mary Douglas's thesis[5] that 'creeping' as a mode of locomotion is regarded as anomalous. What is being said is that just as the Jews must not act like and must separate themselves from the Gentiles, so they must not eat or partake of that which is anomalous. One could say that, while the first sentence makes the 'sociological' point of purity regulations *explicit*, the second expresses this by means of a complex *analogy* between on the one hand *creeping* beasts and nations disobedient to the Law and on the other taking food into the body and having dealings with those outside the body politic. The context makes it clear that, at least at the redactional stage, the sociological sense of such purity regulations was fully acknowledged and understood.

So much for the conventions which associate doing the Law, and more specifically, observing the purity regulations, with separation from the Gentiles. The more positive convention associates observing the Law of purities with holiness and holiness with belonging to Yahweh. What is the meaning of purity regulations in this context? There is a clear link made between observation of purity regulations, avoidance of impurity, of that which is imperfect, not whole, etc., *and* the holiness which is a condition of belonging to God. This linking of purity and holiness as opposed to, say, mercy

116

and holiness, clearly makes certain points about what is of central importance in the Law. As we have said, purity regulations in the Second Temple period were most clearly associated with the Temple cult. Under such circumstances where the link between purity and holiness is stressed, one is in fact being told that it is the priests who first and foremost guarantee the bond between Yahweh and his people. They are the arbiters on matters of purity: just as they administer the cult where purity regulations are most essential for its correct operation.[6]

Simplifying, we can say that, to understand the development of the use of purity regulations in Jewish tradition, we shall have to look at two main clusters of associations, one which links observing such regulations, and indeed observing the Law as a whole, to 'not doing as the Gentiles do', i.e. to separating oneself from the Gentiles; another which asserts that keeping the Law of purities is essential for preserving the bond between Yahweh and Israel, his people; for God's holiness excludes all that is impure and contrary to the Law. How are such conventions in relation to purity developed in the Jewish renewal movements which start at the beginning of the second century B.C.?

Outside the priestly writings of the Old Testament and Ezekiel the principal references to purity occur among the various Jewish sects, specifically the Qumran community, the Pharisees and the Christians. Neusner argues that in 'Second Temple times these sectarian laws about purity would serve to differentiate from those who accept the predominant cult both priests and laymen who rejected the regnant priesthood or its conduct of the cult or its view of purity, and who therefore coalesced to form a sect.'[7] This is true, but it should be added that this inner-Jewish polemic should still be seen in the wider context of the Ḥasidic protest against Hellenism and the foreign adulteration of Judaism. What those who disagreed about the cult and purity were concerned with was not simply an academic liturgical point; it was a matter which went to the heart of Israel's struggle to preserve its identity, to find renewal and liberation. It was not simply a matter of control of the redemptive media over against other Jews, but of controlling them in such a way that they could as a community withstand the pressures of assimilation which bore heavily on all Jews.

The particular developments within which Jesus' sayings and actions are to be located have, that is to say, their origins in the Ḥasidic protest against Hellenism and in particular against the desecration of the Temple by Antiochus Epiphanes. From the beginning they are both Jerusalem and Temple orientated. Nevertheless their concern is for the national renewal of the whole nation and this sets up a certain tension evidenced by the diversity of sectarian groupings. The Pharisees, while apparently attempting to exercise control over the Temple worship, were also concerned with the purification of Jewish everyday life centred on the home, the table and the *ḥaburah*.[8] The Qumran community looked forward to the restoration of the true Temple worship but withdrew into the desert into their separated community where they could preserve the purity of the covenant and themselves form a kind of living Temple, a house of holiness.[9] By contrast the Sadducees seem to have been principally concerned to preserve the traditional form of Temple worship, ready to compromise politically with the ruling powers. The Zealots appear to have been much more concerned with national and religious independence than were the Sadducees, but there is evidence too for their zeal for the sanctuary and for circumcision and laws of purity.[10]

Such then is the broad context within which we may set Jesus' utterances on the subject of purity. Unfortunately much of our evidence for contemporary Jewish belief and practice is too fragmentary for a detailed comparison. What I propose, therefore, is to look in rather more detail at the way purity regulations related to general conventions about the Law and about God's justice, holiness and mercy at Qumran, and to see what light such a comparison may shed on Jesus' teaching. This may help to safeguard us against taking sayings out of their context in a whole system of religious thought, just as it may provide useful suggestions for understanding Jesus' own sayings.

The Qumran community had its origins in the Hasidic movement from which it broke away to establish a desert community based on strict observance of the Law, living in hope of the final destruction

118

of the wicked after the two Messiahs of Aaron and Israel. It is difficult to form an accurate picture of the development of the community's life and beliefs, but it is likely that, with the fading of its immediate hopes of divine intervention, its attention turned to the ordering of its own life and affairs as well as to the interpretation of its own history in relation to the purposes of God.[11] What we shall examine here is the stage of the community represented by the Manual of Discipline or Community Rule (1QS). There is good evidence that this document comes from a relatively late stage in the community's history.

In the Community Rule the notions of purity, pollution, atonement, holiness play an important part.[12] There are references to ritual washings in the community, to specially prepared meals and to the need to avoid contact with goods, food and drink belonging to those outside the community, as well as with the disobedient members of the sect. Equally, within the community there were priests who played a leading role in its ordering of government, just as the community invoked the imagery of the Temple to describe itself. But alongside this emphasis on purity and rites of purification we also find strong stress on the need for repentance, without which no lustration can be of any effect, and on the mercy of God who has chosen the members of the community and plucked them out of sin in which they were otherwise helplessly caught; and a strong ethical, parenetical element in the writings, enjoining the patient endurance of suffering, humility, love, though only for the brethren, and setting these together with prayer, above sacrifices and burnt offerings.[13] The priestly tradition and the prophetic tradition, that is to say, are interwoven in a way which many commentators have felt to be contradictory. This modification of the priestly equation between purity and holiness may well be related to the fact that the community did not control the Temple. Our task will be to see how the conventional associations of the notion have been adapted and interpreted by the community. In this we shall see first how the conventions relating observance of the Law to separation from the Gentiles and to belonging to Yahweh have been modified. Then in the light of that we shall consider the particular use of purity language in Qumran.

119

What distinguishes Qumran's attitude to the Law from that of other groupings in the Judaism of the time is that it is only to the community and its interpreters, notably the Teacher of Righteousness, that the true understanding of the Law has been given. The true meaning of the Law is something hidden and it has been revealed only to the community.[14] The knowledge which is thus given relates to the proper ordering[15] of the community and controls the details of its everyday life. It is the community's task to observe *all* the commandments of the Law.[16] Qumran's interpretation of the Law also relates to the understanding of the community's place in relation to the eschaton, to the particular time in which they are set.[17] The community's understanding of the Law is the very basis of its covenant relationship with God.[18] Only when the true meaning of the Law is grasped is it possible for men to follow the way of perfection and so draw near to the holiness and glory of God.[19] Repentance from their old ways and the rigorous obedience of the Law, properly understood, are what unites the elect to the source of all power and might, the All-Holy one who will finally overthrow and destroy the wicked.

The structure of the community reflects this understanding of Torah. The very word *yahad* (= community) comes from a root *whd* which means both to unify and to separate.[20] The members who enter the community must repent and disavow the world outside, taking an oath to adhere 'to God's truth, to walk in the way of his delight and to separate from all the men of falsehood who walk in the way of wickedness'.[21] Within the community there were ranks, membership of which was decided at the annual assembly and related to a member's progress in the understanding and doing of the Law. Further, there was a sharp distinction between the—ordinary—members of the Covenant, and the—select—Council of the Community. The latter were those who underwent further training and initiation and who thus qualified for the highest rank in the sect's hierarchy. It was to this group that the rules concerning lustrations, common meals and community of property applied which are set out in the Community Rule. These were set apart as holy, to prepare the way of the Lord through the study of the Law.

Set over the whole community were two figures, a priest and a guardian, who was the Teacher, the Maskil.

Thus the structure of the community[22] reflects the esoteric nature of its understanding of the Law. The true revelation is given only to the chosen and must be protected and hidden from the ungodly. Such revelations are thus given within the community only to those who have undergone a long process of separation and purification from any possible taint of wickedness. Thus not only between the world and the community are there sharp boundaries. Such boundaries also exist within the community, acting, as it were, as a series of increasingly fine sieves or filters to exclude wickedness from the heart of the community.

I think this account enables one to see clearly enough how the conventions regarding Torah have been modified at Qumran. Observance of Torah is still associated with separation from the Gentiles, with not doing as the Gentiles do. But observance of Torah now has to be further defined. Observance of Torah is further associated not only with not doing as the Gentiles do, but also with not doing the Law as it is observed by the Wicked Priest or the Pharisees. Positively, doing the Law is further defined in terms of doing the Law as it has been revealed to the Teacher of Righteousness. Hence boundaries are also drawn against other groups within Judaism. Repentance means not only turning away from lawlessness as such but from other Jewish interpretations of the Law. The community is so structured as to reflect these associations of observance of the Law. Only those who have been fully initiated into the esoteric understanding of the Law can be entrusted with the preservation and administration of the Law as interpreted to the *yaḥad* by the Teacher of Righteousness. What has occurred here is that the conventions have required further definition in the light of the conflicting uses made of them within the Jewish renewal movements taken as a whole. Different groupings develop different beliefs which may in time gain conventional status within their community.

Other changes in the conventions can be observed. In Leviticus 20 observance of the Law brings with it possession of the land. Qumran is an emigrant community which has gone into the desert in the expectation of the restoration of the land to the Sons of the

121

Covenant. In the light of Leviticus 20, which relates doing the Law to possession of the land, the experiences of the Jews in the Hellenistic period must be seen as a punishment for sin, or else the convention had to be abandoned. In 1QS the *yaḥad*'s worship is seen, in terms taken from the Temple cult, as atonement for the land, as a necessary condition of its restoration. As such the community has its place within Yahweh's plan for the restoration of Israel and the punishment of the wicked. In the meantime the *yaḥad* is not entirely without its reward, as we shall see when considering the use of purity language. The worship of the community and its study and observation of the Law represent already an enjoyment of God's presence itself.

Let us now, in the light of these remarks about Qumran's use of conventions relating to the Law in general, consider how purity language is used in Qumran. For this purpose we shall look first at the detailed regulations of which we have knowledge to see what their function was in the life of the community.

There is, of course, no reason to suppose that we know the full extent of the purity regulations in force at Qumran or in other groups elsewhere. We do know that new members had to avoid the property, food and drink of non-members, were forbidden to barter with them and allowed only to buy certain articles as deemed fit by their community.[23] On admission members were given a hoe with which to bury their excrement, a linen apron to cover their nakedness during ritual washings, and white garments signifying purity.[24] Admission to the ritual washings may have occurrred on admission or only after a period of testing and trial; admission to the meals and acceptance of a member's goods and property marked further stages in a member's development.[25] Disobedient members of the community were forbidden access to the waters or the community's meals. There were regular times of prayer and a special calendar so devised that none of the festivals would fall on a sabbath. According to Josephus[26] the ranks of the community were also distinguished in terms of degrees of purity, such that seniors must wash if they were touched by juniors. He also notes the elaborate procedure prescribed for relieving themselves[27] and explains that the punishment of exclusion from the community meant the serious risk of starvation because of the prohibitions on taking food and drink which belonged to those outside the community.[28]

In what way did such practices serve to control the members of the community? Members were enjoined to have no dealings with those outside the community, 'not to follow them in matters of doctrine and justice.'[29] Such things are not easy to enforce. Suspicions of Pharisaic influence for example, could easily have destroyed a small community and led to witch-hunts on grounds of false doctrine. The avoidance regulations then had the advantage of being much more easily enforceable, as well as more easily dealt with in terms of set punishments and purification rites. Such regulations would clearly be of crucial importance for small communities living in towns or in rural areas where there would be frequent opportunity for contact and assimilation.

Purity regulations also had their part to play in strengthening the internal structure of the community. The community set great store by respect and deference and the maintenance of a strict hierarchy, but again such offences as answering one's companion with obstinacy and murmuring against the authority of the community are not easily enforceable. By contrast, prohibitions against touching a senior member and spitting in the assembly,[30] as also other restrictions such as silence at meals and in the community house,[31] offer ways of stressing rank and order within the community and checking familiarity and spontaneity without the elaborate inquiries and harsh punishments associated with the more serious offences.[32] This is not to suggest that the more serious offences were never prosecuted, but rather that they represented the extreme threat which must be sparingly used if the community was to survive and prosper.

Nor is it to suggest that ritual offences were used only in this way. In one case clearly they were not, namely the avoidance of the divine name. In the list of offences and punishments this is of the same degree of seriousness as murmuring against the authority of the congregation.[33] The force of such a prohibition is, I suspect, to intensify the need for vigilance and self-discipline at every point of a member's life.

It is I think reasonably clear that the purity regulations are being used here in a way which is recognizably continuous with Leviticus.

Observation of the purity laws separates the community from that which is unclean, which is alien to it. Similarly within the community—and this is analogous perhaps to the different divisions of the Temple—there are divisions and degrees of purity which serve to protect the central 'sanctuary' of the *yaḥad* from alien intrusion. Thus the regulations are controlled by general conventions, common to other forms of Judaism of the period. But in detail, of course, a great deal has changed which reflects the changed situation of the community. Whereas previously purity regulations were observed in order to preserve the purity of the Temple with its central sanctuary and its environs, now observance of purity regulations was designed to protect the community from corruption by alien influence and to strengthen it by inculcating self-discipline, self-control and obedience to its central Council. The association of purity regulations with the Temple worship is not however altogether abandoned, because the community has its place in God's plan for the ultimate restoration of the Temple. Nevertheless, the linking of the regulations with the protection of the community means that there are substantial innovations, both in the explanatory accounts offered and in the details of the regulations themselves.

We can start by referring back to the way observance of purity regulations was related to God's holiness and his election of Israel in Leviticus. There, observance of the distinction between clean and unclean was taken as a sign, a memorial of God's distinction between Jew and Gentile. Similarly not eating teeming and therefore unclean (anomalous) things was related, by analogy, with not mixing with the Gentiles who do not do the Law. Now for Qumran the situation has clearly changed in that there is no longer a clear distinction between Jew and Gentile, between those who do the Law and those who do not. The experience of the community is rather of a situation of conflict with those who observe the Law in a different way from themselves. Hence distinguishing between clean and unclean cannot stand simply as a reminder of God's separation of Jew and Gentile, but instead[34] it is related to God's setting two spirits over men, the spirits of truth and falsehood. That is to say the two groups are not distinguished in terms of their doing and not doing the Law *simpliciter*. The Sons of Light are distin-

124

guished from the Sons of Darkness by a catalogue of virtues and vices. Thus for doing the Law we now read walking in the spirit of truth, which clearly shares characteristics with the prophetic insistence on justice, truth, faithfulness, mercy, etc., which have found strong echoes in the apocalyptic books like Enoch and Jubilees. Purity in these lists is related specifically to worship while impurity is associated specifically with dirt and filth as well as with lust and sexual immorality.[35] Hence we may surmise that the conventional associations have been further specified and interpreted in the following way:

Observance of the Law	linked with	Not doing as the Gentiles do
Observance of the Law as revealed to the Teacher of Righteousness	linked with	Not doing as the Gentiles do nor as the wicked priest at Jerusalem does, etc.
Walking in the spirit of light	linked with	Not walking in the spirit of falsehood
Doing the truth, righteousness, observing purity of worship	linked with	Not lying, pursuing greed, abomination, filthiness and immorality.

There is a further complication however because during this present age both the spirits hold sway over men, and it is only in the final age that the complete separation will take place. Thus it is not just a question of separating oneself from the nations who have been cast out of the land, but there is a continuing struggle for every man to free himself from the influence of the spirit of falsehood. This action of separation anticipates the final judgement and equally determines what will befall the individual at judgement. Moreover again this final separation when the spirit of truth will be poured on the Sons of Light to purify them is compared with washing and purificatory rites.[36] What one might say here then is that we may expect purificatory rites, particularly those relating to the washing away of dirt and filth, to signify and remind the community of the need for the continual struggle against the spirit of falsehood which besets even the Sons of the Covenant. The conventional redefinitions might then be tabulated as follows:

Leviticus: God has separated Jew and Gentile, therefore Jews should separate clean and unclean animals.

Qumran: God has set two spirits over men, therefore the Sons of Light must wash away all dirt.

The two spirits during this life rule over all men so that the Sons of Light must exercise constant vigilance therefore
there must be regular lustrations to signify the need for constant separation from the spirit of falsehood.

This too will conveniently explain why in Qumran washing was the most common form of purity rite. Clearly it was not because water was a common commodity; the community had to go to very considerable lengths to ensure adequate supplies. It is rather, I suggest, because one cannot avoid getting dirty and this signifies very well the community's belief that in this life God has set both spirits over them, while the frequent lustrations both anticipate the final state when God will pour out the spirit of truth fully and signify the need for constant separation from all the works of the spirit of falsehood.

This in large measure, I think, explains the fact which has often puzzled scholars, namely the combination in Qumran of strong emphasis on theological and moral virtues with the frequent practice of purificatory rites. As we saw above emphasis on purification has the function of strengthening discipline within the community. We can now see also that it serves to remind them of the constant need for vigilance, for care in preserving the values of the community which, however much it may set itself apart from the world, is still

126

only too conscious of the dangers of corruption and perversion of its own values from within its own ranks.

One further point may be made in relation to Qumran's practice. It has often been noticed that, whereas contamination for Qumran is automatic, purification is not. Only those who have taken the oath of allegiance 'may enter the water to partake of the pure meal of the Saints—for they shall not be cleansed, unless they turn from their wickedness: for all who transgress this word are unclean.'[37] Now this occurs within a section of the Community Rule which is particularly concerned with the separation of the community from those outside and which may well be taken from an earlier stage of the tradition. This argues caution in trying to fit it too neatly into the pattern which we have discerned so far. Nevertheless some attempt can be made. While it is true that all men are beset by both spirits, it is also true that there is a radical distinction between those who have pledged themselves to the Covenant and those who have not. Lustrations represent the separation of the Sons of Light from the Spirit of Darkness and Falsehood which still besets them. They cannot have the same sense for those who have not pledged themselves. From such men the community must keep itself entirely apart, shunning contact with their goods,[38] as well as their teaching. Thus the function of these regulations is to make a total division between those who take the oath and those who do not. This of course again serves to underline the importance of allegiance to the community and clearly reflects its situation as a voluntary association—'those in Israel who have freely pledged themselves to holiness'[39]—contrasted with the Jerusalem priesthood which was defined by race and birth.

This discussion is of course principally concerned to indicate the kinds of conventional associations which the term 'purity' had in first-century Judaism, specifically at Qumran. To determine what was being said by any particular utterance would require a more detailed discussion. Nevertheless the changes in convention do give us quite a good approximate indication of what was being said about the kind of behaviour due to a God of holiness and purity, about the need to pursue virtue and shun impurity, about the need for discipline and hierarchy within the community and strict avoidance of all that was alien. Fairly clearly too, such injunctions have their place within an overall strategy which seeks to preserve the Jewish tradition both against external Hellenistic influence and against alternative Jewish strategies for survival which pose a threat to Qumran's policies. Furthermore we can say that the force of such purity regulations lies not least in the fact that in using a term like purity they are taking a term which has a very strong affective charge by virtue of its key associations with the Jews' election and with the Temple worship. This is then being applied to the ordering of the community's life and worship which is thus equally invested with high emotional value.

I have chosen to look in some detail at the role of purity in the community of Qumran because of the dangers that lie in making too quick and too simple comparisons between sayings about purity taken from quite different contexts. Only when we see how such sayings and rulings fit into a system of belief and practice can we really understand them. And this involves seeing how certain terms with their conventional associations are used and further defined in the context of a particular community with its organization and structures. I hope that has been shown by the argument above. It also indicates, I believe, the *kind* of considerations necessary for a proper analysis of purity in first-century Judaism, even if Qumran's understanding of purity is quite different from that of Jesus. Thus, if we are to understand what Jesus said about purity we shall have to relate it to what he taught about the Law in general and about the boundaries, internal and external, of society. We shall further have to consider to what extent Jesus accepted, modified or rejected the conventions relating to the notion of purity and to the related notions of Law, holiness, mercy, justice which held in first-century Judaism and which we have seen operating in the Dead Sea Scrolls. This will of course shed light on Jesus' substantial reworking of the conventional associations of the notion of the Kingdom. In all this the aim is, of course, to see how Jesus' treatment of purity relates to those fundamental beliefs about God, man and the world which we have already considered in relation to his preaching of the Kingdom.

There is in fact very little material which might with any reliability be traced back to Jesus on the subject of purity and cultic observance. There are a number of actions or sayings relating to the cult. Foremost among these is the cleansing of the Temple[40] and the various sayings relating to its destruction,[41] but there are also sayings relating to correct sacrifice[42] and swearing in relation to cultic objects.[43] There are sayings and actions relating to the sabbath[44] and there is—I will argue—a specific rejection of the notion of purity in Mark 7:15. Thus the material presents us with an initial question: How are we to make sense of the fact that Jesus both rejected the notion of purity and cleansed the Temple? Let us, then, following the pattern of our discussion of Qumran first consider Jesus' teaching about the Law[45] and community boundaries before giving more detailed attention to the material relating to the cult and purity.

For Jews of the second Temple period the Law, we have seen, was a gift from God, a revelation of his will to his people. By observation of the Law his people were to keep themselves distinct from the nations and by it the bond between God and his people was upheld. Such revelation pertained to the ordering of the life of the community in all its aspects, to the understanding of the community's place in the divine plan for the redemption of Israel and to the knowledge of what was to come. For Jesus too Law was clearly of central importance. He pronounced on a wide range of issues relating to the Law on occasion to substantiate his own views. There are, however, important differences, alongside some similarities, between Jesus' and Qumran's understanding of the Law.

Qumran's understanding of the Law was based on special revelation, granted to the Teacher of Righteousness and to specially trained members of the community.[46] Such knowledge was to be carefully guarded from those outside, whether Jew or Gentile. Now it is also the case that Jesus claimed special knowledge and understanding of the Law. It is also true that in this he distinguished his teaching from that of other contemporary Jewish groups. But Jesus' knowledge of God's will is based not on an inspired interpretation of the *Law*,[47] but on his own understanding of *God's will*, which he may indeed relate to the Law, or justify from the Law, but which is not strictly *derived* from the Law. In this he stands in sharp contrast to contemporary Judaism although charismatic figures whose authority and power are based on their intimate prayer to God may provide some parallels to Jesus' own freedom *vis-à-vis* the Law.[48] Equally, while for Qumran the knowledge granted was to be jealously preserved within the community, Jesus preached openly.[49] Not only that, but such knowledge was communicated in a form which was readily intelligible, which argued the points that he made. The use of Wisdom sayings to substantiate his rulings,[50] the appeal to everyday experience in the parables, the setting of one text of Scripture against another,[51] all this made his teaching widely accessible, open to scrutiny and criticism. It is not a teaching which must be protected from the ignorant and impudent,[52] rather it is itself dangerous;[53] it has power to convince and convict and is recognized as subversive by the Jewish and Roman authorities. All this by strong contrast with the esoteric character of Qumran's teaching.

The contrast between Jesus and Qumran at this point can be developed further. Qumran, we have argued, defined the notion of 'doing the Law' in terms of 'doing the Law as revealed to the Teacher of Righteousness'. Moreover it then contrasted its own practice of the Law, not only with what the nations did, but with what other Jewish groups did. Further, by insisting on secrecy about its own teaching it tried to keep the barriers between itself and other Jewish groups as strong as possible. By contrast Jesus preached openly, trying to win men by his teaching and argument. Thus for him the conventional association of 'not doing as the Gentiles/other Jewish groups do' with 'doing the Law' is weakened in so far as the purpose of doing the Law is to keep oneself apart from the Gentiles and other Jews. The point indeed of Jesus' teaching and, as we shall see, of the behaviour he enjoins is to win over other Jews and Gentiles to his understanding of the Law of God.

The second point of contrast to make between Jesus' understanding of the Law and Qumran's is that whereas Qumran stresses the necessity of fulfilling *all* the points of the Law, Jesus is critical of the Law. Jesus indeed sets himself over against the Law: 'But I say unto you', and he sees the need to discriminate between various aspects of the Law. Again, unlike Qumran, he conceived the Law not as a set of conditions to be fulfilled if a man was to have access to divine power but rather as a divine gift to man which might enable him to find fulfilment. Thus he does not simply insist that these are the commandments of God, which therefore must be fulfilled, whether intelligible or no.[54] Rather he points men to the central matter which is that the intention of these ordinances is that they should enable all men to live as they would individually desire to do.[55] Where there is obscurity or controversy it is this central principle which must decide. This can be seen perhaps most clearly in the sabbath controversies, not least in Jesus' saying: 'the sabbath was made for man, not man for the sabbath'.[56] But it can also be seen to lie behind his sayings about marriage[57] where he shifts the question away from legal debates about what constitutes 'a cause of offence' (Deut. 24:1) to the wider question of the mutual relationship which God has ordained for man and woman (Gen. 1:27; 2:24). Thus the remark about the hardness of men's hearts which was the cause of Moses' ordinance both relates it and subordinates it to the principle of Genesis, at the same time pointing men and women to the greater gift and task which God has set before them. It also, interestingly for our discussion of purity, by implication links the notion of pollution which underlies the legislation of Deuteronomy 24 in relation to marriage to the idea of laws given for the hardness of men's hearts. It is because an adulterous—or re-married—woman is polluted that she must not be taken back. Such regulations were devised for those who could not accept the gift and the demands it made on them. They are then not valid for all time and mask the true nature of the mutual relations between man and woman.

Jesus' legal teaching, that is to say, seeks to realize the intention of the creator in ordering and caring for his world, rather than simply advocating obedience to law because it is the *Law of God*. Thus it does not seek to preserve the created orders willy-nilly, but only in so far as they subserve the creator's fundamental intention of caring for all men.[58] Hence it is legitimate to do good on the sabbath, whether or no it is absolutely necessary for the preservation of life. This cardinal principle of interpretation is then expressed in Jesus' own summary of the Law[59] and in his version of the Golden

Rule.[60] What in particular the summary of the Law suggests is that there is a correlation betwen the love a man bears towards God and that which he bears towards his neighbour. The nature of his relationship to God, which rests primarily on the character of God, is to be reflected also in men's behaviour to one another. A man's grateful acceptance of God's forgiveness and care is to be reflected in his own gracious and caring love of his neighbour. It is this spirit which is to be breathed into all the forms of life which are given him. All this, of course, contrasts sharply with the emphasis on the holiness of God in Qumran, where just as God will draw to himself only those who are willing to undergo purification and discipline, so too the members of the community must separate themselves sharply from the disobedient and impure.

The contrast between Jesus and Qumran at this point brings out further important changes in the conventional association of 'doing the Law' with maintaining the covenant between God and his people. The Law as understood in Qumran is a means of union with a God of holiness. It is necessary to observe the Law because only the pure can approach God and live. What purity is and how it is to be achieved are revealed by God and hence all his revealed Law is to be obeyed. For Jesus, God's will is his will as creator and father for his creatures and sons. It is that by which man shall live together as God intends. Similarly the summary of the Law shows that for Jesus the same virtue of love should inspire relations between men and their fellows as inspires the relations between men and God. Jesus' criticism of the Law is not that it is contrary to God's will, but that parts of it are instituted for those who cannot or will not show the qualities of care and mercy which God intends for his people. This is effectively to abandon the link between doing the Law and union with a God of holiness for a link between 'doing the will of the father' and showing the qualities of mercy and care in one's relations with God and man that are appropriate to a father. This change is developed in Jesus' teaching on questions of the internal and external boundaries of the Jewish community.

In the first place there are a number of sayings which attack the hierarchical nature of Jewish society and advocate simplicity and humility as the model for social relations within the community.

Perhaps the most striking of these are Jesus' sayings about children, especially Mark 10:14,15: 'Of such is the Kingdom of God.' This is also reflected in his more specific attacks on the internal divisions within Jewish society, on the phylacteries of the Pharisees,[61] on those who take the highest seat,[62] etc. These seem to be directed against the correlation between spiritual progress and social status which we noticed earlier in the Qumran community. Against this Jesus sets the necessity for humility, for living out of God's mercy and forgiveness, which characterizes the publican at prayer.[63] Similarly he attacks spiritual leaders who set themselves up over those they lead.[64] Whether these last sayings were originally directed to the disciples or to the Pharisees and scribes is not clear, just as it is mostly very difficult to say with certainty what element if any of the 'community rule' sayings can be traced back to Jesus. Among the most likely is the saying which is also echoed in the Johannine tradition, Mark 9:35: 'if anyone would be first, he must be last of all and servant of all'.[65]

As well as these sayings which attack certain kinds of divisions and ways of marking divisions within Jewish society there are others which deal in personal terms with questions of societal relations which the Law dealt with by legal rulings. Thus on the question of adultery Jesus goes beyond the provisions of the Law which relate to sexual intercourse and makes the whole range of emotions and desires between the sexes a matter for attention.[66] The intention is to bring a far greater range of human behaviour into the light of God's will. Similarly in the commentary which Jesus offers on murder there is a move away from the specific act of killing to embrace a wider range of personal relations.[67] One can contrast the two types of ruling by saying that, whereas the one lays down firm boundaries which mark out the limits of freedom and action between groups and individuals in society, the other makes the whole range of human interaction a matter which is to be lived out in accordance with God's will. In this way the system of rigid boundaries is replaced by a set of personal standards which are at once more demanding and more fulfilling.

If this is true of internal relations and boundaries, what of external ones? The central saying here is Jesus' command to love one's enemies, which may originally have run: 'Love your enemies (and pray for those who persecute you) and you will become sons of the highest who causes the sun to rise on the evil and the good (and causes the rain to fall on the just and the unjust). (Therefore be perfect as your heavenly father is perfect.)'[68] The question is who are the enemies; and what is the nature of the love enjoined?

In the light of what we saw earlier about conditions in Galilee and Palestine in the first century, it is likely that 'enemies' refers fairly generally to those identified with the forces which threatened Jews loyal to their traditions.[69] This is to say Jesus is not addressing his followers by contrast with other Jews or Jewish groups. The majority of Jesus' ethical sayings—with the exception of the discipleship sayings—are directed to a wider audience of Jews. Even so the precise boundaries between Jews and their enemies remain hard to determine. Clearly, for Qumran or for the Pharisees, any one outside the strict observance of the group could have been regarded as an enemy. For the Galilean Jews it is more likely that the 'enemies' referred more specifically to the Romans and Hellenizers, notably the Herods and their officials. The alternative view, that Jesus is here referring to Jewish groups who attacked his followers seems to me to be weak, both because it supposes a tighter grouping among Jesus' followers than we have grounds for in the tradition, and because it misses the polemical note in this saying which is directed aginst those who would hedge themselves off from their enemies, rather than opening themselves up to meet them.

What then is the nature of the love for one's enemies which Jesus enjoins? Can it be simply characterized as an extension of the concept of love of neighbour? Is Jesus merely enjoining Jews to extend love not only to their brother Jews but also to those whom they regard as enemies or is he enjoining a quite different set of attitudes and values?

Clearly where Jewish groups like Qumran are concerned, love is a relationship extended only to the member of the sect, whereas those outside are to be avoided and hated. Moreover even within the sect love is something which is expressed only through very carefully regulated and ordered relationships. Here there is simply no possibility of loving those who disregard the spirit and order of

134

the community. But even for instance the teaching of the later Rabbis about relations with non-Jews does little to extend love of neighbour to those outside. In general love is a characteristic which is to be shown in different ways to different groups within the Jewish community and which may be extended in a cautious way to those outside. By contrast Jesus not only rejects any restriction of love to the community, but underlines the importance and centrality of love of enemies.

Thus the love which is demanded is something more than an extension of the love of the brotherhood to those outside, because it demands a reorientation of the love of the brotherhood. Love is no longer primarily a quality of relationships within the fold, within the walls which hold the dark and threatening powers at a distance; it is something which must prove itself in the engagement with that which is inimical and threatening. Indeed the love which Jesus commands men to show to their enemies is a reflection of their Father's love and care for evil and good alike.

Jesus' teaching in these very critical areas thus shows clearly the way in which he understands the will of God as the will of a loving and forgiving father rather than of a God who will have dealings only with the pure and the righteous and who will exact retribution from the impure and the wicked. Here there is a fairly clear rejection of the conventional associations of God's mercy with his election of a particular people. His love is to all men, just and unjust alike. Similarly we can see how such a view of God makes it very difficult for Jesus to pick up the notion of God's holiness where it is conventionally linked to the idea of his abomination of and destruction of all that is impure. This is of course in line with what we have already argued about Jesus' deleting from the notion of the Kingdom of God its associations with God's destruction and punishment of his enemies.

We can now turn to Jesus' sayings about the cult and purity. We have already noticed that there is an initial problem in understanding how Jesus could both cleanse the Temple and also reject the whole notion of purity. Let us start by looking at the saying in Mark 7:15 in the light of what we have seen about Qumran and Jesus.

135

It is fairly widely agreed that Mark 7:15 is an originally isolated logion which has been incorporated into Mark 7; and that the tradition behind Mark 7 has a fairly complex history, which does not stop with Mark's own editing of it but continues with Matthew.[70] Further than this it is not possible to speak of agreement among scholars. For there is substantial disagreement as to whether this saying is or goes back to an original saying of Jesus, just as there is considerable disagreement as to its meaning. There are those who see this as a clear rejection of Jewish purity laws, or at least of dietary laws, while others deny that it could have had such a meaning. And there are those who deny that Jesus could have uttered such a statement, either because such an abrogation of the Law would have been unthinkable for a first-century Jew, or because it would be unthinkable that the early Church in controversies about dietary laws should not have appealed to such a saying of Jesus if it had existed.[71] What I want to suggest is, first, that the saying is authentic. There is a *prima facie* case for this based on its position at the beginning of a long history of tradition. This is somewhat strengthened if the tradition has softened the saying, a fact which would also explain why it was less prominent in subsequent controversies, viz. because its original sense had been obscured. Secondly, I want to assert that the saying does explicitly reject Mosaic purity laws. These are probably not restricted to dietary laws, though the saying would certainly refer to them. What I want to show is (a) that it can be related coherently to what Jesus taught about the Law and social relations; and (b) that Jesus' teaching on all these points works with ideas and concepts which are familiar first-century Jewish material, but which receive a very distinctive treatment.[72] The point is simply this. Taken in isolation, Jesus' saying Mark 7:15 may seem too far removed from anything we find elsewhere in contemporary Judaism to be accepted as authentic. Seen in relation to his teaching about the Law in general and internal and external boundaries in particular we can see it as part of an important transformation of first-century Jewish thought.

What then does Jesus teach, if we take Mark 7:15 (7:18,20) to be a close approximation to his teaching? Does he reject *any* notion of pollution 'from without' or only specific regulations, e.g. dietary laws? What is the pollution 'from within' which he recognizes?

Formally the saying is classified as a Wisdom saying,[73] formulating a principle in an impersonal way. More specifically the saying is in the typically Old Testament form of a two-membered *Mashal*. The sayings of this kind in the synoptic tradition are usually in parallel form, which is to say that both halves express the same principle in different ways.[74]

When we turn to consider the meaning of the saying, one question strikes immediately. Is the word for 'pollute' used in the same sense in both halves of the saying? In the first half 'pollute' seems to be used in its standard conventional sense, while in the second it appears to be used in a special and somewhat unusual sense. Verse 15a—'There is nothing outside which entering into a man can defile him'—must I think clearly refer to forms of pollution such as 'unclean foods'. Moreover if the phrase 'which entering in' is a Markan addition[75] then the reference may be extended to include *contact* with dirt, dead bodies, certain forms of sickness and the bodily emissions of others. Hence if 'pollute' is used univocally in verse 15b—'only that which is (comes out of) from a man can pollute him'—it would have to refer to *his own* bodily emissions, e.g. semen, spittle, excrement. But this would clearly make nonsense of the whole saying, as it would make use of the notion of pollution which the first half has just rejected. Thus we must assume an ironical or metaphorical use of 'pollute' in the second half.[76] This is, of course, what we should expect if the two halves of the saying affirm the same principle. The first half, that is, categorically rejects any notion of pollution, that is to say, of a reality outside the circle of the faithful which can separate a man from God and so lead to his destruction; the second talks of very different forces which can destroy a man from within.[77] The question now is whether, in the light of what we have seen of the conventional associations of the term purity, we can determine what Jesus was saying in Mark 7:15.

To do that we need to know, we have said, what Jesus' stance was towards these conventions. Did he accept the conventions but reject the beliefs about God which were expressed, for example, in purity sentences in Qumran? Or did he attempt to rework the term so as to fit it for use in his exposition of his own beliefs? In view of the relatively infrequent use of the term in Jesus' sayings it seems certain that Jesus in fact accepted the conventional associations of the term and hence shunned it.

This being so, what is said in the first half of Mark 7:15 is fairly clear. Jesus in accepting the sentence 'Nothing which enters a man from outside can pollute a man' is also by implication rejecting a whole range of other sentences. He is, first, rejecting Levitical and Pharisaical purity regulations which regulate the Jews' conduct to one another and to those outside by means of ritually reinforced barriers. This can be seen in his attitude to divorce, which he rejected even in the case of adultery.[78] Divorce in the case of adultery is, we have suggested, associated with notions of pollution. A woman must be divorced if she has been *polluted* by adultery. Nor may she be taken back subsequently, for the same reason. Jesus' rejection of divorce thus—in his context—represents a rejection of the attempt to control the marriage relationship by the enforcement of tight boundaries and strict sanctions and the advocacy instead of forgiveness to those who have given 'a cause of offence'. Such an emphasis on forgiveness is found repeatedly in Jesus' teaching, perhaps nowhere more clearly than in the reply to Peter's question about forgiveness and the associated parable of the unmerciful servant.[79] Indeed, as we have argued above, this substituting of the qualities of forgiveness and love for fixed boundaries is characteristic of Jesus' teaching on a range of topics. This is not, of course, to suggest that because he rejected purity rules as ways of controlling human behaviour and reinforcing barriers within society he therefore rejected any kind of distinctions in personal and group relations. Rather he sought the true spirit which could transform human relations. What threatened men ultimately were not the forces from without but those forces within societies and human relationships which are the contraries of forgiveness, mercy and love: vengefulness, vindictiveness and hatred.

Similarly Jesus' rejection of purity rules implies a quite different attitude towards the external boundaries of the community from that of Qumran. Whereas in Qumran separation from and hatred of those outside the community was reinforced and regulated by avoidance rules, Jesus abolished the whole basis of such rules and himself broke them clearly in his meals with collaborators and sinners. Again we have seen the ethical counterpart of this in Jesus' command to men to love their enemies, which contrasts of course sharply with Qumran's command to hate them. It is not the wicked and idolaters who threaten the Jewish community ultimately. It is lack of spiritual power which means power to love and forgive and in so doing to outdo evil and wickedness, even if this entails suffering and death. Secondly he is rejecting the network of sentences in which purity sentences are contained, viz. sentences which link obedience to the Law to not doing as the Gentiles do and also to preserving the bond between Yahweh and his people. In particular I would suggest that he is rejecting sentences which assert that God abhors and will destroy all that is impure, outside the covenant between himself and Israel. This is again confirmed by Jesus' positive teaching.

For Jesus, God does not wish to destroy but to forgive and to heal and to restore the lost and fallen. The real power in the world is the divine forgiveness and love which can overcome man's hatred and fear. What is destructive is man's opposition to that spirit of love and forgiveness, his refusal to repent and his active hatred and enmity. It is to all this in its many beguiling forms that man must die if he is to find life. It is this which 'pollutes' a man. This distinction between Jesus and Qumran's teaching on purity is clearly reflected in their differing attitudes to the Law as a whole. Jesus' preaching, missionary ministry, and his authority over against the Law contrasts sharply with the esoteric character of the understanding of Law in Qumran. The power which Jesus preaches is a power which engages with the world of evil and darkness, overcoming it through love and forgiveness. Qumran's power is to be found only within the sanctuary, though ultimately it will break out and destroy the wicked. This suggests a way of understanding what is said in the second half of the sentence, 'only that which is from within a man can pollute him'. The term 'pollution' is clearly being used in a metaphorical sense, which is to say that while the conventional associations of the term are held in mind they are being given a different sense as different values are ascribed to some of the associated terms. If pollution conventionally refers to contact with a reality outside the group which can separate a man from God and hence work his destruction, here it is taken to refer to a power inside a man which can similarly cut him off from God. This is implicitly contrasted with a power which can purify him and which, I suggest, is the loving and forgiving power of God. What then is destructive for a man is not his own nature *per se* but his rejection of that divine love and forgiveness which thus cuts him off from the divine spirit of forgiveness.[80]

But whence does such a spirit come? Where is it experienced? In Qumran power could be appropriated only via a prolonged process of discipline and purgation in which purity rules played an important part.[81] For Jesus the model of the disciple is the child, the publican as opposed to the Pharisee, the man who loses his life, the poor, the forgiven sinner, sitting at table with him. These different figures, who represent personal qualities rather than impersonal standards, emphasize the need for repentance,[82] for receptivity, for humility and above all for learning forgiveness as one is oneself forgiven. In Qumran power was mediated to the initiates by the inspired interpretation of Scripture given by the Teacher of Righteousness and subsequently by those who had undergone purification. For Jesus' followers love and forgiveness were in the first instance mediated through Jesus whose life was centred on an intimate relationship of 'sonship' to the Father. In this respect he was perhaps not unlike Galilean charismatic figures such as Ḥanina ben Dosa and Honi the Circle Drawer, who too showed very little concern for ritual rules, but whose lives were centred on prayer and a sense of the presence of God. Thus in so far as Jesus' followers underwent any training it was a training in prayer and in dependence on the mercy and care of God, a cutting away from all attempts to earn God's rewards, a losing one's life and a receiving it anew from God.

This discussion may also help to explain the apparent contradiction between Jesus' rejection of the purity principle and his other sayings which take a more positive attitude to the cult and the Temple. If, as is sometimes argued, purity is regarded as the sole basis for distinguishing between the sacred and the profane,[83] between holy places and times and the profane world and time, then clearly Jesus' cleansing of the Temple, his concern for the proper observance of the sabbath and the correct way of sacrifice becomes problematical, at most a remainder from his religious past which has not been worked through in the light of his own radical insights. But it is not the case that to reject the notion of purity is to abandon *any* distinction between sacred and profane. What we have argued is that it is to attack *one way* of attempting to uphold that distinction which has indeed a long history in Judaeo-Christianity—for it was never wholly abandoned by the Church—namely the way which saw God, the holy, as a power which would not tolerate or abide the approach of the profane or impure and who therefore had to be carefully separated from it. On Jesus' view the need for such sharp barriers does indeed disappear and this makes for a substantial modification of the distinction. God is no longer restricted to such times and places as are protected from the profane by careful regulations and rituals.

This is not to deny *any* distinction between sacred and secular, just as rejecting purity regulations in respect of human relationships is not to deny that there are any boundaries at all. God is still seen as active, as coming to men in power, in healing, in prayer, in the prophetic word, just as in the priestly view he comes to his Temple. The point is that such power and divine activity is not *limited* to those places and times—and officiants—which are protected and separated from the profane.

Jesus' cleansing of the Temple is not an easy episode to interpret. The reason offered in the synoptics is that its true purpose which was to be a house of prayer has been perverted, and that it has become a den of robbers. This may reflect anger at the way the Temple income sustained those who compromised with the Romans, but it also points to another possible meaning of Jesus' action. It is unlikely that Jesus opposed the Temple cult on 'technical' grounds such as were advanced by Qumran, i.e. incorrect calendar, ritual practice, etc. Whether like Qumran he attempted to apply the Temple imagery[84] to himself is also doubtful, despite the Johannine interpretation of his prophecy of the destruction of the Temple to refer to Jesus' body. What is more likely is that his action

141

was a demonstration intended to initiate a national renewal of prayer and dedication. Even movements of prayer need their centres from which they can go out, because such prayer is a particular encounter with the deity. The point is, however, that the nature of God is not such that he can be worshipped only within the appointed limits of the sacrificial system, but rather that he communicates to men his love for the 'enemies' and the fallen. Thus it may be possible to see in the attack on the money-changers and the sellers of sacrificial animals an attack not only on the rapaciousness and extortion of the Temple cult, but an attack on the cult *qua* sacrificial institution, carefully hedged about with regulations governing access to and participation in the cult.

What all this means in terms of Jesus' response to the religious crisis of his time should be fairly clear. The Pharisees and Qumran intensified the observation of the Law specifically with regard to the purity regulations in order to put strong barriers between themselves and the forces which they believed were threatening Israel's integrity, notably Hellenism as it was mediated through the Romans, the Herods and certain Jewish groups. Jesus' rejection of the notion of purity as a means of regulating relations between men and God and controlling relations inside and outside the group has to be seen as a clear rejection of such strategies over against Hellenism. Rather than intensifying existing norms, as do the Essenes and Pharisees, Jesus' response to the anomic situation of his time is to radicalize the norms. This means both rejecting substantial areas of ethical teaching as well as focusing attention on specific—heightened—demands: as in the summary of the Law and especially the command to love one's enemies. This, we have argued, represents a missionary policy over against the Herodians and the agents of Hellenism, making exacting demands of his followers, which can be understood only in the light of the attempts we have already noted in the last chapter to heighten the self-consciousness of the oppressed and dispirited peoples of Galilee. It is, that is to say, unrealistic to encourage an oppressed and threatened people to love their enemies unless one has given them grounds for confidence and hope. This Jesus did in proclaiming to men that there was a reality greater and more powerful than the forces which oppressed them,

142

a reality which was gracious and forgiving to all men, and which would uphold and sustain them in its service, come what may. It is against this teaching that his rejection of strong barriers, of the intensification of traditional norms, has to be seen. His command to love one's enemies is not in the same sense a strategy for dealing with the situation as was the Essene use of purity regulations. It represents rather a radical change in the fundamental assumptions about God, the world and man which in the course of history would generate many different strategies for dealing with the dark forces which threaten to overwhelm men.

I have tried in this chapter to show the way in which Jesus' teaching about the Law is rooted in a fundamental view of the mercy and love and care of God. This emerges clearly from a consideration of his teaching about the Law in general, about social boundaries and specifically of his rejection of the notion of purity in its cultic sense. The notion of purity in Israel is conventionally linked to the maintenance of tight boundaries and also to certain theological notions about God's power and salvation. We have seen how Jesus' attitudes to Law, society and purity are consistently different from attitudes to such subjects in Qumran. Whereas Qumran is a society closed to the world, carefully structured and organized, carefully guarding its secret power, hedged about with purity laws, Jesus urges men to love their enemies, to pay more attention to love and forgiveness and care than to defending barriers between themselves, proclaims his God openly to the world and discards any notion of purity regulations. While Qumran's view of God is of a holy God who purifies his people and will destroy his enemies, Jesus' view is of a loving God who loves his enemies and seeks out the lost and fallen. Thus we find those basic beliefs which were expressed so powerfully in Jesus' use of the term 'the Kingdom of God' worked out here in the sphere of Law and ethical teaching.

I hope to have shown that such are the conventional associations of purity that Jesus could have used it only at the risk of serious misunderstanding. For though it is theoretically possible that he could have deleted its sacrificial and cultic associations and taken its core-meaning as freedom from moral wickedness, even this would not have conveyed his message if it had then been suggested that

God would have dealings only with the righteous. Moreover, the notion—with all its cultic associations—was so integral a part of different Jewish renewal movements that it is hard to see practically how Jesus might have succeeded in reworking it. Be that as it may, he chose not to rework it, but to reject it. This is both remarkable in the light of its widespread use in contemporary Judaism and, I hope to have shown, readily intelligible in the light of its entrenched associations. The fact that the clarity of Jesus' rejection of the notion was subsequently obscured by the Palestinian church is only too intelligible in the light of the continuing power of the notion in Judaism. It was the Hellenistic church which preserved the saying, even if it then moralized and spiritualized the notion of purity. Jesus by contrast simply discarded it as unusable.

7

Jesus' Theism

Jesus' explicit teaching about God, the world and man has received scant attention of recent years. Whereas scholars like Harnack[1] at the turn of the century saw Jesus' teaching about the fatherhood of God, his care and governance of the world and about the infinite value of the human soul as one of the three keys to his religious consciousness, such views, particularly on the European continent, have become increasingly rare. In England scholars such as C. H. Dodd and T. W. Manson[2] have continued to speak of Jesus' teaching on these subjects, but those who, broadly, have followed Bultmann have taken a very different stance. In his work on the synoptic tradition Bultmann argued strongly against the authenticity of such—wisdom—sayings in the tradition and characterized them as naive and childlike.[3] For Bultmann it was the kerygmatic, existential elements in Jesus' preaching which were of abiding interest; his more speculative teaching was hardly distinguishable from that of contemporary Jews and, if it was genuine at all,[4] provided at most the general background for his own specific existential insights. What I want to argue for in this chapter is something of a synthesis of these two positions. That is to say, I agree with Bultmann in seeing the real weight of Jesus' work as lying in his use of the Jewish prophetic-apocalyptic and legal traditions; but while I think that his more speculative teaching, notably but not exclusively in the wisdom sayings, expresses less clearly the kind of reorientation in the apprehension of God, man and society that is achieved in his preaching of the Kingdom, I want to point to places at least where his use of the wisdom tradition and certain speculative ideas from the apocalyptic tradition allows that basic reorientation to come through more strongly. More precisely what I would suggest is that, just as Jesus reworked the conventional associations of certain key terms taken from the prophetic-apocalyptic and scribal traditions, as well as rejecting other terms, notably purity, outright, so too his handling of certain beliefs relating to God's governance of the world was creative and interestingly original. In particular we shall examine his treatment of the notions of God's fatherhood, of rewards and punishments, of a holy war and of some final judgement and see how he modifies these in the light of his fundamental beliefs about God, man and the world. The originality in his treatment of these notions lies less in his reworking of their conventional associations than in the fact that he gives very different values to the terms, viz. justice, punishments and rewards, etc., from those they received in contemporary Judaism. More simply one could say that these terms in Judaism are associated with certain questions—e.g. whom does God punish, when and how?—to which Jesus gives original answers which relate closely to what we have already seen of his beliefs about God. In some cases, as we shall see, these answers are so original that they effectively deny the applicability of such terms to God's governance of the world at all. Thus, whereas in Jesus' treatment of the notion of the Kingdom of God we saw how he not only deleted certain associations of the term but also replaced them with others, here we often have a clearer idea of where Jesus found contemporary beliefs about God's governance unacceptable than of what he wished to put in their place. His belief in God's mercy and forgiveness led him to reject contemporary doctrines about God's care and governance. He did not however himself always provide fully worked out doctrinal alternatives. The point could perhaps be made by saying that, by giving the kinds of answers he did to questions about God's apportionment of rewards and punishments, Jesus was effectively rejecting one of the most important notions linked with God's righteousness, namely that the righteous God is a God who rewards the righteous and punishes the wicked. But Jesus does not go on to develop this speculatively as Paul does in his treatment of the notion of God's righteousness in Galatians and Romans. Hence in this area we shall see more of the theoretical problems which Jesus posed than of the actual solutions he proposed. However, the fact that such problems are set by the inter-action between his beliefs about God's mercy and forgiveness and contemporary Jewish doctrines about providence provides further corroboration of what we have already argued about Jesus' funda-mental apprehension of God as evidenced in his preaching and teaching about the Kingdom and Law.

As we saw earlier[5] the Wisdom tradition springs from the attempt to derive theological insights and laws from reflection on men's experience in its broadest sense. It is inspired moreover by the belief that there is a divinely-given order in the world, that God rules wisely and justly over his world, however difficult it may sometimes be to receive his rule. We saw however that certain key questions were raised for that tradition specifically by the political and econ-omic undermining of Judaism and its social world by the Ptolemies and Seleucids. How can one speak of the divine distribution of rewards and punishments when the unrighteous prosper and the righteous die in poverty? How can one speak of the divine gover-nance of history when Israel is a puppet of foreign powers? Such questions received answers in the writings of Qoheleth and Ben Sira and also in the more speculative parts of the apocalyptic tradition which drew not inconsiderably on the Wisdom tradition itself. Qoh-eleth denied that it was possible to *perceive* any rationale to God's governing of the world; Ben Sira reaffirmed such a belief at a time of Jewish renewal of the Law; in the apocalyptic writings the answer to such questions was given more and more in the form of special revelations about the course and purpose of history, about the corruption of the world by evil forces and its ultimate redemption, about rewards to be received in another life, about a final restoration of God's rule over the world. In particular, in the apocalyptic tradition judgement was increasingly understood as the destruction of the wicked, salvation restricted more and more to Israel. Equally we saw that along with these very different answers to the questions posed about God's governance of the world, went also very different political stances to foreign rule, ranging from passive acceptance to military opposition. Again however the late apocalyptic writings are filled with a deep longing for the overthrow and destruction of their enemies and the re-establishment of Jewish sovereignty and independence.

How then does Jesus with, if we are right, his very different beliefs about God from those which inspired the apocalyptic writers, with his vision of a loving and forgiving, rather than a judging and avenging God, take and use this tradition? What answers does he give to the problems of the oppression of the just, to the existence of suffering and evil in the world as he knew it?

The initial question which we encounter is that of the authenticity of the sayings relating to these topics which are ascribed to Jesus in the synoptic tradition. There we find sayings which reflect a belief in the continual and sure working of God's providence and care;[6] sayings which encourage men to believe that God will answer their prayers;[7] sayings concerning rewards and punishments,[8] as well as sayings concerned with a future, expected resolution to the present evil age and its oppression of the righteous.[9] Did Jesus utter sayings of all these types?

Prima facie this might seem impossible. How could someone both affirm God's just and providential governance of the world and at the same time look for the overthrow of the dark forces which hold it in thrall? Such views are, if pressed, indeed mutually exclusive and this fact has often led theologians to reject sayings of one class or another. But this may be to assume too quickly that we have the meaning of Jesus' utterances in any of the types of sayings we have just listed. Moreover the very fact that we also find similar conjunctions of sayings in some of the apocalyptic literature[10] should cause us to be cautious about rejecting any of this material out of hand. This is not to say that within the various groups all the sayings are to be taken as authentic. There are for instance very good grounds for excluding large parts of Mark 13. The point I am making is rather the general one that before rejecting any such sayings on the grounds of their mutual incompatibility one should look first for an account of this material which is at least open to the possibility of combining a belief in God's care and providence for the world with a hope for the overthrow of evil and oppression.

Let us start then with the sayings about God's care and providence. Bultmann singles out a number of sayings as breathing the spirit of a 'popular belief in God which, recognizing God's sovereign governance, discerns a distributive justice in the course of the world, as we may take for example Luke 14:11 to mean, which trusts in God's providence, as can be seen in Matthew 6:25–33 (why is there such a complete absence here of any characteristic eschatological motivation?) and bases itself on God's answering of men's prayers as taught in Matthew 7:7–11.'[11] Let us take another look.

Luke 14:11, 'For everyone who exalts himself will be humbled, and he who humbles himself will be exalted,' need not detain us long. Considered as an isolated saying it permits of too many interpretations to be read confidently in any way. When is the rewarding of humility and the punishment of pride to take place? The saying is as conceivable in Qumran as in Ben Sira. At the most it might be said to reflect Jesus' distinctive stress on humility and openness to God's mercy as the way of life.

Matthew 6:25–33 is altogether more complex. We may with Bultmann perhaps exclude v. 27 as an awkward insertion; we may even allow that vv. 31–33 are a secondary elaboration. The question still remains how far it is true that vv. 25f, 28–30 simply express a general trust in God's providence, with no trace of eschatological interest or motivation? It seems clear on the one hand that it does regard the orderly course of nature—the clothing of the lilies, etc.— as the work of God's providence and indeed takes such a belief as its starting-point for what is to come. But the form of the saying in v. 30 which argues *a majori ad minus*[12] makes it clear that the point lies elsewhere. What the argument suggests is that God's care of 'you of little faith' should give *less* cause for wonder than his care for the grass. It does not simply *subsume* God's care for men under the general notion of his care for all living things, as does, for example Psalm 145:15f. The argument is rather that, if God can care for things of such passing worth, then surely he will care for *them*. It is this which as men of little faith they know—yet doubt. Hence the appropriateness of the appeal in v. 33, secondary or no, to seek the Kingdom of God, to discover the mercy and the love of the father, which thus provides the eschatological motivation missed by Bultmann.

The use of 'father' here is itself interesting as it seems consonant with Old Testament usage which associates it with God's adoption of and special care for Israel and also the later inter-testamental usage which restricts God's fatherly care to the righteous in Israel.[13] God is the father of those whom he turns to in his mercy and kindness and who respond to that approach. In this sense his providence is restricted to those who stand in a particular relationship to him. But equally in the sayings here this care is still seen as consonant with, if—humanly speaking—closer to his heart than, his care for his creation which is taken for granted. The question is whether God's mercy and kindness knows any limits; and to what extent men may cut themselves off from such mercy. Is it forcing the sayings too much to say that the appeal to God's—universal—care of nature, in order to encourage the dispirited to believe in the reality of God's love and mercy towards them, suggests too that that love knows no bounds?

Similar comments may be made about the sayings on prayer, e.g. Matthew 7:7–11. Again here the dominant image used is that of a father responding to a son's demands. Here again we have the appeal *a majori ad minus*, this time from the love of a human father who is evil to that of the heavenly father who is—of course—good, and therefore naturally gives good things.

Jeremias[14] has suggested that this means that God will give the eschatological good life. Certainly this is helpful in so far as it again points to this saying as being directed to those who have encountered the eschatological goodness, the mercy of God. Equally it registers a warning against thinking of God's providence too simply in terms of providing for men's material needs. Nevertheless, if pressed, such a suggestion could be misleading. The contrast in the saying is not between the kind of things which a human father and those which a heavenly father would give, but between the confidence one might have in an *evil* father giving good things and in a *good* one giving good things. (Luke has blurred this point by substituting 'holy spirit' for 'good things'.) The argument of this kind of saying is designed to enlighten the—eschatologically—new experience of those addressed by setting it against the familiar and expected and in the contrast showing off its power and meaning. Thus both Matthew 6:25–33 (25f, 28–30) and 7:7–11 seem to require an interpretation in terms of Jesus' proclamation to men of the mercy and love of God and thus have good claims to authenticity. By contrast Luke's stories—at least as they stand—about the friend at midnight and the unjust judge do not contain the *a majori ad minus* argument but stress rather the insistence of the petitioner.[15]

Matthew 6:25ff and 7:7–11 may then be seen as sayings designed to enlarge men's apprehension of God's mercy and grace. They do not however specifically raise the question of what God gives to those to whom he is merciful; nor of whom he is merciful to. Such questions come more closely into view when we consider the sayings about rewards and punishments and the final resolution of the conflict between good and evil.

In certain respects the synoptic sayings about rewards resemble contemporary Jewish sayings on the subject.[16] Both the apocalyptic writers and the Rabbis taught men to look for rewards in the future, in the resurrection: 'Store up knowledge of the Law and fulfilment of the commandments in this life and I will store up a good reward for you in the future world.'[17] Like the apocalyptic writings, the synoptic tradition contains sayings which deny the importance of rewards in this life 'where moth and rust corrupts'.[18] The Rabbis were less unequivocal on this point. The saying in Aboth 3:17 suggests that man stores up treasure for himself in heaven as capital, from whose interest he can live on this earth. The synoptic tradition by contrast affirms that God provides for the basic needs of the righteous and the unrighteous,[19] but rewards only the righteous in heaven; those who receive their rewards now will not enjoy them later.[20] The closeness of the synoptic sayings to other Jewish material gives good grounds for regarding most of these sayings, with the important exception of Matthew 5:46, linked as it is with the distinctive command to love one's enemies, as secondary.

However, while there are these interesting similarities between synoptic sayings and other contemporary Jewish sayings, a more distinct trait in the synoptic material may be discerned if we first look at the wider question of how the relationship between God and man is represented there. Predominantly in the synoptic sayings and parables the relationship is referred to in terms of a relation between father and son,[21] or master and slave,[22] rather than as

151

between master and hireling, though this latter relation is of course found in the parable of the labourers in the vineyard.[23] That is to say, the relationship between man and God is not one which is primarily contractual, subject to certain independent standards and conditions, such that man's behaviour properly earns him certain agreed wages or penalties from God. On the contrary what is demanded of man is simply that which man is created for, that which springs from his fundamental relationship to God and determines his whole life. It is true that the Rabbis too could speak like this: 'If you have learnt much Torah then do not congratulate yourself thereon: for it was for this that you were created.'[24] However, according to Preisker, such a view did not predominate. Moreover in the synoptic sayings it is predominantly doing the will of God which is fundamentally required of man, rather than the more specifically Jewish 'learning Torah'. This difference provides an important clue to the changed way in which the relationship between God and man is envisaged in the synoptic sayings. It means that there is a move away from conceiving that relationship in terms of quantifiable or codifiable codes of behaviour to seeing it in terms of a more personal and fuller relation.

This can interestingly be substantiated by considering the parable which does in fact use the relationship between master and hireling to describe the relation between man and God, the parable of the labourers in the vineyard. As Bornkamm has shown, the narrative goes to considerable pains to spell out the conditions of service under which the labourers are hired. The relationship is clearly a contractual one with certain conditions to be fulfilled by either side: so much work, so much pay. However this carefully devised account of the hiring of the labourers is not the point of the narrative but rather the 'very effective foil' to the wholly surprising course of events at the end.[25] For the *pater familias'* decision to remunerate the last as the first

> breaks through all boundaries of civil order and justice. No scales of remuneration could ever be set up on these principles. Thus the notion of rewards which was so carefully worked into the narrative is rejected because precisely by contrast with all human

concepts of reward and achievement, of justice and fairness, God's sovereignty is to be demonstrated by his goodness (Matt. 20:15f.). This then is the meaning of God's Kingdom (20:1): *God's mercy knows no bounds.*[25]

Thus the central point of the story is to reject the notion of rewards as a regulator of the relationship between God and man. God's relations with men cannot be constrained within such bounds, useful as they may be in some contexts. God in his mercy and goodness wishes to be generous to the least of men, as well as to the first, desires to heal the sick and forgive the sinners as well as to 'reward' the righteous.

Similarly the reaction of the labourers who have worked through the heat of the day holds a lesson about the nature of man's response to God. Like the reaction of the elder son in the parable of the prodigal son,[26] the labourers' remark expresses a deep-seated resistance on the part of the righteous to the graciousness of God's mercy and love. The new vision of God which is offered to men demands as its correlate the humble, grateful acceptance of God's love and mercy, the willing compliance with his gracious ways towards oneself and towards others. The labourers and the elder son represent those whose assumptions about God are founded on an understanding of Law as an impersonal bond between man and God, regulating the conduct of each. Both the stories—especially the prodigal—contain the particular twist that those who react so sourly against God's gracious dealings with the fallen and the weak are those who have all along enjoyed his grace: 'you are always with me, and everything I have is yours', and this must I think clearly be aimed at Jesus' Jewish contemporaries. Again on such a reading the authenticity of these parables seems likely. The vision which Jesus offers men is a vision of the reality of the presence of God which they have long experienced even if they have failed to grasp its true nature. There is, that is to say, an appeal to the tradition over against those who claim to be its true administrators.

Thus to the questions, what God gives to those to whom he is merciful and to whom is he merciful? certain answers are suggested. What God gives men is not a material reward for his service; it is rather the blessing of his own gracious and merciful presence with men. Moreover, we can say that God's giving to men is not conditional on men's efforts, on past performance at all. On the contrary, he extends his mercy to the least of men, to the fallen, the sick, the sinners and the outcast, to all who humbly receive it.

The question however still remains: what of those who reject God's mercy, of those who oppress or persecute the 'little ones', of those whose ways are governed by quite other assumptions about power? How can God be said to rule while his people are oppressed? What will be the ultimate fate of the wicked? Again such topics bring Jesus close to his contemporary Jews, John the Baptist, the Zealots, Qumran. Again we shall see how Jesus with his very different understanding of God gives very different answers to such questions, and indeed leaves certain questions simply unanswered.

The subject of Jesus' teaching about the End is notoriously complex, but it may help to draw out first the comparison with his contemporaries in some detail, and to do this in relation to certain topics. So we shall ask: *who* would be vindicated, according to a given school of thought, in the final resolution of the conflict between good and evil? *How* would they be vindicated? and to what extent might the faithful contribute or work towards the final Resolution? We are concerned, that is, to distinguish various contemporary beliefs about the End.

Let us start with John the Baptist. John announced the imminent judgement of men by God and called men to repent and be baptized as a sealing against God's wrath and to do good works 'worthy of repentance'. For John then those who will be vindicated in the coming crisis are all those who have repented and been baptized and who now do good works, whether Jew or Gentile. Membership of the people of Israel alone will not save a man. Nor are good works conceived strictly in terms of Torah, but in terms of fundamental virtues, sharing one's goods with the poor, just dealings, humane conduct. That is to say, according to Luke[27] John legislated for tax-collectors and Roman soldiers as well as for Jews. How would they be vindicated? Those who repented would be preserved in the coming judgement. The 'stronger one' whom John expected would come baptizing with the Holy Spirit and with fire.[28] He would sift the baptized from the wicked, and the wicked would be destroyed by fire while those who had repented would be purified by the Holy Spirit. A new era would be ushered in where men would live in peace and justice in the sight of God. Essentially the solution of the problem of evil is a practical one. The wicked will be destroyed while those who, though contaminated by evil, repent of their ways will be purified and renewed so that they become worthy members of the new era.

To what extent then might men co-operate with God in the renewal of the earth? Only, for John, in so far as they opened themselves to his renewing work and bore fruits worthy of repentance. One might say simply that the co-operation which was required of men was their co-operation in their own individual reformation. With the exception of John's disciples who assisted him in his baptizing ministry, John's followers do not seem to have formed a cohesive or in any sense organized group or community. They had no specific political or religious programme, but simply awaited the imminent coming of the 'stronger one'.

The Zealots' answers to our questions can be sketched out roughly for our purposes. They too looked forward to the day when the righteous would be vindicated. For them the righteous were those among the people of Israel who remained faithful to its traditions and in particular resisted foreign corruption of those traditions. As those who were 'zealous' for the Law they were particularly concerned with Israel's purity, its privileges, especially with the purity of the Temple. To this end men were called to leave all that they had and to 'follow after' their charismatic leaders in a military campaign against the occupying powers. This 'holy war' would lead to the ultimate overthrow of the Romans and the vindication of Israel. After an initial period of skirmishing in the desert, the whole people would rise against the occupying forces. Setbacks would follow and a period of growing oppression would be ended only by God's miraculous intervention.[29] Thus for the Zealots the final solution was also a practical one, conceived in terms of the political and military defeat of their opponents and the restoration of Israel to full independence, so that the Law might again regulate the life of the people.

155

Such a final resolution lay—ultimately—in God's hands, but the co-operation[30] of the Zealots themselves was equally a necessary condition of such a solution. Whereas for John the end would come with the advent of the heavenly figure of the Son of Man, for the Zealots the Messiah was variously identified as one of their leaders and they themselves were God's agents. Even so their role was more that of bringing about the situation which would lead to God's final intervention than of engineering the final victory itself.

The writings of the Qumran community present again a different picture.[31] In the *War Rule* those who are to be vindicated are members of God's army, the Sons of Light, who will overcome the opposing army of the Sons of Darkness led by Belial. The two forces represent Israel and the nations and God has determined the day when the final battle will occur and salvation come to Israel. Salvation is conceived, as with John and the Zealots, in earthly terms as the restoration of Israel's religious, political and economic independence. In all this there is clearly a close resemblance to the Zealot programme. What is of particular interest is the sharply dualist language used to characterize the two opposing parties. Israel's opponents are not simply those who destroy Israel's traditions and oppress its people; they are under the rule of Satan. In the later versions of the text this is brought out by the contrast between the rule (*memshālāh*)[32] of Belial, or of the Kittiim on the one hand and of the Saints, of Michael, and Israel on the other. God's rule is denoted by the comparable term *malkuth*.

It is not easy to identify the Sons of Light. If the War Rule has a long history and originally predates the Qumran community[33] it may well be that 'Israel' referred to the people as a whole, or to those who sought a renewal of Israel's traditions. In later recensions the term 'the rule of the Saints' may be taken to indicate that the victorious army is to be composed of those who have entered the community of Qumran. The answers to our other questions are more easily given. Vindication will come as the result of a military defeat of the Sons of Darkness which will usher in a new age of earthly blessedness: 'at the season appointed by God, His Exalted Greatness shall shine eternally to the peace, blessing, glory, joy and long life of all the Sons of Light.'[34] As far as the co-operation of the

156

faithful is concerned, this is explicitly described as participation in the battle.

The War Rule is important for our purposes because of the sharp contrast it draws between the rule of the Saints and the rule of Belial. The same kind of contrast is drawn in a theologically more sophisticated way in the sections of the Community Rule: 1QS 3.13–4.26 and 10.9–11.22. In these passages the division of men into two groups occurs by an eternal decision of the Father. The division is effected through the two spirits which God has appointed: the spirits of truth and falsehood. Men are ruled over either by one or the other and at God's visitation they will get their reward: either eternal blessedness or eternal punishment. But while such an ultimate fate is foreordained, in the interim men, because of their weakness, are all plagued in some measure by the spirit of wickedness, so that it is only through God's great mercy that the children of righteousness are saved and justified. Thus here the dualism is developed in terms of a doctrine of predestination. This firmly subordinates the dualism to an overarching monotheism and would appear to open the way for transcending the national character of the division between the Sons of Light and of Darkness in the War Rule for example. However the Sons of Light are in fact still drawn from Israel, although not all Israel is called. To complain, however, as do some commentators that this is less than theologically pure is a trifle quaint. If God is conceived of as arbitrarily choosing some men and damning the rest, there seems to me nothing more or less arbitrary about his choosing only—some—Jews.

Indeed we may see here a development of the association of God's mercy with the election of the people of Israel parallel to the development we traced elsewhere of the association of 'doing the Law' with 'not doing as the Gentiles do'. Just as in Qumran 'doing the Law' becomes 'doing the Law as revealed to the Teacher of Righteousness', which is then linked with 'not doing as the Gentiles do, nor as the wicked Priest does,' etc., so too God's mercy is linked with the election of those members of Israel whom he has chosen and brought under the covenant according to his revelation to the Teacher of Righteousness while those excluded number not only

157

the Gentiles, but also those who follow the erroneous teachings of the Pharisees, etc.

It is then the elect, those over whom the spirit of truth rules, who will be vindicated at God's visitation. The nature of this visitation is portrayed as a healing for those who walk in the spirit of truth, issuing in 'great peace in a long life, fruitfulness, together with every everlasting blessing and eternal joy in life without end, a crown of glory and a garment of majesty in unending light'.[35] This healing is also portrayed as a purification by 'rooting out all spirit of falsehood from the bounds of his flesh and by shedding upon him the spirit of truth (to cleanse him) of all abomination and falsehood'.[36] Such purification will then lead to a life of blessedness on this earth and to a life of joy and blessing and glory in the life beyond death. By contrast the wicked are destined for both eternal torment and ultimate destruction.[37]

It follows then within this predestinarian framework that man's part is at most that of being a receptive object of what God has already decided to work in him. In fact of course this does not preclude the community's most active pursuance of the Law, precisely as a means of separation from the wicked and of purification of the elect. It has often been suggested that there is in this respect a tension between the emphasis on God's grace and justice as the sole cause of sinful man's salvation[38] and the continued stress on works of the Law. Man is sinful, fleshly and so particularly exposed to the influence of the spirit of falsehood, so that only God's grace can save him. But equally God has chosen the Sons of Righteousness to follow in the ways of truth and to this the saints must apply themselves, seeking to understand, to do and to teach that way. I find it hard to see any lack of theological rigour here. The energy with which they follow the Law stems from their gratitude for their election and their obedience to the one who has called them.

The similarities and dissimilarities between Jesus[39] and these various contemporary approaches to the question of the overcoming of evil and falsehood in the world are complex enough to discourage any simple ascription of parentage to one particular source. Like John, Jesus looks forward to the coming of a heavenly figure who will take part in judgement;[40] but on the other hand his own ministry and preaching of the Kingdom is in form in marked contrast to John's ascetic ministry of baptism.[41] Like the Zealots he calls men to follow after him in his ministry of the Kingdom, but the Kingdom will not come by men's military efforts.[42] It grows by itself, though men may be called into its service in mission and in healing and in works of love. Like the War Rule, Jesus sees the Kingdom of God as set in opposition to the Kingdom of Satan, but for him the overthrow of Satan is already in essence achieved[43] and will be carried through not by a military campaign but by healings, exorcisms and preaching. Again, the strong emphasis on God's mercy to the fallen and stumbling which characterizes sections of the Community Rule and the hymns, come close to the view of God's mercy which lies at the heart of Jesus' preaching of the Kingdom; but in Jesus' teaching[44] there is no limit on that mercy such as is set by God's eternal decision according to 1QS. For Jesus God's mercy is not simply to the Sons of Light, but to the fallen, to the sick, the sinners. Indeed Jesus seems explicitly to deny that God sets such boundaries to his mercy. It may be impossible for a rich man to enter the Kingdom of Heaven, but with God all things are possible![45] The question then is, does God in his freedom and mercy receive all men? and how will the conflict between the poor in spirit, the merciful, the Sons of the Kingdom and the world finally be resolved?

As we have said the point at which Jesus' contemporaries seem to come closest to his vision of the mercy of God to sinners is, surprisingly perhaps, in Qumran. But there God's mercy is limited by divine election. The forces of light will be gathered together by the mercy of God and will destroy the forces of darkness, but who is on which side is eternally prescribed. There is a similar contrast indeed in the Gospels between the Kingdom of God and the Kingdom of Satan, but in Jesus' teaching God's mercy is not so much evidenced in gathering the Sons of Light into the fold and protecting them from the forces of darkness[46] as in his overcoming of Satan, in rescuing those who are in the grip of Satan. Thus the 'signs' of the Kingdom are the healings and exorcisms by which men are won over and released and the meals which Jesus shares with the impure and the outcasts. Hence alongside the proclamation of God's active presence in the world goes the assertion that Satan's grip is loosed and that men are being freed. Again what we can see here is the way that Jesus' radical understanding of the mercy of God transforms contemporary notions of spiritual warfare. The image is not altogether foreign to the synoptic sayings; it occurs not only in the Beelzebub controversy but also in the parable of the king going to war.[47] In the first place what distinguishes Jesus' teaching is his confidence that Satan is already overthrown, that his power is broken, a confidence which is drawn from his conviction of the reality of the healing power of God: 'If I by the Spirit of God cast out demons then the Kingdom of God is come upon you.'[48] Secondly the nature of the warfare is changed. It is no longer conceived in terms of spiritual purification, leading to a final military conflict, but rather in terms of receiving healing and forgiveness, preparatory to oneself giving and mediating such healing and forgiveness to others. The cost of such 'warfare' is still great, as the parable of the king going to war makes clear. The action of the disciples in following Jesus will bring on them dire consequences,[49] and can be undertaken only in the confidence that God's mercy and love are stronger than all.

The question then is, if Jesus thus remoulded the idea of spiritual warfare which played such an important part in apocalyptic ideas of the End, what view did he himself have of the final solution. Would all be won over by the mercy of God? What of those who hardened their hearts? Again, if Jesus radically reworked the notion of the holy war, did he perhaps not replace it with, for example, the notion of a final assize which, though often associated with the holy war, is clearly distinct and found in isolation in John's teaching?

The subject bristles with difficulties[50] and will not be resolved in a few paragraphs. I can at best make some tentative assertions. I think it is likely that Jesus expected the End soon and was therefore in this respect mistaken. Sayings like Mark 9:1, 13:30f., Luke 17:20f. make this at least very probable. In this respect he is very close to John, who saw the axe already laid against the root of the tree, although John's expectation was based on his belief in the imminence of the coming of the 'stronger one', whereas Jesus' was arguably based more on the conviction that God had already overthrown

Satan. But were Jesus' expectations in other respects like those of John?

John expected a heavenly figure who would judge (which is to say destroy) the wicked and purify those who had repented, thus establishing God's Kingdom on earth. Jesus certainly seems to have expected a heavenly figure, the Son of Man, who would be present in some capacity at judgement ('confessing and being ashamed of men') but it is less clear whether he conceived the expected Kingdom in purely this-worldly terms or not. The evidence is strong that he believed in some kind of resurrection[51] and in some kind of life after death,[52] but too fragmentary to allow us to construct any very clear picture of Jesus' precise conceptions. It may be that as Qumran expected an earthly Kingdom to be set up whose inhabitants after a long and prosperous life would inherit an eternal crown, so Jesus too entertained some hope which embraced both peace on earth and in heaven. 'Thy will be done, on earth as in heaven'. But if the gate[53] to this earthly-heavenly paradise was to be the judgement brought by the Son of Man, who would pass through?

The synoptic tradition certainly contains a number of sayings which limit entry to the Kingdom, either in numerical terms: 'Many are called but few are chosen'[54] or in terms of certain qualities or actions: mercy, humility, peacemaking as in the Beatitudes.[55] It is doubtful however whether the numerical sayings which have a distinctly predestinarian ring would be considered authentic, whereas sayings like the Beatitudes still leave open the question whether such qualities and actions may not eventually be shared or performed by all.

Some further light may be shed on Jesus' understanding of judgement by considering the Son of Man sayings which are specifically concerned with the future coming of the Son of Man. If Jesus uttered such sayings, as I believe he did, then it is further evidence that he imagined that the course of world history was indeed leading to a final confrontation with a divine emissary accompanied by angelic spirits. However we must be careful not to identify such a figure automatically with John the Baptist's 'stronger one' who judges with fire, or indeed to press the often adduced parallel with Daniel 7 too closely. In both cases the underlying notion of God's

161

righteousness which destroys the wicked, clearly set out in the vision in Daniel 7:9–10, is quite different from Jesus' understanding of God's love and mercy. Nevertheless the idea of judgement, of some division of men is clearly intended in, for example, Mark 8:38. It may not be that of the 'stronger one's' baptism with the Holy Spirit or fire, but what is intended by the Son of Man's 'confessing and being ashamed of men'? The immediate sense is certainly forensic in some way:[56] the Son of Man will act as advocate for or will accuse or not speak up for men. A number of features must be mentioned about the saying itself. The Son of Man is not himself judge but appears before the *Father*, a term which elsewhere is closely related to notions of God's care and mercy and favour to men. The second feature to be noticed is the relation of the Son of Man's actions to men's actions in confessing and being ashamed of Jesus' words and person. In this sense one might say that the Son of Man is doing no more than relaying to the Father the reactions of men to the love and mercy of God as they encountered it in the person and words of Jesus. The correlation of the two suggests that, whatever form the final resolution of the struggle between God's love and men's enmity may take, it will not be one which goes back on the unconditional love and forgiveness which God offers men through the words of Jesus. Equally the setting of the words of Jesus in this apocalyptic context argues their ultimate significance as pointing to or representing the foundation of the new world which is opened to men through his ministry. At most what this tells us is that Jesus looked forward to some final reckoning when men would be confronted with the reality of God's love and glory and in its light be judged. The question whether those whose lives are thus seen to be dark and loveless might still finally be healed and restored remains unanswered as such, but instead men are pointed to the present reality of God's forgiveness. Again as in Jesus' treatment of the notion of rewards and punishments, a notion which is anyway closely related to that of judgement, one can see clearly the way in which the seams of the theological terms Jesus employs are burst by the wine which he pours into them. Contemporary Jewish views of some final assize or visitation, when men will get their deserts, break down when they are so sharply conjoined with the notion of God's love and forgiveness as propounded by Jesus. The fact that the Christian tradition in Mark 13 and Matthew 25 and also rather differently in, for example, 1 Corinthians 15, quickly supplied the missing detail shows how strange and new such a breaking of Jewish notions was, even for those who attempted to follow Jesus. The intention of Jesus' teaching however must be to turn men away from speculation about the final resolution of the conflict between good and evil to the contemplation and service of the present reality of God's grace.

Lastly we must consider whether Jesus called men to co-operate in the overcoming of evil and darkness. How far and in what way were they to engage in 'spiritual warfare', how far were they simply to hold themselves ready for the coming of the Son of Man? Again it is not easy to form a clear impression. The tradition clearly contains material which encourages men to take up their cross and follow Jesus; equally he sends his disciples out on a mission very similar to his own.[57] How far this material has been shaped by the subsequent missionary experience of the Church, how far it is original, it is difficult to say. It certainly suggests that Jesus called some to co-operate in the work of healing and preaching which would bring in or even hasten the End. On the other hand there is a very considerable amount of material, sayings and parables, which exalts the virtues of watchfulness, of waiting, of faithfulness to the hope of the End.[58] Some of this may have been shaped or modified to speak to the Church's anxieties when the expected End failed to materialize,[59] but some may well reflect faithfully Jesus' vivid expectation of a divine inbreaking into the world which would end the present evil age. Again, the material we have lacks sharpness. It is not easy to construct from it a detailed scenario of the events of the End, of the part or parts to be played in them by men. May be—as for example A. Schweitzer believed—Jesus' picture was very simple. He and his disciples would issue a call to repent and believe and then when men had responded God would usher in the new age. May be subsequent editing and development of the tradition have obscured and destroyed the picture that Jesus really had. Or may it be that Jesus' ideas on this point were again less sharp and clearly defined than other contemporary views because of the deep break which he had made with their basic apprehension of God? Indeed Jesus' reported refusal to 'give a sign',[60] to spell out the answer to questions about the End, supports strongly the view that Jesus did not wish to be drawn on such issues but wanted rather to focus attention on the present reality of God's love and grace.

It may be worth venturing a few remarks in this context about the relation between John's and Jesus' teaching on these topics. To what extent and for what reasons has Jesus modified John's teaching? It is, I think, reasonable to take Jesus' baptism by John as an indication that Jesus at that time accepted John's teaching about the end, viz. that those who repented and were baptized and who bore fruits worthy of repentance would—shortly—be vindicated and purified by the stronger one when he came. We may equally accept that John's imprisonment and beheading provided a clear 'disconfirmation' of that teaching. What then seems to have occurred is that Jesus subsequently emerged announcing the coming of the Kingdom in terms rather different from those of John. There is still the expectation of a coming figure and a coming judgement, but this is related to an enthusiastic charismatic ministry, to a call to discipleship and to a proclamation of the forgiveness and mercy of a Father God. The conventional association of God's righteousness with a final judgement and with his establishment of his rule over the world has not been abandoned. What has changed is that certain detailed beliefs about the order of events have been abandoned. Most importantly, the belief has been abandoned that all that is required on the part of man is an act of repentance preparatory to the final intervention of God. Rather, in Jesus' reworking of the notion of a holy war, we see his belief that evil cannot simply be disposed of by a final act of God's judgement, but that it must be dealt with in the present as the power of God's forgiveness and mercy confronts men in his words and preaching. God's judgement will then ultimately reflect this struggle between God's mercy and men's enmity.

Again, as we have seen elsewhere in this chapter, there is no substantial change in the conventional associations of terms. But equally beliefs are being expressed here about God's righteousness and his overcoming of evil which make the conventional association of God's righteousness with a final assize at the least strained; and which must also put serious question marks against the notion that such an assize was imminent. Out of Jesus' experience of the disappointment of John's hopes that God would speedily intervene to destroy the wicked and to uphold and to purify the righteous is born a vision of God's action as a—patient—and forgiving approach to his enemies, healing and restoring, rather than condemning and destroying.

Let us now try to bring together our discussion of Jesus' teaching about God and his care and governance of the world. As we have seen, there are considerable difficulties in reconciling the sayings attributed to Jesus in the synoptic tradition which speak in general, universal terms of God's fatherly care and providence for all living things and those which speak of his rule being finally established only when the Kingdom of Satan is completely overthrown. Nevertheless I have tried to show how, even in those sayings which express a general belief in God's providence, the point of the saying lies in Jesus' assertion of God's care and forgiveness of those whom he is addressing and that there are therefore good grounds for asserting their authenticity. This does not however remove the theoretical problem, though it helps I think to explain how Jesus came to make such diverse statements.

As far as the theoretical problem is concerned I would want to make two general points. In the first place, while the problem of reconciling the belief in God's general care for all things with the belief that Satan is abroad in the world causing sickness, disease and all manner of wickedness cannot be denied, it is equally clear that the *problem itself* is not the subject of any of Jesus' sayings. His concern is a fundamentally practical one, that of overcoming the evil in the world which inhibits or impairs God's rule over it, more specifically of proclaiming the action which God was already taking to overcome such evil; not the theoretical one of explaining how such things could be. This is not to say that, in the traditions on which Jesus drew, such theoretical considerations were not raised. Indeed the introduction of dualist modes of thought into Judaism must be seen as an attempt to explain the Jews' experience of suffering and persecution which ran counter to their doctrines of

God's rule and governance. But whereas in, for example, the Qumran doctrine of predestination we find some kind of theoretical account of how the existence of evil forces in the world is compatible with God's ultimate sovereignty, the synoptic tradition offers nothing comparable.

Secondly, if it is the case that Jesus' orientation towards the problem of evil and suffering is fundamentally practical then we should not be too surprised if in his teaching there are theoretical ends left untied. Belief in the universal care of God for his creatures is used by Jesus largely as a means of illuminating or underscoring the experience and apprehension of God's love and mercy which he tried to communicate and teach to men. Nevertheless it must be recognized that there is a danger here. If such a belief in God's universal care and providence is made central to our account of Jesus' teaching it would seriously distort the picture. Jesus did not I think ultimately envisage God as a God who was sovereignly in charge of all things, if by that is meant exercising, if he wishes, absolute control over the actions and fate of all things and creatures. Such a God might for a while allow Satan to rampage until it pleased him to put an end to it and to settle accounts. By contrast the fundamental springs of Jesus' understanding of God lie in his vision of a God who enters the world as a merciful, loving, forgiving reality, who is in the world healing and overcoming darkness and evil, who—simply—loves his enemies. What it means to pray to such a God, how such a God exercises his rule and governance over the world, how he will ultimately overcome evil and lovelessness and corruption, how men may work and co-operate with such a God, what kind of society and world can be developed on the basis of such belief, are questions to which Jesus gave only preliminary answers. Indeed I have tried to argue that, in his taking up of certain Jewish theological traditions concerning rewards and punishments, concerning spiritual warfare against the enemy and the final judgement, we often see more clearly how such notions fail to serve Jesus' purpose, than we see what positive answers Jesus might have given. The new wine of Jesus' thesis about God bursts the skins of the old bottles; the synthesis has yet to emerge.

Thus it is that Jesus must effectively recast the Jewish doctrine of rewards and punishments because his view of God's mercy and bounty cannot countenance the limits which such a doctrine imposes on God's dealings with man. So too he rejects the Zealot notion of a holy war, because of his deep conviction that God liberates men from the grip of Satan rather than destroying those who are under his sway. Even in his use of the idea of a final judgement, Jesus' sayings, particularly in Mark 8:38 and parallel, create a subtle dialectic between the vision of a future judgement when the Son of Man will plead for or accuse men before his Father and the present response of men to his ministry and preaching. In all this we have beginnings and suggestions as to how a doctrine of God's governance of the world might be developed, but it was left to those who came after him to work this out more thoroughly. How successful such attempts have been is not our subject here, but what we have seen of the nature of Jesus' utterances on this topic should provide important insights for assessing their success.

But while Jesus did not himself work out such a developed theism he did work out the implications of his vision of God in his own personal history and way. Thus while his sayings leave us with a complex set of moral and theological tasks, his own life and ministry, which led him ultimately to the cross, represent a radical development of his vision of God in purely human terms.

8

Jesus' Role in the Transformation of First-Century Judaism

Now that we have seen something of the way in which Jesus re-worked fundamental beliefs which contemporary Judaism held about God, man and the world and of the nature of the response which he made to the social anomie of first-century Judaism we can attempt to characterize the role which Jesus himself played in this process. To this end we shall look both at the ways in which Jesus' contemporaries saw him and at the evidence we have for Jesus' own understanding of himself.

Before turning to this task it may help to summarize what we have already suggested about Jesus' overall strategy with regard to first-century Judaism and its problems. I have argued first that Pharisaism, Essenism and Zealotism all presented fairly detailed *programmes* of resistance and, in part at least, aggression towards Hellenism and its agents and also towards Jewish groups with different strategies. Jesus in his preaching and call to discipleship attacked the basis of current Jewish strategies by challenging the beliefs about God on which they rested, notably the belief that God's justice required that he should destroy the wicked, notably the oppressors of Israel. This can be seen most clearly in his linking his proclamation of the Kingdom of God with his meals with tax-collectors and sinners. Again, whereas Pharisees and Essenes con-structed clearly defined and ritually enforced barriers between mem-bers of the group and non-members and also between different members within the group, Jesus attacked such barriers as a means of regulating behaviour between groups and pointed instead to personal standards as the true guide to human relationships. Such relationships were to be measured above all by the standard of God's love and mercy towards *all* men. Lastly we saw how Jesus in his treatment of more speculative doctrines about God's providence and control of history reformulated doctrines of rewards and punishments, and of the End, in such a way that God and his servants were now seen to be involved in a struggle between love and forgiveness and their contraries, hatred, enmity and vengeance. Again, while many of Jesus' contemporaries appear to have had fairly clear ideas about the course of history leading to some final resolution and intervention of God, in Jesus' teaching, while there is a clear expectation of *some* final resolution, its precise nature and outcome is made to depend on the issue of the present encounter and struggle between love and its opposites. Similarly men are called to a discipleship whose course is equally unspecified even though its end is assured. In all this, we have suggested, we can see more the seeds of a new strategy towards Hellenism and the forces which oppressed Israel than the development of a detailed strategy itself. This is of course partly because the emphasis on personal standards, on the qualities of love and mercy, rather than on a justice operating according to strictly apportioned rewards and punishments, does not permit such a detailed specification of human conduct and behaviour. But it is also I think in the nature of Jesus' particular contribution to the development of his tradition that he is more concerned to make certain fairly fundamental alterations to its general direction than to specify a particular move as such. Thus questions about the nature of the community which can be developed on the basis of such an understanding of God, about control and discipline within it, about its relations with other communities and powers, are dealt with piecemeal rather than systematically. More theoretical questions as we have seen are only broached but in no way resolved. Jesus' response is thus radical and creative in the sense that he is concerned both to set aside the accepted patterns of response of Jewish renewal movements as well as to reach out for new patterns of response, even if their details and consequences can be realized only when the break with the old has been made. What we shall now consider is how far such an understanding of the

169

transformation of Judaism wrought by Jesus is reflected in his utterances about himself.

The question about Jesus' role is formulated deliberately by contrast with questions about Jesus' aims[1] or purposes.[2] Reimarus embarked on a search for the man Jesus by asking what purpose Jesus had for himself. This was partly by contrast with attempts to see Jesus as a divine revealer figure with no *human* purpose at all; but also partly by contrast with attempts to construe Jesus' purpose in terms of some general religious aim, viz. of teaching the doctrines of pure, rational religion. By contrast with this latter view, Reimarus conceived Jesus' 'purpose for himself' in more political, emancipatory terms: specifically he related it to Jesus' plans for liberating the Jews from the Romans. In this he doubtless erred in construing Jesus' purpose in unduly narrow political terms. What is perhaps less often seen is that by focusing attention on Jesus' purpose as he did he narrowed the field of inquiry and omitted questions about the deeper religious apprehensions of Jesus, about the manner in which, as we have argued, he attempted creatively and freely to remould men's vision and apprehension of God, the world and man. It is in this I would argue that Jesus' real contribution to the development of a new religio-social world lies, rather than in any attempts he may have made to play out or influence some expected apocalyptic—or even political—drama.

Thus in turning to Jesus' own understanding of his role we are seeking, first, confirmation that his conception of it is indeed in accordance with his reworking of basic Jewish beliefs about God, the world and man; secondly we shall be wanting to see whether the meaning of Jesus' utterances on this subject is consonant with what we have suggested about the kind of strategy he developed *vis-à-vis* Hellenism and the forces which threatened Judaism.

Two further introductory points occur, one methodological, one theological. First, it hardly needs saying that this is an enormously difficult area in which to make judgement about the authenticity of particular sayings. I think sometimes the critical caution of some scholars has been almost a kind of self-defence against apologetic. They have feared that their own Christian convictions might lead them to attribute to Jesus sayings expressing some kind of messianic self-consciousness, which more detached observers would have discounted. This supposes a rather more direct relationship between this kind of inquiry and Christology than is perhaps appropriate. Even when we have established what Jesus said there is a complex process of analysis to be completed before we can make use of such results in Christology. I shall accordingly be rather more adventurous about attributing sayings to Jesus, not because I feel it is wise to throw scholarly caution to the winds, but because of an interest in seeing what the consequences for our understanding of Jesus' role would be if he had uttered such and such sayings.

Secondly, the question about Jesus' role in transforming first-century Judaism is intended to be a general historical question that any student of religious history might wish to tackle. In this respect it shares certain features with Reimarus's questions about Jesus' purpose for himself. Reimarus certainly intended his question to be destructive of traditional christological thought. Lessing I believe saw that it might lead beyond that to a reorientation in theology which would promote a different view of the relationship between man and God than one of pure passivity and instrumentality on the part of man. This realization bore fruit for example in Bultmann's study of Jesus as the one who brings to expression a new self-understanding in terms of living out of the judgement and forgiveness of God. The question of Jesus' role in the transformation of Judaism may again seem to be directed against traditional views which see Jesus' purpose as being one of reconciling sinners to God by some kind of once-and-for-all cosmic transaction, and even against the transformation of that tradition by theologians such as Bultmann. But equally I would argue, though this would exceed the scope of the present study, that it is by no means without its positive theological implication in enabling us to see God's dealings with men as being mediated through the man who grapples with his society's fundamental assumptions about power. If at the root of all Christology lies the belief in the assumption of humanity in order that it be healed, what such a treatment of Jesus' role may help to promote is deeper reflection on the way in which that humanity is dependent in any given community on a network of commonly held conventions by means of which are expressed cer-

171

tain assumptions about power, about the nature of the world. Only a radical transformation of such assumptions can lead to a radical transformation of man.

Let us now turn to a consideration of the utterances of Jesus and his contemporaries about his role in the Kingdom.

Jesus' preaching of the Kingdom and repentance places him, we have said, among those who looked for a renewal of Israel. Among such groups, renewal was variously associated with certain kinds of figures, leaders, warriors, prophets, priests, teachers. For our purposes we shall have to give first a sketch of those Jewish notions about 'renewal-figures' which seem to come closest to the kind of way in which Jesus talked about himself, to the kind of figure he suggested by his actions and preaching, to the kinds of impressions he made on his contemporaries. We shall then have to ask to what extent Jesus accepted the conventional associations of such terms as he applied to himself in order to see what Jesus was saying in such utterances.

Among the Zealot—nationalist—groups hopes for the restoration of Israel were centred on the charismatic military leader.[3] Such a figure was clearly associated with the great military leaders of the past: Jephta, David, the Maccabees. His role was to gather the faithful, those who were 'zealous' for the Law, for the true traditions of the nation, and to lead them in military struggle against the occupying powers who enslaved the people. Such a struggle could not be brought to a successful conclusion without ultimately the intervention of Yahweh, quite possibly through the sending of a heavenly Messiah figure. Thus the role of Judas was to initiate the struggle and to pursue it to the point when God would finally liberate his people. But equally figures like the priest Phinehas, whose zeal for the Law led him to strike down those who took foreign women, and the associated figure of Elijah the charismatic prophet serve as important models for the Zealot leader.[4]

Such leaders, as Hengel has argued,[5] were not simply military figures. They were inspired charismatic figures who broke radically with existing norms of behaviour and called men to leave all and follow them in the service of the only King, Yahweh. By contrast with such notions of renewal figures among the more activist, ag-

172

gressive nationalist groups we find within the more 'subsiditive' groups[6] notions of heavenly figures who would be sent to intervene on behalf of the faithful. Such figures were associated with prophets and teachers who would announce their coming and prepare the people for the time. This is clearly too vast a field to do more than list the different notions which were, or may have been, current in Jesus' day, but it is important at least to get some overall picture and some idea of how these notions worked, how they related to other expectations.

The term 'Son of Man' clearly belongs here even if we can say very little with any confidence about it. It may of course be that it never designated a particular figure at all and that its treatment as a title rests on a linguistic mistake.[7] Even if this theory is not accepted—and I think it does not do justice wholly to the way the title appears to have been introduced into the synoptic material[8]— we still have difficulties both in delineating and dating the notion. The term in Hebrew or Aramaic may refer to a particular individual as, for example, in the address to Ezekiel; or it may refer to mankind in general. Hence the possibility of considerable elasticity in the use of the term in apocalyptic literature to refer either to some individual redeemer figure or to the community of the redeemed.[9] Again simplifying, this possibility does not seem to outweigh the clear use of the term in the Similitudes of Enoch,[10] in Daniel[11] and 4 Ezra 13 to refer to a heavenly, sometimes pre-existent figure whom God will send to vindicate his saints. This then seems to represent the core meaning of the term. Such vindication is most clearly associated with judgement, with the rewarding of the saints with long life and blessedness and the destruction of God's enemies in fire and eternal torments.[12] It is also apparently associated with some kind of last battle between the forces of darkness and the Son of Man.[13] It is of course controversial whether the title was in existence at the time of Jesus, whether it was coined by him or by the early Church.

As well as such a figure associated with the final vindication of Israel we also find in the Qumran literature the two Messiahs of Aaron and Israel,[14] the priest and the king who will preside at the messianic banquet, having led the community to victory in the final struggle. Here the kingly—military—figure is subordinated to the

173

priest figure who will restore the true worship of Israel and hence re-establish its true relations with God. Such figures are hardly to be seen as heavenly, even pre-existent, figures; they are men whom God will raise up in the last days to rule over his people.[15]

Alongside such redeemer figures are a number of other figures sometimes associated with them who will prepare Israel for the coming redemption. Foremost among these is the prophet,[16] though this term clearly had a range of possible associations. It has roots in two Old Testament passages: Malachi 3:1; 4:1–6 and Deuteronomy 18:15–18. The Malachi passage is associated with the return of Elijah to call the people to repentance in face of the coming of the Lord and as it stands makes no reference to any further messianic figures. The Deuteronomy passage foretells a prophet like Moses and was specifically associated in the tradition[17] with the Exodus and the performance of miracles. In this respect we may notice here the figures, referred to by Josephus, who, promising miracles, led the people into the desert. Notable among them is the figure of Theudas[18] who foretold a new parting of the waters at the River Jordan. Miracles here are clearly associated with the events of the Exodus. The notion[19] is also associated in Qumran with the Messiahs of Aaron and Israel.[20] Hahn[21] has argued that the choice of the Moses typology, as opposed to Elijah, is characteristic of Qumran, because it had already abandoned the people as a *massa perditionis*. The association of the prophet with the Messiahs gives way, he speculates, in later texts to a schema of history which speaks in terms of 'the taking away of the only teacher and the appearance of the Messiahs of Aaron and Israel'.[22] Hahn believes that the eschatological prophet has here been identified with the teacher and that this occurred because of the obvious association of Moses with teaching the Law. However that may be, it is likely that this kind of eschatological prophet was associated both with miraculous signs and with teaching authority.

Lastly, we must consider briefly the role which teachers had in the renewal of Judaism. Clearly what we have just seen of the Teacher of Righteousness is relevant here. A revelation of the hidden meaning of Torah marks the decisive opening of the period of history leading to the end; it is the basis of the life of the community, that by which progress is assessed,[23] the gift which has to be kept from the impure and the wicked.[24] The teaching of the community, which is continued through its council and officers is thus that which serves to mark out the community from the world and the means whereby they can prepare themselves for the coming crisis.

There is doubtless a similarly esoteric function to the Law[25] as taught by the sages at the time of Jesus. There can be no doubt that in attempting to extend the prescriptions of Torah to cover all areas of life the sages were seeking to strengthen observance of the Law and that for them the future of Judaism lay along this path. Renewal here lay in an extension of the Law into all areas of life and in fencing it off from all possible error or contamination. In terms of a response to Hellenism it was essentially a defensive response, if not without its proselytizing sides. Only later, when the basis of Judaism in the Temple was destroyed, did the teachers of the sages come to play a more dominant role. Rabbi Johanan ben Zakkai had effectively to refound Judaism, setting in motion the processes of collecting and compiling the traditions which will in Mishnah and Talmud stake out the bounds of the Jewish world.

Among Jesus' utterances which draw on the traditions we have been sketching, we shall have to consider not only those sayings in which he refers to some figure like the Son of Man, but also those in which he refers to himself in any way, discipleship sayings calling men to follow after him, 'I am come' sayings and indeed 'I' sayings where there is a particular emphasis on the 'I'.

Hengel[26] has argued powerfully that Jesus' discipleship sayings, e.g. Matthew 8:22, bring Jesus close to the Zealot tradition where too the charismatic leader called men to leave all that they had to follow after him. Like such figures Jesus linked such a call with a call to break sharply with existing norms: 'Leave the dead to bury their dead';[27] and this was further, in both cases, clearly linked with an inspired preaching of the Kingdom of God. Nevertheless, as we have seen, Jesus' stance towards the conventional associations of the term 'Kingdom' was highly critical and we should therefore not be surprised to find that here too he reworks many of the conventional associations of 'discipleship' as it had been developed in the Maccabean, Zelotic tradition. Jesus did not call men to follow him

175

in a holy war[28] in the sense of calling them to military revolt against the Romans. Quite the contrary, he taught men to love their enemies and to forgive. What is significant then is that Jesus is identifying himself as one who is active in bringing about the Kingdom by his authoritative call to men to follow after him. The nature of his role in the coming of the Kingdom is illuminated by the fact that the ministry to which he calls men is a wandering, preaching, healing and exorcizing ministry, a struggle against the kingdom of Satan waged with the prophetic and healing word. This still however leaves the questions how Jesus understood his prophetic word and whether he expected some future figure.[29] To answer this question we must look further at other sayings which relate to Jesus' person in the synoptic tradition.

The synoptic Son of Man sayings[30] can be grouped under three heads: future sayings referring to the coming of the Son of Man on clouds with glory; present sayings referring to the earthly life of the Son of Man; and sayings referring to the coming sufferings of the Son of Man. All sayings, which occur in all strata of the synoptic tradition, are in the third person and occur only on the lips of Jesus. While some scholars[31] have rejected all classes, believing that the title was a creation of the early Church, there seem grounds, partly of multiple attestation, partly of coherence with other apocalyptic sayings, for taking the future sayings as authentic and original to Jesus.[32] Assuming that we are right in identifying the core-meaning of the term as referring to a heavenly figure, then in view both of the fact that it is the earthly Jesus speaking and that he refers to the Son of Man only in the third person, it seems reasonable to assume that he is referring to a figure other than himself. Now it is argued by some[33] that it is wrong to isolate the future sayings in this way; that we grasp Jesus' meaning only if we see how he has knitted together the tradition stemming from Daniel 7 and the theology of the suffering servant from Isaiah 53 for which we need to consider the sayings from the other groups. Yet it seems to me that the kind of modification of the Danielic Son of Man tradition which such scholars ascribe to Jesus did indeed occur, but that it occurred in the development of the synoptic tradition rather than in the consciousness of Jesus. This, partly because there is good evidence for believing that the term Son of Man has been introduced during the period of oral transmission into a number of key sayings, notably Mark 10:45,[34] partly because it seems inherently improbable that the earthly Jesus would have sought to apply to himself a title—however modified— whose *core*-meaning related to a heavenly figure. It is however perfectly conceivable that such a process of modification could occur once the post-Easter community had identified the earthly Jesus with the expected heavenly figure.

Jesus then expected the coming of a heavenly figure. The belief, we may reasonably conjecture, was derived in the first instance from John the Baptist's preaching of the 'stronger one' who was to baptize with spirit and fire.[35] To what extent did Jesus modify this belief and how did he see his own relation to this coming figure? In view of the fact that Jesus' ministry was in form substantially different from John's, it is not unreasonable to suppose that Jesus shared rather different expectations about the End and about his own place in the events of the End.

Jesus' choice[36] of the title Son of Man does not in itself tell us very much. Like John's 'stronger one' the Son of Man term is strongly associated with judgement, with the vindication and purification of the righteous and the destruction by fire of the wicked. Where we do, however, gain both an insight into the particular meaning which the term may have had for Jesus and of his own place in relation to the Son of Man is in the sayings which contrast men's response to his words with the Son of Man's response to them when he comes. Key among such sayings is Luke 12:8f with its parallel in Matthew 10:32, of which Mark 8:38 and its parallel Luke 9:26 is a doublet. In this saying, which I take to be essentially authentic,[37] the Son of Man's confessing and denying ('being ashamed of', Mark)[38] men before (the angels of) God is paralleled with men's denying and confessing Jesus (me) before men. It is reasonable to suppose here that the term Son of Man is itself being qualified and further defined by being associated with Jesus (and his words), just as Jesus' ministry is being defined in relation to the Son of Man.

As I have already argued the notion of the Son of Man confessing and denying men before (the angels of) God is clearly connected with the final judgement. It is however not altogether clear whether the Son of Man is thought of as a witness, variously accusing or pleading for men, or as judge himself. The latter seems to be more the sense of the Markan version, the former that of the Q-saying.[39] But whatever the precise role of the Son of Man in judgement, the important thing for our purposes is that the standard of judgement is to be man's response to Jesus. This can only mean, I think, that judgement here is conceived not, as in John the Baptist's preaching of the 'stronger one', in terms of purification for those who bear fruits worthy of repentance and destruction by fire for those who do not, but rather in terms of the rejection of those who reject Jesus' offer of forgiveness and grace and acceptance of those who accept.[40]

If this is correct then what of Jesus' relation to the coming Son of Man? Does Jesus come to prepare the way for the Son of Man by calling men to repent and to do works worthy of repentance? In so far as John's call to repentance was a call to those who had slipped from careful observance of the Law to return to a more rigorous (albeit simplified) observance, Jesus' call is distinct. His purpose is to show and proclaim to men the living reality of God's acceptance and forgiveness and to call them to follow him. Such actions on Jesus' part and on the part of his followers are then related to judgement in the sense that those who hear and respond to Jesus' words are 'already judged'. Even if that is to introduce later Johannine accounts of the matter, the point can be made by saying that the emphasis on men's confessing or denying *Jesus*, as opposed to his gospel or preaching indicates more than a simple preparatory role for Jesus. In him God's righteousness and mercy are already present.[41]

One further point in the saying requires attention. What is required of men is that they should confess Jesus *before men*. Jesus calls men not only to acknowledge him and accept the proffered forgiveness, but to testify publicly in favour of the forgiving reality which he mediates. Thus the situation of Jesus before men in the first half of the verse is the same as men's situation before God in the second. Jesus is on trial before men. The standards, the 'law' which he proclaims is rejected by man and his followers must argue for it. The Kingdom is being done violence to and violent men press in upon it.[42] The way of Jesus is not a victorious progress but a way of suffering and trial.[43] This is also expressed in sayings like Mark 10:38 where Jesus expects a baptism, a cup, judgement, trial, testing. The 'holy war' to which Jesus calls men is one in which love and forgiveness will struggle with the powers of enmity and hatred, ready to bear the ultimate cost of such obedience. Thus Jesus' suffering and death are wholly consistent with the role which he suggests here for himself. Such suffering and death are what men are called to (Mark 8:34f) who follow him, sharing his fate. It is what is involved in the mediation to men of God's loving forgiveness and mercy.[44]

It is possible to see here how the notion of the coming heavenly judge figure such as John's 'stronger one' has been modified in line with Jesus' reworking of contemporary Jewish notions of judgement, even such as were expressed by John. Judgement is no longer conceived of as an act whereby the righteous, i.e. those who have held themselves apart from the enemies of God, however conceived, are vindicated and his enemies condemned and destroyed at the final reckoning. By contrast judgement for Jesus is related to the process of God's overcoming by his forgiving, long-suffering love the enmity, pride, lovelessness and fear of men, by which process he will restore and heal a lost world. In line with this understanding of judgement, the twin figures of a prophet of repentance and a heavenly judge yield to the picture of an earthly mediator of God's righteousness and forgiveness calling men to follow him in his struggle against enmity and darkness and of a future figure who will ratify the work of the mediator and of those whom he has called.

Jesus' consciousness of his role in this drama can be further documented by those sayings which refer to him as in some sense a prophet,[45] a term which we have seen had a number of differing associations. At its core it refers to a figure who will come before God's intervention. His purpose and task is variously to prepare the people for God's coming by calling them to repent, by performing miracles which will inaugurate God's saving action, by teaching them the true understanding of the Law. The difficulty is that there are elements in the tradition which correspond to all these prophetic types so that it is not at all easy to decide questions of authenticity.

Within the Gospels, both John and Jesus are referred to as prophets. Jesus' saying about John: 'Why then did you go out? To see a prophet? Yes, I tell you and more than a prophet.'[46] is clearly an early saying. The qualification 'more than a prophet' is explained by reference to Malachi 3:1 which, as we have seen, is one of the two sources for the notion of the eschatological prophet. Even if, as is probable, this explanation is secondary it may very well give the sense of 'more than a prophet'. John's message of repentance in face of the coming judgement fits well with the figure in Malachi.

Did Jesus recognize John as the eschatological prophet? The question is obviously important, for if he did then we would have to assess his understanding of his own role in the light of that conviction. There can, I think, be little doubt that Jesus' baptism by John gives strong evidence for such a conviction *before* his own ministry. Equally his own ministry of preaching, healing and exorcism shows that he developed an eschatology substantially different from that of John. This we have suggested is related to the 'disconfirmation' of John's expectations brought about by his death. Two possible accounts of Jesus' relation to John may then be offered. Either we may suppose that Jesus, without necessarily explicitly rejecting John's movement and preaching, effectively started a new movement with rather different hopes and beliefs after John's imprisonment, or else we can suppose that he saw his own ministry as something added to John's overall schema. The former view is to be preferred both on the grounds that there is evidence of tension between John and Jesus[47] and that this pattern of emergence of 'milennial' movements is well testified to in other cultures where figures who have been involved in a subordinate role in one movement may subsequently emerge as leaders of later movements with rather different programmes.[48] If it is the case that Jesus' movement is to be viewed as effectively a separate movement from John's but one which may be expected to have analogous traits, then John's designation as a prophet gives us a clue that this is the kind of role in which Jesus may have cast himself too. This, whether the saying in Matthew 11:9 goes back to Jesus or to the Q community.

Certainly there is evidence in the gospels that Jesus' contemporaries saw him in this role. Mark 6:15, probably a redactional insertion into the pericope[49] about Herod's reaction to Jesus, gives an account of popular reactions to Jesus: 'Others said, "It is Elijah." And others said, "It is a prophet, like one of the prophets of old." ' The reference to Elijah points fairly clearly back to the Malachi text with its expectation of an eschatological prophet of repentance. The alternative view is less easy to give any precise sense to. The best one can say is that it indicates a consciousness that Jesus' role is different from that of the prophet of repentance, perhaps laying stress on his declaration of the nature of the divine will. Luke 7:16, 39 also gives some evidence for the way Jesus' miracles might lead people to see him as a 'great prophet'.

Beyond this evidence that Jesus' behaviour struck his contemporaries as prophetic, there are some sayings attributed to Jesus himself: Mark 6:4: 'a prophet is not without honour, except in his own country'; Matthew 12:39: 'An evil and adulterous generation seeks for a sign; but no sign shall be given to it except the sign of the prophet Jonah.' As well as these sayings there are two which link Jesus' death directly or indirectly to the killing of the prophets: Luke 13:33: 'it cannot be that a prophet should perish away from Jerusalem'; Matthew 23:29f.: 'Thus you witness against yourselves, that you are sons of those who murdered the prophets.' As well as this evidence from the synoptic Gospels, there are a number of interesting passages in the fourth Gospel. In John 6 after the feeding of the multitude Jesus is acclaimed as 'the prophet who is to come into the world'. Other references occur more or less clearly in John 7:40f.; 4:19, 25; 3:2.[50]

The material here is admittedly diverse and some of it is fairly clearly secondary and redactional. It would be hard to argue that the notion of Jesus as a prophet had contributed very substantially to the development of Christology in the New Testament period. Nevertheless the existence of such a tradition in John and the synoptics may lead us to suppose that we have here 'a very early christological tradition of the primitive church'[51] which subsequently faded as the Son of Man Christology developed in various ways. The tradition was retained in so far as it served to give evidence of the popular impact which Jesus made, in so far as it was linked

181

with his own death. But can we say if this tradition went back originally to Jesus?

A number of indications suggest that it might have. In the first place there are actions of Jesus which seem to be consonant with such a self-understanding. As we have seen, typically the kind of prophet Josephus refers to claimed to work miracles which were to be the prelude to the expected intervention of God. These miracles, the parting of the waters of the Jordan, the destruction of the walls of Jerusalem, the discovery on Mount Gerizim of the Temple vessels traditionally hidden there by Moses, had associations with the events of the Exodus and may have been seen then as a prelude to the repossession of the land by the prophet[52] and his followers— evidence one might note for a further modification of the notion of a holy war. Of Jesus' recorded actions two most obviously fall into this category: the feeding of the multitude in the desert[53] and his action in cleansing the Temple.[54] Certainly in the account in the Fourth Gospel the feeding of the multitude is regarded by them as a prophetic sign; Jesus however evades attempts to force him into a messianic role. The subsequent discourse notes the similarity between Jesus' actions and the manna in the wilderness, while stressing the transcendent nature of Jesus' bread. Whether both the awareness of the similarity between Jesus' actions and those of messianic prophets *and* the suggestion that they are nevertheless of a different character accurately reflect Jesus' view of the matter is hard to say. At least these traditions, which may be early, point again to the fact that Jesus' actions had a prophetic character. Again, Jesus' cleansing of the Temple is fairly closely related to the prophecy of Malachi: 'Behold I send my messenger to prepare the way before me, and the Lord whom you seek will suddenly come to his temple.'[55] Jesus' action can be seen as preparatory, perhaps as intended to precipitate the Lord's sudden coming. In Mark's account Jesus' action raises the question of prophetic authority,[56] which Jesus discusses in relation to the Baptist.

Now it is of course difficult to know how accurate these stories are, but their wide attestation suggests that they must have some considerable substance and, as we have seen, they make good sense within the context of a ministry that is—broadly—prophetic, even if Jesus' conception of the kind of divine action he was inaugurating varied very considerably from the militaristic conceptions of a figure like Theudas.

Do we have any further evidence for Jesus' view of his role? One obvious source of such evidence is the 'I' sayings of the synoptic tradition. It has recently been argued by Arens that of the sayings of the form 'I am come to . . .', at least Mark 2:17b: 'I came not to call the righteous but sinners'; and Matthew 11:19: 'the Son of Man came eating and drinking, and they say, "Behold, a glutton and drunkard, a friend of tax-collectors and sinners" ' represent the *ipsissima vox* of Jesus. The saying in Mark 10:45a is, Arens believes, better preserved in Luke in the form: 'I am among you as one who serves' (Luke 22:27).[57] In another recent study of the use of *ego* by Jesus in the synoptic Gospels, Howard concludes that only in Matthew 5:22, 28, 34 do we have an emphatic *ego* which refers specifically to Jesus in an authentic dominical saying.[58]

On the basis of these findings we can say something about the sense of such sayings. The formula 'I am come' on the lips of Jesus would, according to Jeremias,[59] indicate primarily purpose: 'My calling in life (*Lebensberuf*) is to . . .'. This by contrast with subsequent understanding of the phrase to mean that Jesus has come (forth)[60] from heaven, the Father, etc. It is of course important that 'purpose' is not understood here too individualistically, but as related to the divine purpose in the restoration of Israel, the bringing in of the Kingdom. If that is allowed then one has in these sayings important evidence for Jesus' understanding of his prophetic role. Unlike the expectations of the Messiah in Jubilees and Ethiopian Enoch who would 'come for the sake of and to dwell among the righteous of Israel',[61] Jesus comes for the sinners,[62] to offer them God's forgiveness and acceptance. He comes moreover not as a Messiah to reign over his kingdom, but as one whose task is to win over the sinners, to call men into the struggle against enmity and hatred. The calling of *sinners* means, that is to say, that the role of the prophet is not to call the faithful to prepare for the coming judgement, not to gather the elect, but to initiate the process whereby evil and enmity are judged and overcome.[63]

The implications of this are brought out further by the saying in

Matthew 11:19, where the reference to the Son of Man is secondary. Here Jesus contrasts himself with John as the one who feasts in contrast to the ascetic Baptist. As we have argued,[64] this is to associate Jesus' preaching of the Kingdom with eschatological joy and fulfilment. In relation to his understanding of his own role it must, I think, point to a consciousness that the judgement and forgiveness which is mediated through his words and actions is not simply an announcement of what is to come but *is* already the reality and power of God. In this way the Malachi prophecy of a figure preaching repentance in the face of the coming judgement is transformed into the notion of a prophet in whose words the judging and forgiving God is already present.

Finally in the 'I say unto you' sayings of the antitheses of the Sermon on the Mount, we may detect a further development of the notion of the prophet like Moses in Deuteronomy 18:15. Jesus' authority and freedom to proclaim a radically modified version of God's will[65] clearly marks him out as a figure like the Teacher of Righteousness, whose proclamation of the Law forms the basis for a new community within the Jewish tradition. But the sharp contrast which Jesus makes between his teaching and that of Moses betrays a consciousness of the newness of his message. He is not simply the prophet of repentance recalling men to the laws of their fathers; nor is he the founder of a new community based on a special revelation of the meaning of the Law; he proclaims a new Law consonant with the judgement and mercy of God which he brings to men.

Thus I think it is possible to trace in these sayings a coherent understanding of Jesus' prophetic role which draws on both the traditions of Malachi 3 and Deuteronomy 18 but reinterprets them in the light of Jesus' modified understanding of God's judgement and mercy which we also met in Jesus' modifications of the notion of the coming of the Son of Man. What Jesus says about his role is that it is to mediate God's righteousness and forgiveness through prophetic word and action and through the proclamation of God's will and to call men to follow him in his struggle against enmity and darkness. Such action however, precisely because it mediates forgiving love, is also a readiness to stand trial, to be exposed to and to bear the rejection of love, even to the point of death.

In conclusion we may ask how Jesus' utterances about himself relate to the kind of strategy *vis-à-vis* Hellenism and social anomie which we have seen so far in relation to his preaching and teaching. What we have argued is that Jesus was critical of attempts by his contemporaries to maintain and reinforce the Jewish tradition in the face of its steady erosion by alternative values and beliefs. Instead he sought a renewal of the tradition by giving it a new direction: cutting away attempts to multiply the detailed prescriptions of the Law and directing them instead to personal standards as a means of regulating conduct; rejecting the belief in God's punitive justice and emphasizing instead God's mercy, his will to heal, to forgive, to overcome enmity with love. In the same way, we have just seen, he sees his own prophetic role not simply as one of warning men to take the necessary action to avoid disaster in the imminent judgement of God, but as proffering them now the forgiveness of God and calling them to follow him in his ministry of love to the lost, the poor and the enemy. And, as we have suggested, this means that we must not look in Jesus' work and teaching for an elaboration of *detailed* responses to Hellenism, social anomie, etc., but rather see his work as the basis for subsequent attempts to translate these fundamental apprehensions about God, man and the world into social terms. The question now is, can we relate what we have seen of Jesus' own understanding of his own role in this process to our general thesis about his transformation of Judaism in the first century?

I think contemporary parallels make it fairly clear that, in calling men to follow him, Jesus was intending to emphasize his own charismatic authority. Similarly in contrasting himself with Moses and the scribal tradition, Jesus was both laying claim to authority for his teaching and also stressing its radically innovative character. Furthermore, in linking men's response to his teaching and person with the Son of Man's response to men, Jesus was stressing that the new teaching and beliefs which he proclaimed were linked to the coming age and hence superseded the old. In all this he was clearly picking up elements from the tradition—notably the apocalyptic and Zealot traditions—and applying them to his own teaching, thereby giving a certain affective charge and force to his utterances.

So far what we have said relates principally to Jesus as a source of authority and initiative, portraying him as a key figure in *initiating* the changes which it is necessary for Israel to undergo. As such it relates primarily to his teaching, his declaration of God's forgiveness to men, to his call to them to follow him in his ministry. But, as we have seen, his own actions, his meals, his healings and exorcism are an essential part of the context of that teaching such that they cannot be separated from it.

We may however question whether the *meaning* of Jesus' utterances about himself can be exhausted by considering what it says about his initiatory role in the transformation of Judaism. Y. Talmon[66] has distinguished importantly between a leader's function in *initiating* social change and in *symbolizing* it. A leader may hold together a group of people by interpreting the traditions of his own people and of colonizing powers, by popularizing them, combining disparate elements and systematizing them. But often when such leaders die or lose their drive the movements disintegrate almost immediately. On the other hand, according to Talmon, in many cases leaders function as a 'symbolic focus of identification' rather than as sources of authority and initiative which come from the group itself. This function may be exercised by absent or even dead leaders. In some notable instances the influence of a leader and his integrating power have increased enormously after he left or was removed from his scene of operation. Death, imprisonment or mysterious absence have increased their stature and enhanced their authority. This distinction is clearly of great relevance to Jesus. If we see Jesus, as did Reimarus very largely, as primarily a leader with a set political and religious purpose, then like Reimarus and Schweitzer we shall focus attention on his efforts to bring about a new age, to overcome the oppression of his fellows by military or religious means. Now these may not be insignificant in so far as Jesus healed, exorcized, preached the Kingdom of God and gave his own teaching about the will of God. Nevertheless we are left with the strong feeling that this does not exhaust the significance of the man and his life and death. Both Reimarus and Schweitzer indeed recognized other aspects of Jesus' teaching, but they were unable to relate this very significantly to his more active and purposive behaviour and intentions.

Now what I have been trying to argue throughout the last four chapters is that the central importance of Jesus' life and work is not to be found in any particular programme or design that he had, but rather in his reworking of fundamental assumptions about God, man and the world. Similarly when we come to consider his own role in this process I would want to argue that his importance lies less in his initiatory leadership, in the moves he made to initiate significant social change, and more in the way in which he embodied those assumptions and apprehensions of love and power which he proclaimed.

In what sense and in what way did Jesus himself symbolize the new order which he strove to bring in? Talmon talks about leaders in millennial contexts functioning 'as a symbolic focus of identification rather than as sources of authority and initiative'. The point, though it is not spelt out, is, I take it, that leaders in this sense are both identified or identifiable with a particular group as well as representing in some perhaps surprising way the fulfilment of their goals. They are, that is to say, typical and yet untypical; they gather up the experience of the group and yet give it a surprising direction. In this respect they are perhaps more like the lens through which the experience is passed; but both analogies are important. The prophet is the focus of attention in so far as it is in his story that the experience of the group is reworked; he is the lens in that the interest of the group does not or should not simply stop with him but should itself be directed on past him to the goals and fulfilment which he already embodies.

In Jesus these two features of identification and transformation are particularly clearly marked. He identifies himself with the poor, the persecuted, those who hunger and thirst after righteousness. His call to men to leave all and follow him stresses his poverty, marks out his identification with the poor and uprooted among the Galilean peasantry. Whether or not the saying in Matthew 11:28f. is genuine, it certainly shows how Jesus was seen as sharing the lot

187

and experience of those who are gentle and lowly of heart. At another level too Jesus identifies himself with the aspirations and hopes of such people, in his use of kingdom language and in his preaching and in his ministry. In his meals with the outcast and the sinners too he shares with them, identifies with them. The fact that he can be taken for a Zealot shows again the way in which he could be seen by his contemporaries.

However while Jesus can thus be seen as a man of his time, identified with a particular group of Galilean peasantry, identified with the cause of the Jews under foreign domination and oppression, his own life and demeanour mark him out from his contemporaries, set him apart as a 'prophet, and more than a prophet'. What in particular makes him untypical and surprising is the way in which he points to his own ministry of healing and forgiveness, of association with sinners as the way of redemption for his people. For his contemporaries the way to redemption lay via the destruction of Israel's enemies, not via the forgiveness and invitation to the feast of those who wittingly or unwittingly were their instruments, i.e. those who collaborated with the foreign powers or neglected the carefully established boundaries between Jews and Hellenists. Further, we have suggested, Jesus made no secret of the fact that this way of forgiving love was a way of suffering, one deeply costly to all who would tread it yet the one—narrow—way which led to ultimate victory and glory. Moreover, Jesus in thus embodying or symbolizing the way of forgiving love, pointed to himself not simply as an example for men to follow, or as a source of inspiration for them, but as the very point where God's love meets them: Whoever is ashamed of me and of my words . . .

Thus in this lowly, humble, poor man who proclaims God's presence and victory in his own ministry of healing and forgiveness the poor of his time could find comfort, hope and a vision of fulfilment. God's power and glory could be shown, could come alive in this man with his own particular story and way and it could do the same for those who could and would follow. The fact that few in his life were ultimately prepared to follow him all the way matters less than the fact that his story and preaching burned themselves into the minds of those who heard him and went about with him and that after his death they found the power and strength which in his lifetime only he had truly known and that the community of those on whom this power 'fell' were thus launched on a way of discipleship in which they would attempt in the most bewildering variety of ways to be true to that loving power. It was the power of this story of Jesus and his way, whether in its various 'synoptic' forms or in the more terse form of the kerygma which Paul inherited which 'founded' the Church; but it was Jesus himself in his own suffering and love who made these stories possible.

List of Abbreviations

General abbreviations used in the Notes and Bibliography are listed here; for abbreviations for particular works cited, see the Bibliography under relevant authors.

Ant.	Josephus, *Antiquitates Judaicae*
Ass. Mos.	*Assumptio Mosis*
Bell.	Josephus, *De bello Judaico*
Ber.	Berakoth
CD	Cairo Documents (Damascus Rule)
CRINT	*Compendia Rerum Iudaicarum ad Novum Testamentum* (see Bibliography under 'C')
ET	*Expository Times* (Edinburgh, T. & T. Clark)
E.T.	English translation
Evang.Theol.	*Evangelische Theologie* (Munich, Kaiser)
IEJ	*Israel Exploration Journal* (Jerusalem)
JBL	*Journal of Biblical Literature* (Society of Biblical Literature)
JTS	*Journal of Theological Studies* (Oxford, Clarendon Press)
NTS	*New Testament Studies* (Cambridge, Cambridge University Press)
Nov.T.	*Novum Testamentum* (Leiden, Brill)
I QM	Qumran War Rule
I QS	Qumran Community Rule
4 Q Test	Qumran Testimonia
RGG[3]	*Die Religion in Geschichte und Gegenwart*, 3rd edn (Tübingen, Mohr)

SJT	*Scottish Journal of Theology* (Cambridge, Cambridge University Press)
Str. B.	ed. (H. L. Strack) and P. Billerbeck, *Kommentar zum Neuen Testament aus Talmud und Midrasch* (Munich, Beck, 1922ff)
TDNT	*Theological Dictionary of the New Testament* (Grand Rapids, Eerdmans)
TZ	*Theologische Zeitschrift* (Basel, Reinhardt)
ZNW	*Zeitschrift für die neutestamentliche Wissenschaft* (Berlin, de Gruyter)
ZRGG	*Zeitschrift für Religions-und Geistesgeschichte* (Köln, Leiden, Brill)
ZThK	*Zeitschrift für Theologie und Kirche* (Tübingen, Mohr)

Notes

Where a book or article appears both in the Notes and in the Bibliography, full publication details are given only in the Bibliography.

Chapter 1: Putting the Questions

1. Hermann Samuel Reimarus was from 1728 Professor of Hebrew and Oriental Languages at the Akademisches Gymnasium in Hamburg where he also lectured on philosophy, mathematics and natural science.

2. In 1737 he published his commentary on the life and works of J. A. Fabricius; in 1750–52 his edition of Dio Cassius; in 1756 a philosophical treatise; in 1760 a study in zoology. For a fuller bibliography see *Hermann Samuel Reimarus (1694–1768): ein 'bekannter Unbekannter' der Aufklärung in Hamburg*, pp. 149f.

3. His best known work was his *Abhandlung von den vornehmsten Wahrheiten der natürlichen Religion* (Treatise on the most sublime truths of natural religion). It was this work which caused many to doubt the rumours that he was the author of Lessing's *Fragments*.

4. *Apologie oder Schutzschrift für die vernünftigen Verehrer Gottes*.

5. Lessing published the first fragment in 1774 and a further four in 1777; see Lessing's *Werke*.

6. *Vom Zwecke Jesu und seiner Jünger*, *LW* vol. xxii, p.267ff. Lessing declares that he feels obliged to offer this further fragment in order to enable critics of the fragment on the resurrection to see more clearly the context from which it was taken. But, he adds, he is conscious of having replaced a smaller offence with a far greater one.

7. Lessing would appear to be using an earlier draft of the final version of the manuscript published by G. Alexander. The final version is

more systematic, but Lessing's text seems closer to the moment of discovery.

8. *LW* vol. xxii, p. 212.

9. In the final version of the manuscript this point is developed more fully. Elsewhere in dealing with the history of philosophers and teachers we are compelled to distinguish between the system of the teacher and that of his pupils. So too with Jesus: 'To presume therefore without further thought or proof that the apostles departed in no point from the teaching of their master ... would be to make our catechism the primary yardstick of our faith; and that would be the end of all honesty in our inquiry. All *theologia positiva* is historical and exegetical. What matters is the *res facti*, what the founders of a new sect said and wrote, and how their words are to be understood.' (*Apol.* vol. ii, p. 21)

10. *LW* vol. xxii, p. 212f.

11. Cf. Lessing's typically two-edged comment to Goeze: 'the first book is based wholly on Wolffian definitions and if in all that follows the strict mathematical method is less evident, then that is clearly the fault of the material which was not patient of such treatment.' *9th Anti-Goeze. LW* vol. xxiii, p. 242.

12. John Locke's *The Reasonableness of Christianity* is a book of very considerable originality and importance, notable in its own right for a genuine spirit of inquiry, cf. especially the quotation from the Second Vindication given in the introductory essay of the 1836 edition.

13. Cf. the distinction he makes, *Apol.* vol. ii, p. 6, between the general and positive aspects of Jesus' teaching: 'Even in Jesus' teaching not everything is of the same ilk. He appears above all, if we presuppose the positive religion of the Jews, in a twofold form: on the one hand, in so far as he preaches a general religion and is a teacher of the whole human race; on the other hand, however, in so far as he intended particularly to reform corrupt Judaism and to lead it, as its Mosaic constitution would allow, into the ways of rational religion.'

14. A. Schweitzer, *The Quest of the Historical Jesus*. See p. 3f for a discussion of the doctrine of the two natures and its effects on theologians' understanding of Jesus.

15. Op. cit. p. 25f.

16. *Beantwortung der Fragmente eines Ungenannten insbesondere vom Zweck Jesu und seiner Jünger*. References here are to the 2nd edition of 1780.

17. Op. cit. pp. 17–19.

18. Op. cit. p. 51.

19. Op. cit. p. 19.

20. Op. cit. p. 219: 'Jesus wanted to overthrow these prejudices of the Jews about the Messiah, as he had previously stated on a number of occasions, also by his own shameful death; otherwise he could easily have escaped in these four or five days.'

21. Cf. the often-quoted phrase of Tyrrell's: 'The Christ that Harnack sees, looking back through nineteen centuries of Catholic darkness, is only the reflection of a Liberal Protestant face, seen at the bottom of a deep well.' George Tyrrell, *Christianity at the Cross-roads*, p.44, quoted in D. M. Baillie, *God was in Christ*, p. 40.

22. A. Schweitzer, op. cit., p. 397.

23. Lessing's correspondence of the time shows him more concerned to challenge the Neologists, those who attempted to form some kind of synthesis between religion and philosophy, than the orthodox. Lessing referred to the work of such theologians as a 'patchwork of ham-fisted half-philosophers'. *Sämtliche Schriften*, ed. K. Lachmann and F. Munker, vol. xviii, pp. 101f. See too my 'Lessing's Change of Mind', *JThS* N.S. xxix (1978).

24. Such a view of Lessing's work as a whole has been strongly argued by one school of German interpreters, cf. F. Mehring's *Die Lessing Legende*, and more recently P. Rilla, *Lessing und sein Zeitalter*. See also a most useful survey of recent East German work on Lessing in H. Scheller, *Kamenz und Lessing*.

25. *LW*, vol. vi, pp. 61–83.

26. See above n.15.

27. Published in German in 1892. Weiss had delayed publication out of respect for his father-in-law, Albrecht Ritschl.

28. A good summary of this position can be found in the—late—work of A. von Harnack, *What is Christianity?*

29. See for a short summary of this position, A. Ritschl, *Instruction in the Christian Religion*, section on Kingdom in *Three Essays*.

30. It is interesting to note that few of the major works of this period of German scholarship were translated into English until recently; some remain untranslated. The following are the dates of the German and English editions respectively of the major books: J. Weiss, *Jesus' Proclamation of the Kingdom*, 1892, 1971; W. Wrede, *The Messianic Secret*, 1901, 1971; W. Bousset, *Kyrios Christos*, 1913, 1970; K. L. Schmidt, *Der Rahmen der Geschichte Jesu*, 1919, no E.T.; M. Dibelius, *From Tradition to Gospel*, 1919, 1930; R. Bultmann, *The History of the Synoptic Tradition*, 1921, 1963. Perhaps the intervention of the First World War

proved decisive in some cases; but it is odd that English scholars, much of whose work was directed against these books, should have been content to leave their students largely in ignorance of the published views of the men they attacked.

31. A. Hausrath, *Neutestamentliche Zeitgeschichte*, quoted in W. G. Kümmel, *The New Testament: The History of the Investigation of its Problems*.

32. Cf. the foreword to the first edition.

33. *Jesus Predigt in ihrem Gegensatz zum Judentum*. Göttingen, Vandenhoeck & Ruprecht, 1892.

34. Cf. G. Bertram, *Die Leidensgeschichte Jesu und der Christuskult*; R. Bultmann, 'The Study of the Synoptic Gospels' in *Form Criticism: Two Essays on New Testament Research* by R. Bultmann and K. Kundsin.

35. Now available in R. Morgan, *The Nature of New Testament Theology*, pp. 68–116.

36. The misrepresentation of this book by English-speaking scholars would provide a fascinating short study in itself. In his long discussion of it in *The Life of Christ in Recent Research*, W. Sanday attacks it for the arbitrariness of its hypothesis (viz. the attribution of the idea of the messianic secret to the Christian community and to Mark) as against more straightforward and reasonable explanations which would ascribe the idea to Jesus. More recently however Wrede has been hailed as a forerunner of a particular kind of redaction criticism, namely, one which declares it to be impossible to know anything about Jesus, but which finds comfort—and employment—in the examination at least of what the Evangelists believe. Such a view splendidly overlooks the fact that if it is impossible (I would prefer 'difficult') to disentangle Jesus' views from what Mark made of them, it is, given Mark's editorial methods, also wellnigh impossible to disentangle Mark's handling of the tradition from the tradition he received. It further overlooks the fact that not to know anything about Jesus or the tradition which preceded Mark is to be placed at a grave disadvantage when it comes to trying to place Mark's theology in the context of the development of early Christian thought.

37. J. Wellhausen, *Das Evangelium Marci*; *Das Evangelium Mathaei*; *Das Evangelium Lucae*; *Einleitung in die drei ersten Evangelien*.

38. London, Lutterworth, 1938.

39. London, 1935, rev. ed., 1946.

40. Weiss, *Proclamation*, pp. 84–92.

41. Bousset, *Jesus im Gegensatz*, but cf. his later remarks in *Jesus*, where he

speaks of 'All that appears to us strange, fantastic and childish in Jesus', p. 97.
42. Bousset, *Jesus im Gegensatz*, quoted, Kümmel, *Investigation*, p. 232.
43. Ernst Troeltsch, *Gesammelte Schriften*, vol. ii, 'Das Wesen der Religion und die Religions-Wissenschaft', pp. 452 ff. Now available in English in E. Troeltsch, *Writings*.
44. Cf. his portrayal of this development in *The Mysticism of Paul the Apostle*.
45. *Kyrios Christos*, p. 151.
46. W. Bousset, *Das Wesen der Religion*, pp. 192–201.
47. *Kyrios Christos*, p. 158.
48. K. Barth, *The Epistle to the Romans*.

Chapter 2: Religion and Change

1. E. Troeltsch, *Gesammelte Schriften* pp. 452–6.
2. Dodd, *Parables*, p. 34.
3. Ibid., p. 35.
4. Ibid., p. 36.
5. Ibid., p. 38.
6. Ibid., p. 47.
7. Recently N. Perrin has protested against this, as he terms it, misunderstanding of Jesus' language of the Kingdom *as a concept*, in *Jesus and the Language of the Kingdom*, pp. 32ff. He argues that we should speak of it rather as a—tensive—symbol. The discussion below gives some indication of why I feel that the language of 'symbol' has its own dangers. I hope to develop these points elsewhere with Alan Millar.
8. Dodd, *Parables*, p. 79.
9. Ibid., pp. 118f.
10. Ibid., p. 79.
11. Ibid., p. 70.
12. Ibid., p. 71.
13. Bultmann, *Jesus*, p. 16: 'The ideas are understood in the light of the concrete situation of a man living in time; as his interpretation of his own existence in the midst of change, uncertainty, decision; as the expression of a possibility of comprehending this life; as the effort to gain clear insight into the contingencies and necessities of his own existence'. Contrast Perrin, *Language*, p. 111: 'Bultmann resolutely refused to speak of Jesus' understanding of his own situation, of his

understanding of his existence, or indeed of anything else that depended upon a claim to know something about the thought processes of Jesus.' Bultmann's resoluteness in this respect dates, I think, from his turn towards a Reformation understanding of Paul and the *viva vox evangelii*, post-1926. Fuchs's work, praised by Perrin, but criticized by Bultmann in his Akademie Vortrag (*Das Verhältnis der urchristlichen Christusbotschaft zum historischen Jesus*), is a legitimate extension of Bultmann's work on the synoptic tradition and Jesus which led to his *Jesus and the Word*, completed in German in 1925.

14. Bultmann, *Jesus*, pp. 138–54.
15. Cf. G. Ebeling's similar characterization of christological statements as 'homological' in *Theology and Proclamation*, pp. 32, 82.
16. 2nd ed., London, 1978.
17. Op. cit. pp. 122f. The account is taken from M. B. Srinivas, *Religion and Society among the Coorgs of South India*, and contains some inaccuracies and omissions in transcription: there were three brothers; they were chewing betel leaves and areca-nut (a combination which together signifies hospitality, social commerce and leisure, respect: cf. Srinivas pp. 46, 66, 74, 80, 91, 94, 104, 112, 114, 119–21, 152, 205); what they said when she had been tricked was: you have eaten *enji* (i.e. something defiled by spittle); *and you have lost your caste*. They then force her to become the deity of the Poleyas (a caste of untouchables whose name is formed from the root *polé* meaning ritual impurity in general).
18. Douglas, *Purity*, p. 123.
19. Ibid., p. 124.
20. Ibid., p. 123.
21. Ibid., p. 123.
22. M. Douglas, *Natural Symbols*, p. 113.
23. Those who would like to learn more of Dr Millar's theory are invited to write to him at The Dept. of Philosophy, Stirling University, Stirling FK9 4LA, for a typescript account.
24. M. Wilson, *Religion and the Transformation of Society: A Study in Social Change in Africa*, p. 56.

Chapter 3: The Study of the Synoptic Tradition

1. Cf. above pp. 1–8 and the Fragment 'Of the Purpose of Jesus and his Disciples'.
2. For the nineteenth century, cf. above all Schweitzer, *Quest*; for form-

criticism see R. Bultmann 'Study'; for the history of interpretation see N. Perrin, *The Kingdom of God in the Teaching of Jesus*. For general surveys, see W. G. Kümmel, *Investigation* and H. J. Genthe, *Kleine Geschichte der neutestamentlichen Wissenschaft*. Göttingen, Vandenhoeck & Ruprecht, 1977.

3. *LW*, vol. xxiii, pp. 120–39.
4. *Die synoptische Frage*.
5. Though contrast the views of e.g. B. C. Butler, *The Originality of St. Matthew*; W. R. Farmer, *The Synoptic Problem*; H. H. Stoldt, *Geschichte und Kritik der Markus-hypothese*.
6. Cf. A. Ritschl, *Instruction*.
7. Weiss, *Proclamation*, pp. 92ff.
8. Cf. W. Bousset's sharply deterministic formulation of this view: in its environment nascent Christianity *had to* take on this form of Kyrios-Faith and Kyrios-Worship. There was no alternative. See above, Ch. 1, n. 43.
9. Ch. 1, n. 33.
10. W. Wrede, *The Messianic Secret*, pp. 11–49.
11. The foundational works of form-criticism are those of M. Dibelius, *From Tradition to Gospel*; K. L. Schmidt, *Der Rahmen der Geschichte Jesu*; and R. Bultmann, *The History of the Synoptic Tradition*.
12. This may occur either because forms which were formerly found over a wide area are now preserved only in a particular cultural setting; or else because particular sociological settings, e.g. the Jewish debate about Torah, only occur within a particular culture.
13. It is important to restrict the meaning of the term *Sitz im Leben* to the *kind* of situation in which, for example, a parable was uttered, as distinct from the actual occasion on which it was uttered. Cf. the rather misleading use of the term in Dodd, *Parables*, p. 111, etc.
14. This is sometimes thought not to be a *formal* classification, which is doubtless strictly correct but in practice unhelpful, cf. E. B. Redlich, *Form Criticism*, pp. 51f quoting B. S. Easton, *The Christ before the Gospels*, p. 74: 'What *form* difference is there between the "logion"—"whosoever exalteth himself shall be humbled"—the "apocalyptic word"— "whosoever shall be ashamed of me, the Son of Man shall be ashamed of him"—and the "church rule"—"whosoever putteth away his wife and marrieth another committeth adultery"?' One might reply that while the grammatical forms are similar if not identical (the third sentence has a present tense in its main clause) the logical form of the sentences is distinct. The first is, probably, in the nature of a general

law based on observation and experience; it may possibly however be an apocalyptic prediction but here classification is admittedly difficult. The second is a prediction and belongs to a class of visionary, inspired oracular utterances; the third is prescriptive and is offering a definition of conduct with binding force. It is however quite misleading to conclude: 'Thus all the attempts made to classify the sayings are of no use in form criticism'. In practice some consideration of the subject-matter will often be necessary to determine what the literary form is as indeed is recognized clearly by Bultmann: 'The dominical sayings can be divided into three main groups, according to their actual content, though formal differences are involved as well' (*HST*, p. 69). Furthermore, while it is quite obviously true that the Evangelists were not form-critics it is equally misleading to say: 'And in fact there is no evidence that the Evangelists were interested in classifying sayings to the extent that Bultmann suggests.' This is beside the point; but it might suggest that they were also not able to distinguish one kind of saying from another and that would be wrong. Finally Redlich's blanket assertion: 'oral tradition cared not for such things as form or the history of form' rests, I suppose, on a confusion between self-conscious awareness of form which is characteristic of literary cultures, for example in the use and development of the sonnet form, and unreflective use of forms in predominantly oral cultures. Again it is sad to relate that these criticisms were published long before Bultmann's major work in the field appeared in English.

15. For a simple but clear account of such classifications see R. H. Fuller, *A Critical Introduction to the New Testament*, pp. 81ff.

16. Bultmann, following Bousset, distinguished between the earlier *Palestinian* church and the subsequent *Hellenistic* church, cf. *HST*, p.5: 'an essential part of any inquiry concerning the one chief problem of primitive Christianity, the relationship of the primitive Palestinian and Hellenistic Christianity.' Recent criticisms of this way of describing the development of primitive Christianity are discussed at the end of this chapter.

17. *HST*, p. 6, and the detailed discussions at pp. 61ff; 81ff; 125ff; 145ff; 179ff, also 'Study' p. 29: 'the laws by which the further development of material takes place, i.e. a certain orderliness in change by which a body of tradition is always controlled in its growth'.

18. 'Study', p. 60.

19. Unlike those who, like Dibelius and some English scholars, have seen the method as allowing one to make judgements only about the *Sitz*

im Leben of a particular saying in the Church, cf. *HST*, p. 5: 'By contrast with M. Dibelius I am indeed of the opinion that form-critical work precisely because of the relationship of literary forms to the life and the history of the primitive Christian congregation not only presupposes critical judgements on matters of fact in its literary critical presuppositions, but also must necessarily lead to such critical judgements about matters of fact (for instance in relation to the authenticity of a saying, to the historicity of a report, etc.).' There follows the sentence already quoted above in n 16. To be fair, Dibelius does offer thoughts about the historicity of the paradigms, cf. *From Tradition*, pp. 59–64.

20. Cf. e.g. N. Perrin, *Rediscovering the Teaching of Jesus*, pp. 15ff. Of the extensive literature on this subject I have consulted E. Käsemann, *Essays on New Testament Themes*, pp. 34–7; H. Conzelmann, article 'Jesus Christus' in *RGG³*, vol. iii; M. D. Hooker 'Christology and Methodology' (*NTS*, 1971); D. G. A. Calvert, 'An Examination of the Criteria for Distinguishing the Authentic Words of Jesus' (*NTS* 1972); R. S. Barbour, *Traditio-Historical Criticism of the Gospels*; D. A. Mealand, 'The Dissimilarity Test', *SJT* (1978). The last mentioned gives a very balanced account of the case.

21. 'Study', p. 61.

22. *HST*, pp. 125ff, cf. Barbour, *Criticism*, n 20, p. 6

23. Cf. M. D. Hooker in *The Son of Man in Mark*, pp. 6ff: 'If we place a saying or tradition to the *credit* of the Church, are we necessarily obliged to *debit* it from our picture of Jesus? . . . To reduce the number of "authentic" *logia* to such an extent may produce a picture of Jesus which is so unbalanced as to be misleading, for we shall have elim-inated not only later accretions, but also the material which could possibly be common to Jesus and the Church, and which may explain the continuity between them', quoted by Barbour, *Criticism*, pp. 6f, who rightly observes that the same point can be made *mutatis mutandis* about material which could have come from contemporary Judaism.

24. *HST*, pp. 108ff.

25. *HST*, p. 128, para 2. I have given my own translation.

26. Cf. esp. the chapter on the Near and Far God.

27. Cf. the discussion of this thesis by C. H. Dodd, 'The Framework of the Gospel Narrative' (*ET*, 1932), and D. E. Nineham, 'The Order of Events in St Mark's Gospel—an Examination of Dr Dodd's Hypothesis' in *Studies in the Gospels, Essays in Memory of R. H. Lightfoot*, pp. 223–39; A. T. Hanson, 'The Quandary of Historical Scepticism',

in *Vindications*, pp. 74–192; D. E. Nineham, '. . . *et hoc genus omne*—an Examination of Dr A. T. Hanson's strictures on some recent Gospel study', in *Christian History and Interpretation. Studies presented to John Knox*, pp. 199–222.

28. In fact Bultmann himself minimized the importance of the wisdom sayings in Jesus' teaching, see below, ch. 7. His achievement was to see that any account of Jesus' teaching which wanted to do justice to him, would have to give full weight to his legal teaching *and* his eschatological message, and that this meant above all that one would therefore have to *understand* eschatology, rather than simply dismiss it as something quite alien to our age, as variously Schweitzer and Harnack had done. Cf. his treatment of the interpretation of eschatology in *Jesus*, esp. pp. 27–55; 133–219, and in *Jesus Christ and Mythology*, esp. pp. 22ff.

29. All too often scholars have overlooked the fact that Bultmann himself wrote a book on Jesus and was seriously interested in the interpretation of Jesus' sayings. For a positive estimation of his work in this respect cf. Schubert Ogden's Introductory Essay in R. Bultmann, *Existence and Faith*, pp. 9–21.

30. Cf. especially the preface to the 2nd edition of Karl Barth, *The Epistle to the Romans*, pp. 2ff.

31. The much discussed 'new quest' for the historical Jesus which was inaugurated in 1953 by Käsemann's essay, 'The Problem of the Historical Jesus', *ENTT*, pp. 15–47, was, despite Bultmann's own protest, a continuation of the work which Bultmann had done on the synoptic tradition but had broken off under the influence of Barth—though Bultmann saw his own book on Jesus as a contribution to their common cause (see Bultmann's letter to Barth of 10 December 1926 in *Karl Barth – Rudolf Bultmann Briefwechsel 1922-6*)—and his study of the Reformers' exegesis of Paul.

32. Cf. the excellent account of the method in H. Zimmermann, *Neutestamentliche Methodenlehre*, pp. 214ff. Also N. Perrin, *What is Redaction Criticism?* and J. Rohde, *Rediscovering the Teaching of the Evangelists*.

33. Cf. J. H. Drury's remarks in his otherwise illuminating study of Luke, *Tradition and Design in Luke's Gospel*, p. 43: 'It simply changes the subject of historical study from Jesus to the (much more accessible) evangelists'.

34. *Q. Die Spruchquelle der Evangelisten.*

35. Cf. Schulz, *Q*, pp. 47ff, developing Dibelius' analysis of paraenetic material in Q which has been developed christologically; Dibelius,

From Tradition, p. 245, instances the temple narratives: Matt. 11:25–30; 23:34–39; 11:7ff; Luke 7:24ff.

36. 'Sachkritische Urteile' (*HST*, p.6).

37. Schulz, *Q*, pp. 47, 57, 177, etc. There is a telling admission, p. 43, n. 199, that Hengel's work has now made an absolute distinction between Judaism and Hellenism unacceptable. The question is whether Schulz's work, most of which was carried out in seminars going back to 1960, does not still move along the lines laid down by Bousset in presupposing a development of later *Hellenistic* Jewish Christian congregations out of *earlier Palestinian* Jewish Christian congregations. He rightly denies that it is possible to trace a single line development from one group to the other (p. 43) but he still operates (pp. 47ff) with an overall picture of the differences between *Hellenistic* Christianity and *Palestinian* Christianity.

38. *From Tradition*, p. 246.

39. See the work of D. Lührmann, *Die Redaktion der Logienquelle*; also P. Hoffmann, *Studien zur Theologie der Logienquelle*; also the useful review article by U. Luz, 'Die wiederentdeckte Logienquelle' in *Evang. Theol.* (1973).

40. Cf. e.g. the *Compendia Rerum Iudaicarum ad Novum Testamentum*.

41. E. Bickermann, *From Ezra to the Last of the Maccabees*.

42. M. Hengel, *Judaism and Hellenism*, London.

43. See now too M. Hengel, *Jews, Greeks and Barbarians*, an expanded version of two contributions to appear in the *Cambridge History of Judaism*.

44. Though cf. the review article by Louis H. Feldman, 'Hengel's *Judaism and Hellenism* in Retrospect' in *JBL* (1977).

45. 'Zwischen Jesus und Paulus. Die "Hellenisten", die "Sieben" und Stephanus (Apg. 6:1–15; 7:54–8,3)' in *ZThK* (1975).

46. The settling in Jerusalem of Greek-speaking Jews from religious motives may be connected with the belief that Israel was 'the land of the living' in the sense that 'only there could the dead entertain hope of being raised from their graves.' Cf. R. P. Gordon, 'The Targumists as Eschatologists' in *Congress Volume Göttingen, 1977*. See also his reference to the practice of secondary burial in Palestine for Jews who had died outside.

47. A question which Schulz, whose method is to postulate a separate community for each of the—two—theological systems of belief which he believes he can find in the Q tradition, does not put. But Schulz's basic assumption is questionable. While there must be a certain basic

sympathy between a community and the tradition which it preserves, it would be most unlikely that there was a straight equation between the two. The very fact of development within a tradition must be explained in part at least by a certain discrepancy between the community's standpoint and that of the material which it preserves. Clearly this does not rule out other factors which may also lead to development: the community's need to respond to different situations, persecution, the problems of community discipline, other forms of religious propaganda.

Chapter 4: Developments in Judaism to the Time of Jesus.

1. For what follows see especially E. Bickermann, *From Ezra*; M. Hengel, *Judaism*; also F. E. Peters, *Harvest of Hellenism*.
2. Hengel, *Judaism*, vol. i, pp. 12–18.
3. Bickermann, *From Ezra*, p. 15; Hengel, *Judaism*, vol. i, pp. 32–55.
4. Hengel, op. cit., pp. 39–47.
5. Ibid., pp. 18–32.
6. Cf. Eccles. 4:1,7,14; Hengel, *Judaism*, vol. i, pp. 118f; contrast E. Rivkin's rather too optimistic view of the rule of the Aaronides during the Ptolemaic period, *The Shaping of Jewish History*, pp. 21–41.
7. Hengel, op. cit., pp. 23f.
8. Ibid., p. 27.
9. Ibid., p. 24.
10. Bickermann, *From Ezra*, pp. 55–7.
11. Hengel, op. cit., pp. 25f.
12. Ibid., pp. 58f.
13. Rivkin, *Shaping*, c. 2.
14. H. Kreissig, *Die sozialen Zusammenhänge des judäischen Krieges*, p. 92, has protested against the tendency of many scholars to find an exclusively religious explanation for unrest in Palestine in this period. 'No one would without qualification regard ancient popular movements in Greece, Rome, Egypt as religious movements, although religious questions played a limited role in every case. So why is it justified in the case of Judaean popular movements always to look first and solely for religious factors and to accept social and other factors as at the most incidental?' Like many Marxist accounts of cultural and religious movements it is fascinating because it throws light on the social realities of the time; but equally it is frustrating because of the way it filters out from its consideration men's concern for and devotion to

moral and religious values, except as these are related to economic structures. Thus it is illuminating to point out that for peasant farmers independence, control over their land and its produce, is a matter of fundamental importance; but it is misleading to underestimate the importance to them of their religious traditions and the values which they incorporate. What does it mean for a Jew with his traditions about liberation from the 'house of bondage' and about the strength and sanctity of family ties to have to sell his family into slavery? Kreissig is also far too sweeping in his condemnation of some scholars: cf. his attack on Hengel, admittedly written (presumably) before the publication of *Judaism*: 'Hengel's method of finding a text in the Old Testament for every event in Judaea is ultimately unscientific because it ignores acute problems of the time' (p. 92).

15. See the final section of this chapter for a discussion of G. Theissen's account of social anomie in Palestine in first century A.D.

16. Hengel, op. cit., pp. 78–83; *CRINT*, pp. 945–70; Kreissig, *Zusammenhänge*, pp. 90–1, cautions against too enthusiastic accounts of Jewish literacy at this period.

17. *CRINT*, pp. 908–44.

18. Bickermann, *From Ezra*, pp. 153–65.

19. The views expressed here are taken from Rivkin, *Shaping*, ch. 2; cf. and contrast M. Smith, *Palestinian Parties and Politics that Shaped the Old Testament*.

20. See below pp. 112–28.

21. See J. Neusner, *The Idea of Purity in Ancient Judaism*, and M. Douglas, *Purity*, ch. 3.

22. G. Schenk, art. *'dikaiosune'* in *TDNT*; G. von Rad, *Old Testament Theology*.

23. Hengel, *Judaism*, vol. i, pp. 78ff; E. E. Urbach, *The Sages: Their Concepts and Beliefs; CRINT*, pp. 908–44.

24. Cf. the concern with the purification of the Temple in the Zealot movement, M. Hengel, *Die Zeloten*, pp. 211–29.

25. E.g. Ps. 73:3,12—even if the Psalmist finds comfort in the circumstances of their demise, 73:18f.

26. Hengel, op. cit., pp. 115–30.

27. Eccles. 7:23f; cf. 1:17f, 8:16f; Hengel, op. cit., p. 118.

28. Eccles. 3:16f.

29. Eccles. 7:15; notions of covenant, election, the distinction between Israel and the nations are not to be found in the book.

30. Eccles. 3:1–16, especially v.11.

204

31. Hengel, op. cit., pp. 124f.
32. Notably in the development of beliefs in different 'ages' in apocalyptic literature, see below p. 74, and in the speculations on the 'times' in Qumran, see W. Paschen, *Rein und Unrein*, pp. 125–34.
33. Sir. 19.20; cf. again for this section Hengel, op.cit., pp. 131–53.
34. Sir. 44.
35. Sir. 45:26.
36. Sir. 50:27.
37. Sir. 39:27; Hengel, op. cit., pp. 114ff.
38. Sir. 39.23.
39. Sir. 1:1–10; ch. 24 with specific reference to the Temple, v.10, and to the 'book of the covenant of the Most High God, the Law which Moses commanded us', v.23; Hengel, op.cit. pp. 139–57ff.
40. Sir. 36:1; 43:27; Hengel, op.cit., pp. 146–8; vol. ii, p. 94, n. 259.
41. Baruch 3:23,28. For the argument here see Hengel, *Judaism*, vol. i, pp. 169ff, who follows R. Meyer, *Tradition und Neuschöpfung im antiken Judentum*.
42. Baruch 4:3.
43. Hengel argues this by analogy with the 'Stoic idea of the unity of the world *nomos* and the moral law ordering the life of the individual. To accord with the "cosmic" significance of the law, the pious man had to put it into practice without omission and without qualification in his everyday life, so that his whole life was directed by it. Of exemplary significance here was the transference of ritual Levitical holiness, which was a matter for the Temple and those concerned with Temple worship, to the whole life of the faithful, including the laity. The realization of this demand which was also an Essene ideal (see below pp. 223f) and goes back to common Hasidic roots, probably led to the foundation of the first Pharisaic ḥabūrōth.' *Judaism*, vol. i, p. 170.
44. Lev. 20:22ff., see below pp. 112–28.
45. I am assuming here only that it is possible to give a—broad—account of the linguistic conventions which held at the time by comparing different beliefs held at different times from the Wisdom to the apocalyptic literature. There is of course a major scholarly debate about whether the 'roots' of apocalyptic lie in Wisdom, e.g. G. von Rad, *Wisdom in Israel*, pp. 263–83 or in prophecy, cf., for example, P. D. Hanson, *The Dawn of Apocalyptic: the historical and sociological roots of Jewish apocalyptic eschatology*; D. S. Russell, *The Method and Message of Jewish Apocalyptic, 200 BC–AD100*; for a rather different account, cf. P. von der Osten-Sacken, *Die Apokalyptik in ihrem Verhältnis zu Prophetie*

und Weisheit. Perhaps, as Hengel suggests, 'the entire controversy about the derivation of apocalyptic from prophecy or wisdom is basically an idle one, because, in their opposition to the spirit of the Hellenistic age, both had become inseparably bound up with each other.' *Nachfolge*, p. 52.

46. Dan. 12:2.
47. Sir. 38:21, cf. Hengel, *Judaism*, vol. i, p. 153; vol. ii, p. 96, n. 286.
48. Dan. 11:34; 12:10.
49. Dan. 7:22, 27.
50. Dan. 2.
51. Dan. 7.
52. Enoch 85–90.
53. Dan. 11:34; 12:1, 10.
54. Dan. 12.2f; Enoch 67:4–13.
55. See below pp. 157f.
56. e.g. Dan. 2:7: dreams; Dan. 8; 9:21ff; 10:4ff, etc.: visions.
57. Hengel, *Judaism*, vol. i, pp.210–18.
58. For surveys of this period see A. Schalit, *König Herodes*; H. W. Hoehner, *Herod Antipas*; M. Stern, 'The Reign of Herod and the Herodian Dynasty', *CRINT*, pp. 216–307; and 'The Province of Judaea', *CRINT*, pp. 308–76. See also G. Theissen, *The First Followers of Jesus*, pp. 65–76.
59. Theissen, *Followers*, pp. 65f: 'Any survey of the first century of Roman policy in Palestine must find fault with it for contributing to the instability of the situation by changes of direction and an inadequate presence in both the political and military spheres.'
60. Josephus, *Ant.* 18.38; cf. Hoehner, *Antipas*, pp. 91–100.
61. *CRINT*, p. 286, where Stern refers to the absence of Antipas's image from his coins in contrast to those of his brother Philip.
62. Hoehner, op.cit., pp. 84ff.
63. Ibid., pp. 251–4; *CRINT*, pp. 284ff.
64. *CRINT*, p. 275.
65. Ibid., pp. 277–81.
66. This is important as against views like those of Kreissig, *Zusammenhänge*, *passim*, which would stress too sharply the element of class-struggle in the unrest of this period. Inter-dynastic rivalry and resentment of foreign rulers and their harsh puppets were equally important. Against this see G. Theissen, "Wir haben . . .'; Hengel, *Zeloten*, p. 46, takes a middle position and speaks of 'for the most part

members of socially disadvantaged classes, who among other things
fought for a divinely willed re-ordering of the distribution of wealth.'

67. *CRINT*, pp. 92f.
68. On the development of scribes and their relation to the sages see S.
    Westerholm, *Jesus and Scribal Authority*, pp. 20–39, and the literature
    there.
69. *CRINT*, pp. 259f.
70. Ibid., pp. 372–4.
71. *Bell.* 2.405, 407; cf. *CRINT*, pp. 330–6.
72. *CRINT*, p. 332; G. Theissen, 'Wir haben . . .', p. 182.
73. *CRINT*, p. 572.
74. Ibid., pp. 570f.
75. Ibid., pp. 646–64; B. Golomb and Y. Kedar, 'Ancient Agriculture in
    the Galilee Mountains' in *IEJ* (1971); cf. F. C. Grant, *The Economic
    Background of the Gospels*, pp. 55–64.
76. *CRINT*, pp. 680–90 gives a useful survey of the production and cir-
    culation of goods in Palestine. See too Kreissig, *Zusammenhänge*, pp.
    56–74. For industry in Jerusalem, see J. Jeremias, *Jerusalem in the Time
    of Jesus*, pp. 3–30.
77. See Kreissig, *Zusammenhänge*, *passim*, and Theissen, 'Tempel'.
78. 'The loss of the coastal plain following Pompey's drastic reorganiza-
    tion of the affairs of Judaea and Syria, must have meant the creation
    of a very considerable class of landless Jewish peasants, as Schalit has
    seen. This phenomenon may serve as a key to an understanding of
    the entire development of the agrarian problem in Judaea down to
    the great rebellion of 70 C.E. Indeed combined with the seismic effect
    of the sudden and massive loss of commerce caused by the cutting off
    of the coastal towns and the Decapolis from the Judaean State which
    must have thrown a considerable number of Jews back on agriculture,
    this situation (widely ignored by historians) would have done much
    to foment the stormy revolutionary atmosphere of the subsequent
    period.' *CRINT*, p.637.
79. Golomb and Kedar, 'Agriculture', pp. 137f.
80. *CRINT*, pp.641–6; Kreissig, *Zusammenhänge*, pp. 26–36.
81. S. Zeitlin, *The Rise and Fall of the Judaean State*, p. 269 (quoted by
    Theissen, 'Wir haben . . .', p. 183), suggests that this process of the
    growth of large estates was promoted also by famine.
82. Theissen, 'Wir haben . . .', p. 192.
83. Matt. 21:30–40.

84. Kreissig, *Zusammenhänge*, pp. 36–51, cf. Applebaum's discussion of this, *CRINT*, p. 662.
85. Matt. 18:25.
86. M. Shebiith 10:3.
87. *Bell.* 2:427.
88. *CRINT*, p.662.
89. '*sub Tiberio quies*', Tacitus, *Historiae* 5.9, but the crucifixion of two 'thieves' with Jesus may suggest political unrest at that time.
90. R. Meyer, *Der Prophet aus Galiläa*. Cf. most recently D. Hill, 'Jesus and Josephus' "messianic prophets"' in *Text and Interpretation. Studies in the New Testament presented to Matthew Black*, pp. 143–54. See below ch. 8.
91. In this respect Hengel and others have stressed the dynastic connections of Zealot leaders, Hengel, *Die Zeloten*, p. 338.
92. See Theissen, 'Wir haben . . .', pp. 188–96. He defines 'anomie', a term originally coined by E. Durkheim, in words quoted from W. Rüegg, *Soziologie*, Funk-Kolleg 6, Frankfurt 1969, 40. 'It refers to a state in which individuals are no longer in a position to behave in a manner conformable to the norms of their group.'
93. As religious phenomena these movements 'are not themselves anomic phenomena, but have a point of contact with anomic behaviour, in order to overcome anomie.' 'Wir haben . . .', p. 188, n. 63.
94. Theissen, 'Wir haben . . .', p. 190.
95. J. le Moyne, *Les Sadducéens*.
96. Hengel, *Die Zeloten*, pp. 211–29.
97. See below pp. 124, 128.
98. It is an open question whether one should regard the members of the *haburoth* as distinct from the Pharisees. Certainly in the respect that the *haburah* represents a particular development during the course of Pharisaic history we should make some distinction. In any case we should be careful not to over-emphasize the unity of the Pharisaic tradition, cf. Westerholm, *Jesus*, pp. 13ff.
99. A. Oppenheimer, *The 'Am Ha-aretz*, pp. 52–5.
100. Oppenheimer, op. cit., pp. 69ff; 83ff.
101. Ibid., p. 20, is too emphatic here.
102. J. Bowker, *Jesus and the Pharisees*, p. 61, states rightly that 'for those who had ordinary lives to pursue in town and country . . . The possibilities of contracting uncleanness were so many that if no condition of suspended uncleanness (*tebul yom*) existed life would come to a halt . . .' Even so, certain regulations relating to corpse impurity may well have borne more heavily on those who had to deal with

animals—of course one must equally not press the distinction between town and country too hard.

103. Bowker, op. cit., pp. 30f.
104. Kreissig, *Zusammenhänge*, pp. 88–92.
105. Hoehner, *Antipas*, p. 53.
106. Hengel, 'Zwischen Jesus . . .' p. 163 and n. 47; cf. Oppenheimer's critical discussion of the question, *'Am Ha-aretz*, pp. 4ff.
107. Cf. Vermes, *Jesus the Jew: a historian's reading of the Gospels*, pp. 52–7, and the critique of this kind of presentation in Oppenheimer, *'Am Ha-aretz*, pp. 4ff; 200–17.
108. E.g. Matt. 12:9; 13:54; Mark 5:22; Luke 4:16.
109. Oppenheimer, op.cit., pp. 200–17.
110. But cf. Kreissig's cautions here, Zusammenhänge, pp. 112–13.
111. Hill, 'Prophets'.
112. A. Büchler, *Types of Jewish-Palestinian piety from 70 B.C.E. to 70 C.E.: the ancient pious men*; G. Vermes, 'Ḥanina ben Dosa' in *Post-biblical Jewish Studies*.
113. The Zealots' actions *vis-à-vis* the Temple do not betray any particular concern with fastidious observances of purity regulations, Hengel, *Die Zeloten*, pp. 223ff.
114. Cf. Kreissig's summary, *Zusammenhänge*, p. 92: 'What passed by word of mouth among the people, was passed on from parents to children, were—as one can see from analogies of all times and peoples—the mythical and legendary stories of the patriarchs, of King David and the brave Maccabees, of the redeemer, who was expected all over the Hellenistic world.'
115. Judas the Galilean's name, given to him by a nationalist father, may provide some evidence for this; discussion of these figures in Hengel, *Die Zeloten*, esp. pp. 69f, 152–81.
116. See n.16 above.
117. 1 Macc. 2:41.
118. Vermes, op. cit. (see n.112 above), p. 186.

Chapter 5: Jesus' Preaching of the Kingdom

1. The literature on this subject is too substantial to detail here. For some recent interesting treatments see N. Perrin, *Language*, and the works discussed there. I have chosen not to concentrate on the parables, whose sense, despite the work of Dodd and Jeremias, seems to me still fundamentally elusive, and which therefore, as indeed Dodd

saw, require some prior understanding of Jesus' teaching about the Kingdom as a key to unlock their meaning, see Dodd, *Parables* pp. 34–80. Instead I shall base my interpretation on Jesus' sayings as they were uttered in the context of his ministry.

2. The Markan summary of Jesus' message (Mark 1:15) is doubtless Mark's own creation; but there is enough evidence for Jesus' teaching about watchfulness, etc., to suggest that this gives at least an accurate indication of the traditions on which Jesus was drawing. On Jesus' teaching about repentance in its contemporary context see especially H. Braun, ' "Umkehr" in spätjüdisch-häretischer und in früh-christlicher Sicht,' in *Gesammelte Studien zum Neuen Testament und seiner Umwelt*, 2nd edn, 1962.

3. For the following discussion see Bultmann *HST*, pp. 108–30.

4. As we have just seen Bultmann includes parables in his lists of apocalyptic-prophetic sayings because of their sense, rather than be-cause parables as such are prophetic.

5. Such a reintroduction of Jewish conventional associations of the term 'kingdom' would be expected in the light of the radical nature of the changes Jesus made in this respect. The thesis that there was a progressive Judaizing and Qumranizing of the tradition, see E. Stauf-fer, *Jesus war ganz anders*, and H. Hübner, *Das Gesetz in der synoptischen Tradition. Thesen zur progressiven Judaisierung und Qumranisierung der syn-optischen Tradition*, is both intriguing and I think patient of further amplifications in terms of the reintroduction of conventional associ-ations of terms which had been previously deleted by Jesus.

6. The classic statement of this view was made in Dodd, *Parables*, and was essentially upheld by J. Jeremias, *The Parables of Jesus*, who how-ever suggested a greater range of meaning to the parables than had Dodd, and spoke of a 'sich realisierende Eschatologie'.

7. H. M. Kleinknecht, art. *basileus* in *TDNT*.

8. This is, for example, a notable feature of enthronement psalms, cf. e.g. Ps. 72:1.

9. G. von Rad, art. *basileus*, in *TDNT*.

10. N. Perrin, *Language*, p. 17.

11. von Rad, art.cit., distinguishes three distinct Old Testament traditions in which kingship language occurs.

12. Cf. the alternative accounts offered of the introduction of a monarchy in Israel in 1 Sam. Noteworthy in the light of later, especially Zealot, traditions is 1 Sam. 8:7 where God says to Samuel of the people's

request for a king: 'They have not rejected you [i.e. as charismatic ruler], but they have rejected me from being king over them.'

13. Ps. 78:1.
14. 2 Sam 7; Amos 9:11.
15. Dan. 7:13f. The Kingdom is to be 'given to the people of the Saints of the Most High', 7:18,27, rather than to a monarch as such.
16. Both in Dan. 2, with its vision of a great image made of different metals representing different kingdoms, and in the vision of the beasts in Dan. 7. Similar notions are to be found in the contrast between the kingdoms of Satan and of God, *Ass.Mos.* 10.2 and in 1 QM, see below p. 156.
17. Dan. 7:11, cf. Dan. 7:9.
18. Ps. 101:8.
19. Dan. 7:9f. 'The fire is a symbol of judgement and is associated in the Old Testament with theophanies' (Ps. 50; 97; cf. Mal. 3:2; Isa. 30:27–28.) N. Porteous, *Daniel. A Commentary*, 2nd rev. edn, p. 108.
20. Hengel, *Die Zeloten*, especially pp. 79–150.
21. Josephus, *Ant.* 18.2f.
22. Josephus, *Ant.*, 18.4f.
23. Josephus, *Bell.*, 2.117–19.
24. Hengel, *Die Zeloten*, pp. 93–114.
25. Ibid., pp. 100–02.
26. Ibid., pp. 127–9; cf. Josephus, *Ant.*, 18.5.
27. Hengel, op.cit., pp. 98–103.
28. Cf. Ber. 14b, 15a: 'R. Johanan said: "If one desires to accept upon himself the yoke of the kingdom of heaven in the most complete manner, he should relieve himself and wash his hands and put on *tephillin* and recite the Shema^c and say the *tephillah*: this is the complete .nowledgement of the kingdom of heaven." ' Cf. Bowker, p. 125.
29. It is reasonable to see here a consistent development from the early theology of *Jubilees*, cf. Bickermann, *From Ezra*, pp. 59ff, and *Baruch*, cf. Hengel, *Judaism*, pp. 169–75, especially p. 170, see p. 205 (n. 43) above.
30. See J. Becker, *Das Heil Gottes*, pp. 74–83.
31. IQS 9.11.
32. See below, ch. 7.
33. Matt. 3:1–12, etc.
34. Matt. 3:8f.
35. Luke 3:10–14.
36. Cf. G. Theissen, 'Die Tempelweissagung Jesu.' *TZ* (1976) 152: '"Rad-

ically theocratic" I take to refer to any movement in which God's rule is played off against the theocratic mediators.'; Hengel, *Die Zeloten*, pp. 93–150; *Josephus-Studien* p. 180, 'Eine theokratische Ideologie des Freiheitskampfes.'

37. Theissen, *Followers*, p. 36.

38. Cf. Hengel, *Die Zeloten*, pp. 235–51 and *Nachfolge*, pp. 18ff; 37f; 41ff, on the charismatic character of Judas, John the Baptist and Jesus.

39. Theissen, *Followers*, pp. 4f, makes this point well in relation to Burckhardt.

40. Matt. 8:22: 'Leave the dead to bury their dead.' Cf. Hengel, *Nachfolge*.

41. N. A. Dahl, *Jesus in the Memory of the Early Church*, p. 172 quoted in Hill, 'Prophets', p. 144.

42. Hengel, *Die Zeloten*, p. 334, however sees no reason to suppose that '*sub Tiberio quies*' excludes the continuance of the minor actions (*Klein-krieg*) in the desert.

43. It is perhaps interesting to recall Semler's attempt to solve this prob-lem in terms of a dual mode of teaching (*eine doppelte Lehrart*), where what Jesus said meant one thing to one kind of people, another to another, see above pp. 5f. This recognizes both the fact that Jesus must have used terms which already had an established meaning in his community if he was to communicate *at all*, and also the fact that he intended to say something different when he used them. But it offers no account of how this could be.

44. See above pp. 34f.

45. See above p. 101. The point is taken up in W. O. Walker, 'Jesus and the Tax-Collectors' in *JBL* (1978).

46. Dibelius, *From Tradition*, pp. 37f.

47. Ibid., p. 61.

48. Ibid., p. 62.

49. Bultmann bases this judgement on the 'the quite impossible appearance' of the Scribes of the Pharisees and on the fact that while it is the disciples who are addressed, Jesus himself answers, something which also reflects the Church's consciousness of itself as the mediator between the world and Jesus; Bultmann, *HST*, p. 18.

50. Bultmann, *HST*, p. 50.

51. Contrast Dibelius, *From Tradition*, pp. 65, 130f.

52. Matt. 11:2–6.

53. Cf. Isa. 29:18f; 35:5f; 61:1.

54. Mark 3:23–30.

55. Vermes, *Jesus*, pp. 69–78; 'Hanina'.

56. See here the stories of Ḥanina ben Dosa, Vermes, loc.cit., and the synoptic sayings: 'This kind cannot be driven out by anything but prayer (and fasting).' (Mark 9:29.)

57. Matt. 6:9ff.

58. G. Fohrer, art. 'Mahlzeiten II', *RGG*[3].

59. B. Hentschke, art. 'Opfer II' *RGG*[3].

60. Matt. 8:11, etc.

61. Zeph. 3:13; En. 62:14; Slav. En. 42:3f; Apoc. Bar. 29:4f; 1QS 6:1f.

62. N. Perrin, *Rediscovering*, pp. 102–8.

63. Bultmann's account of the apophthegmata, see above p. 102, may provide some grounds for arguing for their frequency, at least for believing that they were regarded as typical. See too Perrin (n. 62).

64. R. Otto, *Kingdom*, esp. pp. 47–93; 333–76.

65. Matt. 11:18f.

66. e.g. Mark 2:16f.

67. 1QS 5:13.

68. Hengel, *Nachfolge*, pp. 18–27.

69. O. Betz, 'Jesu Heiliger Krieg', *NovT* (1957–8); cf. M. Black, *Josephus-Studien*, p. 54, and 'Uncomfortable Words: The Violent Word', *ET* (1969–70).

70. Matt. 5:44f.

71. Matt. 21:28–32; 22:1–10; cf. John 3:21f.

72. Matt. 9:17.

73. Matt. 8:11f.

74. Matt. 11:28–30.

75. Luke 18:9–14.

76. R. M. Benson, S.S.J.E., *The Final Passover*, ch. 8, quoted in *Corda in Caelo*, arr. S. C. Hughson, p. 71.

Chapter 6: Jesus and the Law of Purity

1. In what follows I have drawn principally on H. Braun, *Spätjüdisch-häretischer und frühchristlicher Radikalismus*; W. Paschen, *Rein und Unrein*, and J. Neusner, *Purity*; see also G. Alon, *Jews, Judaism and the Classical World*, and E. Feldman, *Biblical and Post-Biblical Defilement and Mourning: Law as Theology*. The major difficulty in any study of this period is to give a balanced assessment of one's sources. It is, in particular, very difficult to establish what the Pharisees of Jesus' day taught, because of the late date at which our sources were written down. Hence I have followed Paschen in concentrating on the teaching of

213

the Qumran Community, where the evidence is strongest and fullest. However, interesting evidence of how Jesus' teaching challenged Jewish conventions is provided by the handling of Jesus' sayings by the Jewish-Christian communities which preserved the synoptic tradition, particularly those traditions which lie behind Matthew's Gospel.

2. Neusner, p. 27. See also Rivkin, *Shaping*, ch. 2.

3. See Neusner's list, *Purity*, p. 26.

4. In the Pentateuch, the purity regulations are portrayed as part of the ordinances first given to Moses and relating to the Israelite cult, as opposed to all foreign ones (Lev. 20:25). By contrast the P creation narrative describes God's work as 'good' and Noah is expressly commanded to eat of every living and crawling thing (Gen. 9:3 P); cf. Paschen, *Rein*, p. 57.

5. Douglas, *Purity*, pp. 56f.

6. But Smith, *Parties*, argues that under Nehemiah, the Greek *tyrannos*, the layman already gains prominence.

7. Neusner, *Purity*, pp. 26f.

8. Neusner, *Purity*, pp. 64ff, 'the main point was keeping the purity laws outside of the Temple, where the priests had to observe purity when they carried out the requirements of the cult' (p. 65).

9. 1QS 8: 4–10; 9: 3–6.

10. Cf. M. Hengel, *Die Zeloten*, pp. 151ff; contrast however Neusner, *Purity*, p. 40.

11. See J. Maier, 'Zum Begriff *yahad* in den Texten von Qumran' in *ZAW* (1960).

12. See Braun, *Radikalismus*, vol. i, p. 29 n. 5, and 33ff for detailed references. Paschen, *Rein*, 85ff, offers an analysis of the purity vocabulary in the Scrolls.

13. See, for example, Braun, *Radikalismus*, vol. i, pp. 43ff.

14. 1QS 11: 5. On the esoteric nature of the community's (*yahad*'s) understanding of Law see Paschen, *Rein*, pp. 116ff.

15. See Paschen, *Rein*, pp. 100f, for a discussion of 'order' (*tkn*) in 1QS.

16. Braun, *Radikalismus*, vol. i, 28, n.2, points to the frequency of 'all' in 1QS, listing at least 192 occurrences.

17. Paschen, *Rein*, 125–34.

18. G. Vermes, *DSSE*, pp. 35f.

19. Cf. Paschen's discussion of 'the purity of glory' (1QS 4: 5), p. 121f, where he quotes J. Maier, *Die Texte vom Toten Meer*, Bd. II, Munich, 1960, p.20: 'It refers to that stage of cultic (-ethical) purity, which permits access to the kabod-sphere (around God's throne)'.

20. Cf. Maier, 'Zum Begriff *yaḥad* . . .' p. 148f.
21. 1QS 5: 10f.
22. For the structure of the community, see Vermes, *DSSE*, pp. 16ff.
23. 1QS 5: 14–17.
24. So at least Josephus tells, whose evidence on the score of purity regulations is to be taken seriously, as it runs counter to his own tendency to portray the Essenes as a kind of Stoic group. See Josephus, *Bell.*, II, 137.
25. For a discussion of the regulations concerning lustrations, meals and property, see Paschen, *Rein*, pp. 91ff.
26. *Bell.*, II, 150.
27. *Bell.*, II, 147ff.
28. *Bell.*, II, 144.
29. 1QS 5: 15f in Vermes' translation.
30. 1QS 7: 7 and 17.
31. Josephus, *Bell.* II, 132: 'No clamour or disturbance ever pollutes their dwelling' refers to this regulation specifically in terms of purity.
32. 1QS 6: 27–7: 2.
33. 1QS 7: 18, seems to suggest that the latter case may be open to reclassification as 'trembling against' as opposed to 'murmuring against' and hence be less final than the mention of the Divine Name.
34. 1QS 3: 13—4: 26.
35. 1QS 4: 9–11. See P. Wernberg–Møller, *Manual of Discipline, ad loc.*
36. 1QS 4: 21.
37. 1QS 5: 13.
38. On the fear that food bartered or sold to those outside might be used in idolatrous worship, see Paschen, *Rein*, p. 96, referring to CD 12, 8–11; 1QS 5: 14.
39. 1QS 5: 6,8.
40. Mark 11:11, 15ff.
41. Mark 13:1f; 14:58; 15:29.
42. Matt. 5:23f.
43. Matt. 23:16ff (secondary?).
44. Mark 2:23ff; 3:2ff; Matt. 12:5, 11; Luke 13:10ff; 14:1ff.
45. For recent major discussions of the subject with comprehensive bibliographies see K. Berger, *Die Gesetzesauslegung Jesu. Teil I: Markus und Parallelen*; Hübner, *Gesetz*; R. J. Banks, *Jesus and the Law in the Synoptic Tradition*.
46. 1QS 4: 6.
47. So, e.g., Hengel, *Nachfolge*, pp. 26f.

48. See Vermes, 'Ḥanina', p. 179.

49. I assume here that passages such as Mark 4:11f are secondary.

50. E.g., in Matt. 5:43ff; see discussion below.

51. As in the question of marriage and divorce.

52. Mark 9:40, preferring the form 'he that is not against us is for us' to its alternative—contradictory—formulation in Matt. 12:30. Cf. W. L. Knox, *The Sources of the Synoptic Gospels*, vol. i, p. 24, n. 1.

53. Cf. J. B. Metz's use of the notion of 'dangerous' memories: *Befreiendes Gedächtnis Jesu Christi*; 'The Future in the Memory of Suffering' in *Concilium* (1972).

54. Cf. the saying attributed to Rabbi Joḥanan ben Zakkai about purity regulations: 'The dead body does not really defile; the water does not really purify; but God has said, I have ordained an ordinance, I have decreed a decree; it is not permitted to you to transgress my decree.' Num. R. Huḳḳat, xix. 8.

55. Cf. Matt. 7:12, which Matthew gives as the climax to the Sermon on the Mount.

56. Mark 2:27.

57. See the discussion in Hübner, *Gesetz*, pp. 113f, and Banks, *Law*, pp. 113f.

58. O. Michel, 'Jesus der Jude', in *Der historische Jesus und der kerygmatische Christus*, pp. 310–16.

59. Berger, *Gesetz*, pp. 508ff; Hübner, *Gesetz*, pp. 42ff; Banks, *Law*, pp. 146ff.

60. Matt. 22:37–40.

61. Matt. 23:5, secondary?

62. Matt. 23:2, secondary?

63. Luke 18:10.

64. Matt. 23:8–10.

65. Cf. John 13:12–17.

66. Matt. 5:27–30.

67. Matt. 5:21–26.

68. Matt. 5:43ff. It is widely agreed that the antithetical form in which it is presently contained is secondary and to be attributed to Matthew. Equally it is likely that vv.46f have been added as a second reason for the command, the first and original reason being given in v.45. V.48 is then either a gloss on v.45 or the original ending of the saying, possibly in a slightly modified form (cf. Luke 6:36 but this is possibly adapted to follow on Luke's version of Matt. 5:45 in Luke 6:35). For discussion of these points see Bultmann, *HST*, p. 144; J. Dupont, *Les*

Béatitudes, vol. i, 2nd edn, p. 191; H. Schürmann, *Das Lukasevangelium*
I, 345, 357; T. W. Manson, *The Sayings of Jesus*, p. 50; D. Lührmann,
'Liebet eure Feinde (Luke 6:27–36/Matt. 5:39–48)', *ZThK* (1972);
Schulz, *Q,* 127f.

69. This is not the view generally taken; cf. e.g., L. Schottroff, 'Non-
violence and Love of One's Enemies' in *Essays on the Love Commandment*,
p. 15, who argues that 'even the historical Jesus himself could hardly
have spoken of "enemies" and "your persecutors" without thinking
of his own conflicts and those of his disciples.' But this supposes that
the conflicts between the Jerusalem Jews and Jesus were his primary
concern, rather than seeing them as the outcome of the attitudes he
proclaimed to the Jews' enemies. In the first instance this may have
brought him more into conflict with the Zealots than with Jerusalem;
see Hoffmann, *Studien*, p. 76; Lührmann, p. 437; M. Hengel, *Was Jesus
a Revolutionist?*; N. Perrin, *Rediscovering*, pp. 148, sees the saying as
having been directed to the group gathered together in the table
fellowship of the Kingdom. This is correct in so far as it is this group
who were most likely to be responsive to such teaching; but it would
not be right to define 'enemies' by contrast with this group.

70. For discussion of the tradition-history of Mark 7, see Paschen, *Rein*,
153ff; Berger, *Gesetz.*, 461ff; Hübner, *Gesetz*, 142ff; Banks, *Law*, 132ff.
See also W. G. Kümmel, 'Äussere und innere Reinheit des Menschen
bei Jesus' in *Das Wort und die Wörter. Festschrift für G. Friedrich*, pp. 35ff,
which gives a full discussion of the literature. Both Paschen and
Hübner suggest that the version of the saying in Mark 7:18,20 also
represents a traditional form of the saying which in some respects,
notably its positive formulation, may come nearer to the original
saying.

71. See the discussion of these questions by Hübner, *Gesetz*, pp. 158f;
171f; Banks, *Law*, pp. 141f.

72. Contrast however Berger, *Gesetz*, pp. 465ff, who relates it to Philonic
Judaism; but this is again to treat the saying too much in isolation.

73. R. Bultmann, *HST*, p. 74.

74. In Mark 10:25 however the point of the saying lies in the contrast
between the two halves. Paschen, *Rein*, p. 181, referring to J. Jeremias
and E. Linnemann, suggests that the emphasis in such sayings lies
however on the second member; they are 'hecklastig' 'tail-heavy'.

75. So e.g., V. Taylor, *The Gospel according to St. Mark*, London, Macmillan,
1952, p. 343; Paschen also omits the phrase, *Rein*, p. 174.

76. This point seems to be missed by Paschen who argues that the word

is used univocally, *Rein*, p. 182, although his own interpretation hardly holds to this. It might just be possible to construe the saying along such lines as this if it were thought that Jesus was asserting—symbolically—that the danger from within was greater than that from without, cf. M. Douglas's account of the Coorgs, above pp. 25ff, but this would be quite impossible to square with the rest of Jesus' teaching.

77. Cf. H. Merkel, 'Markus 7:15—das Jesuswort über die innere Verunreinigung', *ZRGG* (1968) who therefore wants to dismiss the second half as a later Hellenistic addition.

78. The Matthean 'exception', Matt. 19:9, is clearly secondary.

79. Matt. 18:23–35.

80. Is this the meaning of the strange saying about the blasphemy against the Holy Spirit, Mark 13:29?

81. Nor is Jesus simply advocating the pursuit of certain virtues which one may learn by instruction and experience as might be suggested by the use of the Hellenistic *Lasterkatalog* in Mark 7:21f, but the reception of a Divine Power which can overcome evil.

82. Cf. H. Braun, 'Umkehr', p. 84f, who contrasts Qumran's demand to their followers to give up their possessions, in the context of entering the security of the community, with Jesus' demands to the Rich Young Ruler to sell all that he has and cast himself on God's care.

83. E.g. E. Käsemann, *ENNT* p. 39: 'He is removing the distinction (which is fundamental to the whole of ancient thought) between the *temenos*, the realm of the sacred and the secular and it is for this reason that he is able to consort with sinners.'

84. In this respect Qumran too sees its prayers as equivalent to the Temple worship, a *commercium* with the divine on behalf of the land.

Chapter 7: Jesus' Theism

1. Harnack, *Christianity*, ch. 1.

2. Cf. e.g. C. H. Dodd, *The Founder of Christianity*, especially ch. 4; T. W. Manson, *The Teaching of Jesus*, Part 2.

3. R. Bultmann, *HST*, pp. 101ff; see also his *Jesus*, p. 115.

4. Bultmann's views on this subject are expressed rather differently in his *Theology of the New Testament* vol. i, pp. 22ff, esp. p. 23 where he refers to Matt. 6:25, 34; 10:29f as sayings of Jesus.

5. See pp. 70ff.

6. Matt. 6:25–33 and par.; Matt. 10:29f and par.

7. Matt. 7:7–11 and par.; Luke 11:5–8; 18:1–8.
8. Matt. 5:12 and par.; 6:19–21 and par.; Mark 10:21 and parr.; Matt. 19:27ff and parr.; 20:2; 24:45–51 and par.; Mark 9.41. The word *misthos* occurs specifically in Matt. 5:7; 6:14; 10:32, 39; 25:29. Punishments are referred to in Matt. 11:20–24; 13:40f; 10:28 and par.; 18:8f and par.; 18:23–35; 23:37–39; Mark 12:9 and par.; Luke 12:47–48; 13:1–5; 16:9; E. Würthwein & H. Preisker, art. *misthos* in *TDN7*.
9. As well as Mark 13 and parr. cf. esp. Mark 9; Luke 17:20f; 17:23–24 and par.; 19:42–44; Matt. 25:31–46.
10. Cf. 1 Enoch 1–5.
11. Bultmann, *HST*, p. 104.
12. Bultmann, *HST*, pp. 76f.
13. Cf. J. Jeremias, pp. 11ff.
14. Op.cit., p.38. The appeal to 'established eschatological linguistic usage' must be balanced carefully against the actual use in the context of the saying.
15. It may well be that in Luke 11:5–8 the original *a majori ad minus* conclusion has been replaced by the saying 11:9–13 = Matt. 7:7–11, which does of course contain such a conclusion. Equally it is possible that in Luke 18:1–8 an original *a majori ad minus* conclusion has been reworked to stress now both the insistent crying of the elect and the speed with which the judge will come.
16. Würthwein, *misthos*; on Jesus' teaching on rewards see also Bo Reicke, 'The New Testament Conception of Reward', in *Aux Sources de la Tradition Chrétienne. Mélanges offerts à Maurice Goguel*, pp. 195–206; G. Bornkamm, 'Der Lohngedanke im Neuen Testament', in *Studien zu Antike und Urchristentum*, pp. 69–92, and the literature cited there.
17. See Str.-B. IV, 1.490ff.
18. Matt. 6:19–21.
19. Matt. 5:46.
20. Matt. 6:1–6.
21. Matt. 7:7–11; (10:34–36); Luke 15:11–32; Matt. 21:28–32.
22. Matt. 6:24; Luke 12:47–48; 17:7–10; Matt. 24:45–51 and par.; 25:14–30 and par.
23. Matt. 20:1–16.
24. Aboth 2.8, attributed to Johanan ben Zakkai.
25. Bornkamm, 'Lohngedanke', p. 82; cf. N. Perrin, *Rediscovering*, pp. 116–18 (my italics).
26. Luke 15:11–32.
27. Luke 3:12ff.

28. Matt. 3:11 and Luke 3:16.

29. See Hengel, *Die Zeloten*, pp. 277–96.

30. See Hengel, *Die Zeloten*, pp. 127–32, referring to Josephus, *Ant.* 18.5.

31. Cf. for this section especially Becker, *Heil*, pp. 37–189.

32. Cf. Becker, *Heil*, pp. 78f.

33. This is Becker's view, but it is not widely held, cf. G. Vermes, *Perspective*, pp. 51–4; Y. Yadin, *The Scroll of the War of the Sons of Light against the Sons of Darkness*, pp. 244–6. More recently P. R. Davies, *1QM, the War Scroll from Qumran. Its Structure and History* has argued for a composite document consisting of three sections.

34. 1QM 1.8f.

35. 1QS 4.6f.

36. 1QS 4.20f.

37. 1QS 4.11ff.

38. Cf. 1QS 11.12ff.

39. I am assuming here, as argued at least briefly above, pp. 90f, that, while the more elaborate apocalyptic prophecies of Mark 13:5–27 and parr. are not genuine, many of the other prophecies are.

40. Mark 8:38 and parr.

41. This contrast was brought out powerfully by R. Otto, in *Kingdom* esp. pp. 67–93.

42. Cf. Hengel, *Nachfolge*, pp. 23ff.

43. Luke 10:18; Mark 3:22–27 and parr. (cf. the additional material in Q: Matt. 12:26–28 and par.).

44. Again, excluding Mark 4:11f, which does exhibit such a tendency but is almost certainly secondary.

45. Mark 10:25–27.

46. Cf. the discussion of *'yaḥad'* above, pp. 120f.

47. Mark 3:22–27; Luke 14:31–33.

48. Matt. 12:28.

49. Mark 8:34f.

50. A useful account of the issues is to be found in W. G. Kümmel's 'Die Naherwartung in der Verkündigung Jesu' in *Heilsgeschehen und Geschichte, Gesammelte Aufsätze 1933–1964.*, pp. 457–70.

51. Mark 12:18–27 and parr.

52. Luke 16:19–31.

53. The Lucan form of the saying, Luke 13:23f, about the narrow gate suggests that there will be many who will not be able to pass through; the Matthean version, Matt. 7:13f, offers men a choice of two ways, one leading to life, one to destruction. The Matthean version certainly

reflects a view of the Christian community as set apart from the rest of men who are engaged on the works of destruction. Whether Luke's version is a simplification of this more original Q saying or whether it is closer to an orginal saying of Jesus, it is difficult to say. If the latter is true, then this still leaves the question open whether it originally stressed the difficulty of man's entering the Kingdom and the need of moral effort in this direction or whether the original saying was more paraxodical like the saying about the rich man entering the Kingdom. See Schulz, *Q*, pp. 309–12.

54. Matt. 22:14.
55. Matt. 5:3ff; Luke 6:20ff.
56. Cf. C. K. Barrett, 'I am not Ashamed of the Gospel', in *New Testament Essays*.
57. Mark 8:34 and parr.; 6:6–13 and parr.; Luke 10:1–16; Matt. 9:35–10:16.
58. E.g. Luke 12:35–38; Mark 13:33–37; Matt. 24:43–44 and par.; 24:45–51 and par.; 25:1–13; Luke 21:34–36. Cf. Bultmann, *HST*, pp. 118ff.
59. Cf. E. Grässer, *Die Naherwartung Jesu*, for a useful summary of the discussion.
60. Matt. 12:38ff.

Chapter 8: Jesus' Role in the Transformation of First-Century Judaism

1. Cf. most recently B. F. Meyer, *The Aims of Jesus*. Meyer's use of the term owes a good deal to the existentialist tradition. 'Aims' are 'the key to' a man's 'historic selfhood' which 'they both fashion and express'. It is a question ultimately about Jesus' authenticity which has to be settled by reference to an attempt 'to locate the pattern or form or determining principle of Jesus' career' (p. 111).
2. Cf. the discussion of Reimarus in ch. 1 above.
3. Hengel, *Die Zeloten*, pp. 235–51; *Nachfolge*, pp. 18–27; 37–40.
4. Hengel, *Die Zeloten*, esp. pp. 160ff, and *Nachfolge*, pp. 18ff.
5. Hengel, *Nachfolge*, pp. 9–17.
6. Theissen, *Followers*, p. 36, E.T, 'Support', uses this expression to characterize those groups whose social uprootedness led them to hope and pray for help from Yahweh; cf. Theissen, 'Wir haben. . .', pp. 187f.
7. G. Vermes appendix, 'Son of Man' in M. Black, *An Aramaic Approach*

to the Gospels and Acts, Oxford, OUP, 1967, pp. 310–28; cf. M. Hooker, 'Is the Son of Man problem really insoluble?' in *Text and Interpretation*.

8. Cf. e.g. E. Arens' excellent discussion of the Son of Man *elthon* sayings in *The Elthon Sayings in the Synoptic Tradition*, pp. 117–93.

9. This has often been explained in terms of 'corporate personality' but contrast the views of J. Rogerson, 'The Hebrew Conception of Corporate Personality: A Re-Examination', *JTS* (1970). On the question of corporate and individual meanings of the term, see also F. Hahn, *The Titles of Jesus in Christology*, pp. 17ff.

10. But it is of course not certain that these passages existed at the time of Jesus.

11. In so far as we have the title here at all: one like unto a Son of Man. It seems more likely that Dan. 7 is the *source* of what is admittedly an odd linguistic usage, than an instance of the title itself. If this is so, then it tends to confirm the point that the apocalyptic use of the term is specifically connected to the notion of an individual, a heavenly redeemer figure; so, too, Hahn, *Titles*, pp. 17–19.

12. Dan. 7:26f; 12:2f.

13. 4 Ezra 13:8–11.

14. 1QS 9:10f.

15. Cf. discussion of Holm's views of the reaction between the eschatological prophet and the two Messiahs below.

16. See Hahn, *Titles*, pp. 352–65.

17. Meyer, *Prophet*; Theissen, 'Tempel', and Hill, 'Prophets'.

18. Acts 5:36.

19. The florilegium from cave four provides evidence for the use of Deut. 8:18 by the community: 4QTest 5ff.

20. Cf. 1QS 9: 10f.

21. Hahn, *Titles*, p. 362.

22. CD 19:35f.

23. 1QS 5:21–24.

24. 1QS 5:14.

25. See above ch. 6 on the esoteric understanding of the Law in Qumran.

26. Hengel, *Nachfolge*, pp. 18ff; 37ff; 41ff.

27. Matt. 8:22.

28. See above ch. 5, p. 107, and Betz, 'Krieg'; M. Black, 'Matt. 10:34'; and 'Judas'.

29. The question is put by John's disciples to Jesus: 'Are you he who is to come, or shall we look for another?' (Matt. 11:3) and 'answered' precisely in terms of Jesus' preaching and healing activity. While the

use of Isaianic prophecies clearly expresses the view that Jesus' ministry was part of the eschaton, it does not fully answer the question whether Jesus expected some further figure.

30. R. Bultmann, *TheolNT*, pp. 28–32. I make no attempt to list the relevant literature.

31. E.g. H. Conzelmann, *Jesus*.

32. This is of course Bultmann's view, *TheolNT*, p. 30.

33. Notably J. Jeremias, *New Testament Theology*, I, pp. 257–76. The view has also been much canvassed by English scholars.

34. Arens, *Elthon*, pp. 117–61.

35. Matt. 3:11. There is a useful discussion of Jesus' relation to the Baptist in J. Becker, *Jesus und Johannes der Täufer*. Cf. also D. R. Catchpole, 'On Doing Violence to the Kingdom', in *Journal of Theology for Southern Africa*, who on the basis of a reconstruction of the earliest text of Matt. 11:12 argues that in Jesus' view what characterized John and him *alike* was the preaching of the nearness of God's Kingdom. Catchpole does not in that context however discuss variations between the two in terms of their understanding of the nature of the Kingdom and the manner of its coming. In a subsequent article 'John the Baptist, Jesus and the Parable of the Tares' in *SJTh* Catchpole has argued again for the similarity between John and Jesus in relation to their expectation of the End and the 'need for an immediate response so that the disaster of belonging to the category of chaff or weeds might be averted and replaced by the security of belonging to the category of the wheat'.

36. It is of course possible that John used the title to refer to his own 'stronger one' and that this was subsequently dropped in the tradition because of the convention that the title Son of Man was uttered only by Jesus.

37. Partly on the grounds of its distinctiveness from other Jewish utterances of this kind, partly because of its multiple attestation, partly because of its coherence with the way Jesus reworks Jewish notions of righteousness and judgement elsewhere; partly too because it makes sense of the development of the tradition in respect of the Son of Man sayings, if we see here the germ of the subsequent elaboration by the Church of the conception to include notions of forgiveness (Mark 2:10, parr.) and suffering (Mark 8:31, etc.). Its authenticity has been challenged most substantially by E. Käsemann, 'Sentences of Holy Law in the New Testament' in *New Testament Questions of Today*, but

contrast K. Berger, 'Zu den sogenannten Sätzen heiligen Rechtes' in *NTS* (1970–1).

38. On the terminology here see Barrett, 'I am not Ashamed', pp. 116–43.

39. Clearly there is evidence in the tradition of Dan. 7, Eth. En., 4 Ezr. for the association of the Son of Man with judgement in varying roles, but this cannot in any case be determinative of the precise meaning here.

40. For this reason I find it hard to accept the authenticity of Luke 12:49: 'I came to cast fire upon the earth; and would that it were already kindled!', if as does, e.g., Arens, *Elthon*, pp. 82ff, one takes it to refer to the fire of judgement, an image which is certainly very closely associated with destruction. Of course, it might be argued that this saying too, in the context of Jesus' teaching, meant something very different from what the Baptist taught, but for this one would require more evidence than we have that Jesus had reworked the notion of fire.

41. This point is clearly developed in the Son of Man saying Mark 2:10 which, though early, is probably a creation of the Church, but one consistent with the theological tendency of our present saying.

42. Matt. 11:12f.

43. Again this is made more explicit in the Son of Man sayings which refer to Jesus' suffering: Mark 8:31; 9:31; 10:33ff. While in their present form these sayings are doubtless much formed by historical recollection of the details of Jesus' passion, it may be possible to get back to an earlier stage behind Mark 8:31 of the form: 'The Son of Man must suffer many things and be rejected' and another behind Mark 9:31: 'The Son of Man will be delivered into the hands of men (in Aramaic: 'Sons of Men')'; cf. J. Roloff, 'Anfänge der soteriologischen Deutung des Todes Jesu (Mk. X. 45 und Lk. XXII.27)', in *NTS*, p. 39, n.3.

44. Cf. here the associations in Mark of the Son of Man saying 8:38 with the discipleship sayings 8:34ff. On the relation to Jesus' death see Roloff, art. cit.

45. For a full bibliography see F. Schnider, *Jesus der Prophet*. Of particular interest: C. H. Dodd, 'Jesus as Teacher and Prophet', in *Mysterium Christi*, pp. 53–66; and works referred to in footnote 17 above.

46. Matt. 11:9.

47. Matt. 11:1–6, esp. v.6: 'Blessed is he that takes no offence at me'.

48. See P. Worsley, *The Trumpet Shall Sound. A Study of 'Cargo' Cults in Melanesia*.
49. It has its doublet in Mark 8:28.
50. More detailed discussion of this Christology in T. F. Glasson, *Moses in the Fourth Gospel*; W. A. Meeks, *The Prophet-King—Moses Traditions and the Johannine Christology*.
51. Hahn, *Titles*, p. 383.
52. Hill, 'Josephus', p. 147.
53. H. Montefiore, 'Revolt in the Desert?' in *NTS* (1962).
54. Theissen, 'Tempel', pp. 154ff.
55. Mal. 3:1f.
56. Mark 11:27–33, cf. Hill 'Prophets', p. 150.
57. Arens, *Elthon*, pp. 28ff; 222ff; 117ff. He also claims Luke 12:49 as an *ipsissimum verbum* of Jesus. I have indicated above, n. 40, why I consider this unlikely.
58. V. G. Howard, *Das Ego Jesu in den Synoptischen Evangelien*, pp. 247ff. 'In the "But I say unto you" of the antitheses of the Sermon on the Mount there is contained a claim to absoluteness which in its depth and radicalness has its nearest analogy in the Jewish idea of the Messiah.' The notion of a claim to absoluteness is hardly a very useful hermeneutic tool, but Howard is correct in stressing the claim to *authority* in Jesus' saying. Again I doubt whether 'the Jewish idea of the Messiah' provides the closest analogy, but rather the figure of a prophet like Moses of Deut. 18:15, though there is also an explicit contrast.
59. J. Jeremias, 'Die älteste Schicht der Menschensohn-Logien', in *ZNW* (1967).
60. The Fourth Evangelist has developed this christological 'trajectory' most fully in his use of the term Son of Man.
61. Jub. 1.17, 24f, 28; 1 En. 45.4; 62.14; 105.9, refs. and discussion in Arens, *Elthon*, p.330.
62. Arens argues that the negative 'not the righteous' is to be understood dialectically: 'not so much the just—hence, no exclusion—as the sinners'. 'It breaks the exclusivist circle!', *Elthon*, pp. 54,331.
63. In this respect it is interesting to see how the ancient motif of the suddenness of God's judgement, to be found as early as Job and again in the Malachi text, 3:1, is reworked in Jesus' saying about the coming of the Kingdom, Luke 17:20f. The suddenness of judgement is not associated with some final apocalyptic drama but with Jesus' call to the sinners to repent and leave all and follow him.

225

64. See above ch. 5, pp. 104–6.; cf. Dodd, *Parables*, 50f.
65. See above ch. 6, pp. 129–35.
66. Y. Talmon, 'Pursuit of the Milennium: The Relation Between Religious and Social Change' in *Reader in Comparative Religion: An Anthropological Approach*, p. 528.

Bibliography

Abbreviations in brackets after date

Alon, G., *Jews, Judaism and the Classical World*. Jerusalem, Magnes P., 1977.

Applebaum, G., 'Economic Life in Palestine' in *CRINT*, pp. 631–700.

Arens, E., *The Elthon Sayings in the Synoptic Tradition*, Göttingen, Vandenhoeck und Ruprecht, 1976. (*Elthon*)

Baillie, D. M., *God was in Christ*, London, Faber, 1948.

Banks, R. J., *Jesus and the Law in the Synoptic Tradition*, Cambridge, CUP, 1975. (*Law*)

Barbour, R. S., *Traditio-Historical Criticism of the Gospels*, London, SPCK, 1972. (*Criticism*)

Barrett, C. K., 'I am not Ashamed of the Gospel', in *New Testament Essays*, London, SPCK, 1972, pp. 116–43. ('I am not Ashamed . . .')

Barth, K., *The Epistle to the Romans*, Oxford, OUP, 1933. (*Romans*)

Karl Barth–Rudolf Bultmann, *Briefwechsel*, 1922–1966, Zürich, TVZ, 1968.

Becker, J., *Das Heil Gottes*, Göttingen, Vandenhoeck und Ruprecht, 1964. (*Heil*)

Becker, J., *Jesus und Johannes der Täufer*, Neukirchen-Vluyn, Neukirchener V., 1972.

Benson, R. M., *The Final Passover*, London, Longmans, Green, 1884.

Berger, K., *Die Gesetzesauslegung Jesu. Teil I: Markus und Parallelen*, Neukirchen-Vluyn, Neukirchener V., 1972. (*Gesetz*)

Berger, K., 'Zu den sogenannten Sätzen heiligen Rechtes', in *NTS*, 17 (1970/71), 10–40.

Bertram, G., *Die Leidengeschichte Jesu und der Christuskult*, Göttingen, Vandenhoeck und Ruprecht, 1922.

Betz, O., 'Jesu heiliger Krieg', *NovT*, 2(1957–8), 116–37. ('Krieg')

Bickermann, E., *From Ezra to the Last of the Maccabees*, New York, Schocken, 1975. (*From Ezra*)

227

Black, M. 'Uncomfortable Words: the Violent Word (Matt. 10.34)', *ET*, 80 (1969–70), 115–18. ('Matt. 10:34')

Black, M., 'Judas of Galilee and Josephus's "Fourth Philosophy" ' in *Josephus-Studien* (q.v.), 45–54. ('Judas')

Bornkamm, G., 'Der Lohngedanke im Neuen Testament', in *Studien zu Antike und Urchristentum*, Munich, Kaiser, 1970, pp. 69–92. ('Lohngedanke')

Bousset, W., *Jesus Predigt in ihrem Gegensatz zum Judentum; ein religionsgeschichtlicher Vergleich*, Göttingen, Vandenhoeck und Ruprecht, 1892 (*Jesus im Gegensatz*)

Bousset, W., *Jesus*, London, Williams & Norgate, 1906.

Bousset, W., *Kyrios Christos*, Nashville, Abingdon Press, 1970.

Bousset, W., *Das Wesen der Religion*, Halle, Gebauer-Schwetschke, 1904.

Braun, H., *Spätjüdisch-häretischer und frühchristlicher Radikalismus*, Tübingen, Mohr, 1957. (*Radikalismus*)

Braun, H., 'Umkehr in spätjüdisch-häretischer und in frühchristlicher Sicht', in *Gesammelte Studien zum Neuen Testament und seiner Umwelt*, 2nd edn., Tübingen, Mohr, 1962. ('Umkehr')

Bowker, J., *Jesus and the Pharisees*, Oxford, OUP, 1973.

Büchler, A., *Types of Jewish-Palestinian piety from 70 B.C.E. to 70 C.E.: the ancient pious men*, London, Jews' College, 1922.

Bultmann, R., *Existence and Faith*, London, Collins, 1961.

Bultmann, R., *The History of the Synoptic Tradition*, Oxford, Blackwells, 1963. (*HST*)

Bultmann, R., *Jesus and the Word*, London, Collins, 1958. (*Jesus*)

Bultmann, R., *Jesus Christ and Mythology*, London, SCM, 1960.

Bultmann, R., 'The Study of the Synoptic Gospels' in *Form Criticism : Two Essays on New Testament Research* by R. Bultmann and K. Kundsin. Tr. F. C. Grant. New York, Harper, 1934. ('The Study')

Bultmann, R., *Theology of the New Testament*, London, SCM, 1952. (*TheolNT*)

Bultmann, R., *Das Verhältnis der urchristlichen Christusbotschaft zum historischen Jesus*, Heidelberg, Winter, 1962.

Butler, B. C., *The Originality of St Matthew. A Critique of the Two-Document-Hypothesis*, Cambridge, CUP, 1951.

Calvert, D. G. A., 'An Examination of the Criteria for Distinguishing the Authentic Words of Jesus', *NTS*, 18 (1971/2), pp. 209–19.

Catchpole, D. R., 'On Doing Violence to the Kingdom', in *Journal of Theology for Southern Africa*, 25 (1978), pp. 50–61.

Catchpole, D. R., 'John the Baptist, Jesus and the Parable of the Tares', *SJTh*, 31(1978), pp. 557–70.

Compendia Rerum Iudaicarum ad Novum Testamentum, ed. S. Safrai and M. Stern. Assen, van Gorcum, 1974.

Conzelmann, H., Article, 'Jesus, Christus', in *RGG*[3]., vol. iii, col. 623. Philadelphia, Fortress, 1973. ('Jesus')

Dahl, N. A., *Jesus in the Memory of the Early Church*, Minneapolis, Augsburg, 1976.

Davies, P. R., *1 QM, the War Scroll from Qumran, Its Structure and History*. Rome, Biblical Institute, 1977.

Dibelius, M., *From Tradition to Gospel*, London, Nicholson & Watson, 1934. (*From Tradition*)

Dodd, C. H., 'The Framework of the Gospel Narrative', in *ET* 53 (1932), pp. 396ff.

Dodd, C. H., *The Founder of Christianity*, London, Collins, 1971.

Dodd, C. H., 'Jesus as Teacher and Prophet', in *Mysterium Christi*, ed. G. K. A. Bell and A. Deissmann, London, Longmans, Green, 1930, pp. 53–60.

Dodd, C. H., *The Parables of the Kingdom*, London, Nisbet (1935), rev. edn. 1946. (*Parables*)

Douglas, M., *Natural Symbols*, London, Penguin, 1973.

Douglas, M., *Purity and Danger*, London, Routledge, Kegan Paul, 1978. (*Purity*)

Drury, J. H., *Tradition and Design in Luke's Gospel*, London, Darton, Longman and Todd, 1976.

Dunn, J. D. G., 'Prophetic "I"-Sayings and the Jesus Tradition: The Importance of Testing Prophetic Utterances within Early Christianity', *NTS*, 24 (1977–78), pp. 175–98.

Dupont, J., *Les Béatitudes*, I, 2nd edn, Paris, Gabalda, 1969.

Easton, B. S., *The Christ Before the Gospels*, New York, Scribners, 1930.

Ebeling, G., *Theology and Proclamation*, London, Collins, 1966.

Farmer, W. R., *The Synoptic Problem. A Critical Analysis*, New York, Macmillan, 1964.

Feldman, E., *Biblical and Post-Biblical Defilement and Mourning: Law as Theology*, New York, Yeshiva UP, 1977.

Feldman, L. H., 'Hengel's *Judaism and Hellenism* in Retrospect', in *JBL*, 96 (1977), pp. 371–82.

Fohrer, G., art. 'Mahlzeiten II', *RGG*[3]., vol. iv, cols. 607f.

Fuller, R. H., *A Critical Introduction to the New Testament*, London, Duckworth, 1966.

Glasson, T. F., *Moses in the Fourth Gospel*, London, SCM, 1963.

Golomb, B., and Kedar, Y., 'Ancient Agriculture in the Galilee Mountains', *IEJ*, 21(1971), pp. 136–40. ('Agriculture')

Gordon, R. P., 'The Targumists as Eschatologists', in *Congress Volume Göttingen 1977*, Leiden, Brill, 1978.

Grant, F. C., *The Economic Background of the Gospels*, Oxford, Oxford UP, 1926.

Grässer, E., *Die Naherwartung Jesu*, Stuttgart, Katholisches Bibelwerk, 1973.

Hahn, F., *The Titles of Jesus in Christology*, London, Lutterworth, 1969. (*Titles*)

Hanson, A. T., 'The Quandary of Historical Scepticism', in *Vindications*, London, SCM, 1966.

Hanson, P. D., *The Dawn of Apocalyptic. The historical and sociological roots of Jewish apocalyptic eschatology*, Philadelphia, Fortress, 1975.

Harnack, A. von, *What is Christianity?*, London, Williams & Norgate, 1901. (*Christianity*)

Hausrath, A., *Neutestamentliche Zeitgeschichte*, Heidelberg, Bassermann, 1868–74.

Hengel, M., *Judaism and Hellenism*, London, SCM, 1974. (*Judaism*)

Hengel, M., *Jews, Greeks and Barbarians*, London, SCM, 1980.

Hengel, M., *Nachfolge und Charisma*, Berlin, Töpelmann, 1968. E. T. *The Charismatic Leader and his Followers*, Edinburgh, T. & T. Clark, 1980. (*Nachfolge*)

Hengel, M., *Was Jesus a Revolutionist?*, Philadelphia, Fortress, 1971.

Hengel, M., *Die Zeloten*, Leiden, Brill, 2nd edn, 1976.

Hengel, M., 'Zwischen Jesus und Paulus. Die "Hellenisten", die "Sieben" und Stephanus (Apg. 6,1–15; 7,54–8,3)', in *ZThK*, 72 (1975), pp. 151–206. ('Zwischen Jesus')

Hentschke, B., art. 'Opfer II', *RGG*³., vol. iv, cols. 1641ff.

Hill, D., 'Jesus and Josephus, "messianic prophets" ', in *Text and Interpretation (Studies in the New Testament presented to M. Black)*, eds. E. Best and R. McL. Wilson, Cambridge, CUP, 1979, pp. 143–54. ('Prophets')

Hoehner, H. W., *Herod Antipas*, Cambridge, CUP, 1972. (*Antipas*)

Hoffmann, P., *Studien zur Theologie der Logienquelle*, Münster, Aschendorff, 1972. (*Studien*)

Hooker, M. D., 'Christology and Methodology', in *NTS*, 17(1970/71), pp. 480–7.

Hooker, M. D., 'Is the Son of Man problem really insoluble?' in *Text and Interpretation* (see Hill, 'Prophets').

Hooker, M. D., *The Son of Man in Mark*, London, SPCK, 1967.

Howard, V. G., *Das Ego Jesu in den Synoptischen Evangelien*, Marburg, Elwert, 1975.

Hübner, H., *Das Gesetz in der Synoptischen Tradition. Thesen zur progressiven Judaisierung und Qumranisierung der Synoptischen Tradition*, Witten, Luther Verlag, 1973. (*Gesetz*)

Hughson, S. C., arr. *Corda in Caelo*, London, SPCK, 1957.

Jeremias, J., 'Die älteste Schicht der Menschensohn-Logien', in *ZNW*, 58 (1967), pp. 159–72.

Jeremias, J., *Jerusalem in the Time of Jesus*, London, SCM, 1969.

Jeremias, J., *The Parables of Jesus*, London, SCM, rev.edn. 1963.

Jeremias, J., *The Prayers of Jesus*, London, SCM, 1974.

Jeremias, J., *New Testament Theology*, London, SCM, 1971.

Josephus-Studien. Untersuchungen zu Josephus, dem antiken Judentum und dem Neuen Testament, ed. O. Betz, K. Haacker and M. Hengel, Göttingen, Vandenhoeck und Ruprecht, 1974.

Käsemann, E., *Essays on New Testament Themes*, London, SCM, 1964. (*ENTT*)

Käsemann, E., 'Sentences of Holy Law in the New Testament', in *New Testament Questions of Today*, London, SCM, 1969, pp. 66–81.

Kleinknecht, H. M., art. *basileus* in *TDNT*, vol. i, pp. 564f.

Knox, W. L., *The Sources of the Synoptic Gospels*, ed. H. Chadwick, Cambridge, CUP, 1953–57.

Kreissig, H., *Die sozialen Zusammenhänge des judäischen Krieges*, Berlin, Akademie V, 1970. (*Zusammenhänge*)

Kümmel, W. G., 'Äussere und innere Reinheit des Menschen bei Jesus', in *Das Wort und die Wörter. Festschrift für G. Friedrich*, ed. H. Balz and S. Schulz, Stuttgart, Kohlhammer, 1973, pp. 35ff.

Kümmel, W. G., 'Die Naherwartung in der Verkündigung Jesu', in *Heilsgeschehen und Geschichte, Gesammelte Aufsätze, 1933–64*, Marburg, Elwert, 1965.

Kümmel, W. G., *The New Testament : The History of the Investigation of its Problems*, London, SCM, 1973. (*Investigation*)

Lessing, G. E., *Werke*, ed. J. Petersen and W. V. Olshausen, Berlin, Bong, 1919. (*LW*)

Lessing, G. E., *Sämtliche Schriften*, ed. K. Lachmann and F. Muncker, Stuttgart, Göschen, 1886.

Locke, John, *The Reasonableness of Christianity*, London, Hatchard, 1836.

Lührmann, D., 'Liebet eure Feinde (Lk. 6, 27–36/Mt. 5, 39–48)', in *ZThK*, 69 (1972), pp. 412ff.

Lührmann, D., *Die Redaktion der Logienquelle*, Neukirchen-Vluyn, Neukirchener Verlag, 1969.

Luz, U., 'Die wiederentdeckte Logienquelle', in *Evang.Theol.* 33 (1973), pp. 527–33.

Maier, J., 'Zum Begriff *yaḥad* in den Texten von Qumran', in *ZAW*, 72 (1960), pp. 162–65.

Manson, T. W., *The Sayings of Jesus*, London, SCM, 1961.

Manson, T. W., *The Teaching of Jesus*, Cambridge, CUP, 1967.

Mealand, D. A., 'The Dissimilarity Test', in *SJT*, 31 (1978), pp. 41–50.

Meeks, W. A., *The Prophet-King: Moses Traditions and the Johannine Christology*, Leiden, Brill, 1967.

Mehring, F., *Die Lessing-Legende*, Frankfurt/Main, Ullstein, 1972.

Merkel, H., 'Markus 7.15 – das Jesuswort über die innere Verunreinigung', in *ZRGG*, 20 (1968), pp. 352ff.

Metz, J. B., 'The Future in the Memory of Suffering', in *Concilium*, vol. vi, No. 8 (1972), pp. 9–25.

Metz, J. B., *Befreiendes Gedächtnis Jesu Christi*, Mainz, Matthias-Grünewald, 1970.

Meyer, B. F., *The Aims of Jesus*, London, SCM, 1979.

Meyer, R., *Der Prophet aus Galiläa*, Leipzig, Lunkenbein, 1940. (*Prophet*)

Meyer, R., *Tradition und Neuschöpfung im antiken Judentum*, Berlin, Akademie V, 1965.

Michel, O., 'Jesus der Jude', in *Der historische Jesus und der kerygmatische Christus*, ed. H. Ristow and K. Matthiae, Berlin, EVA, 1960, pp. 310–16.

Montefiore, H. W., 'Revolt in the Desert?', in *NTS*, 8 (1961/62), pp. 135–41.

Morgan, R., *The Nature of New Testament Theology*, London, SCM, 1973.

Moyne, J. le, *Les Sadducéens*, Paris, J. Gabalda, 1972.

Neusner, J., *The Idea of Purity in Ancient Judaism*, Leiden, Brill, 1973. (*Purity*)

Nineham, D. E. '. . . *et hoc genus omne* – an Examination of Dr A. T. Hanson's strictures on some recent Gospel study', in *Christian History and Interpretation. Studies presented to John Knox*, Cambridge, CUP, 1967.

Nineham, D. E., 'The Order of Events in St Mark's Gospel – an Examination of Dr Dodd's Hypothesis' in *Studies in the Gospels. Essays in Memory of R. H. Lightfoot*, Oxford, Blackwell, 1957.

Oppenheimer, A., *The 'Am Ha-aretz*, Leiden, Brill, 1977.

Osten-Sacken, P. von der, *Die Apokalyptik in ihrem Verhältnis zu Prophetie und Weisheit*, Munich, Kaiser, 1969.

Otto, R., *The Kingdom of God and the Son of Man*, London, Lutterworth, 1938. (*Kingdom*)

232

Paschen, W., *Rein und Unrein*, Munich, Kösel, 1970. (*Rein*)

Perrin, N., *Jesus and the Language of the Kingdom*, London, SCM, 1976. (*Language*)

Perrin, N., *The Kingdom of God in the Teaching of Jesus*, London, SCM, 1963.

Perrin, N., *Rediscovering the Teaching of Jesus*, London, SCM, 1967. (*Rediscovering*)

Perrin, N., *What is Redaction Criticism?*, London, SPCK, 1970.

Peters, F. E., *The Harvest of Hellenism*, London, Allen and Unwin, 1972.

Porteous, N., *Daniel: a commentary*, London, SCM, 2nd. edn. 1979.

Rad, G. von, art. *basileus* in *TDNT*, vol. i, pp. 565–71.

Rad, G. von, *Old Testament Theology*, Edinburgh, Oliver & Boyd, 1962–5.

Rad, G. von, *Wisdom in Israel*, London, SCM, 1972.

Redlich, E. B., *Form Criticism*, London, Duckworth, 1956.

Reicke, Bo, 'The New Testament Conception of Reward', in *Aux Sources de la Tradition Chrétienne, Mélanges offerts à Maurice Goguel*, Neuchatel, Delachaux & Niestlé, 1950, pp. 195–206.

Reimarus, H. S., *Abhandlung von den vornehmsten Wahrheiten der natürlichen Religion*, Hamburg, 1754.

Hermann Samuel Reimarus: ein "bekannter Unbekannter" der Aufklärung in Hamburg, Göttingen, Vandenhoeck und Ruprecht, 1973.

Reimarus, H. S., *Apologie; oder Schutzschrift für die vernunftigen Verehrer Gottes*, ed. G. Alexander, Frankfurt/Main, Insel, 1972. (*Apol.*)

Rilla, P., *Lessing und sein Zeitalter*, Munich, C. H. Beck, 2nd edn, 1977.

Riches, J. K. 'Lessing's Change of Mind', *JThS* NS, 29 (1978), pp. 121–36.

Ritschl, A., *Instruction in the Christian Religion*, in *Three Essays*, P. Hefner, Philadelphia, Fortress Press, 1972. (*Instruction*)

Rivkin, E., *The Shaping of Jewish History*, New York, Scribner's, 1971. (*Shaping*)

Rogerson, J., 'The Hebrew Conception of Corporate Personality: A Re-Examination', in *JTS*, NS, Vol. 21 (1970), pp. 1–16.

Rohde, J., *Rediscovering the Teaching of the Evangelists*, London, SCM, 1968.

Roloff, J., 'Anfänge der soteriologischen Deutung des Todes Jesu (Mk. X.45 und Lk. XXII.27)' in *NTS*, 19 (1972/3), pp. 38–64.

Russell, D. S., *The Method and Message of Jewish Apocalyptic, 200 BC–AD 100*, London, SCM, 1964.

Sanday, W., *The Life of Christ in Recent Research*, Oxford, Clarendon Press, 1907.

Schalit, A., *König Herodes*, Berlin, de Gruyter, 1969.

Scheller, H., *Kamenz und Lessing*, Kamenz, 1971.

Schenk, G., art. *dikaiosunē*, in *TDNT*, vol. ii., pp. 192ff.

233

Schmidt, K. L., *Der Rahmen der Geschichte Jesu*, Berlin, Trowitsch, 1919.

Schnider, F., *Jesus der Prophet*, Göttingen, Vandenhoeck und Ruprecht, 1973.

Schottroff, L., 'Non-Violence and Love of One's Enemies', in *Essays on the Love Commandment*, Philadelphia, Fortress, 1978.

Schulz, S., *Q. Die Spruchquelle der Evangelisten*, Zürich, TVZ, 1972. (*Q*)

Schürmann, H., *Das Lukasevangelium*, I, Freiburg, Herder, 1969.

Schweitzer, A., *The Mysticism of Paul the Apostle*, London, A. & C. Black, 1931.

Schweitzer, A., *The Quest of the Historical Jesus*, London, A. & C. Black, 2nd edn, 1936. (*Quest*)

Semler, J. S., *Beantwortungen der Fragmente eines Ungenannten insbesondere vom Zweck Jesu und seiner Jünger*, Halle, 1779.

Smith, M., *Palestinian Parties and Politics that Shaped the Old Testament*, New York, Columbia UP, 1971. (*Parties*)

Srinivas, M. N., *Religion and Society among the Coorgs of South India*, Oxford, OUP, 1952.

Stauffer, E., *Jesus war ganz anders*, Hamburg, Wittig, 1967.

Stern, M., 'The Reign of Herod and the Herodian Dynasty', in *CRINT*, pp. 216–307.

Stern, M., 'The Province of Judaea', in *CRINT*, pp. 308–76.

Stoldt, H.-H., *Geschichte und Kritik der Markus-hypothese*, Göttingen, Vandenhoeck und Ruprecht, 1977.

Talmon, Y., 'Pursuit of the Milennium: The Relation Between Religious and Social Change', in *Reader in Comparative Religion: An Anthropological Approach*, ed. W. Lessa and E. Vogt, 2nd edn, New York, Harper & Row, 1965.

Taylor, V., *The Gospel according to St Mark*, London, Macmillan, 1952.

Theissen, G., *The First Followers of Jesus*, London, SCM, 1978. (*Followers*)

Theissen, G., 'Die Tempelweissagung Jesu. Prophetie im Spannungsfeld von Stadt und Land', in *TZ*, 32 (1976), pp. 144–58. ('Tempel')

Theissen, G., ' "Wir haben alles verlassen" (MC. X.28). Nachfolge und soziale Entwurzelung in der jüdisch-palästinischen Gesellschaft des 1. Jahrhunderts n. Chr.', in *NovT*, 19 (1977), pp. 161–96. ('Wir haben ...')

Troeltsch, E., *Gesammelte Schriften*, Tübingen, Mohr, 1912–25.

Troeltsch, E., *Writings*, ed. R. Morgan and M. Pye, London, Duckworth, 1977.

Urbach, E. E., *The Sages: Their Concepts and Beliefs*, Jerusalem, Magnes P, 1975.

Vermes, G., *The Dead Sea Scrolls in English*, London, Penguin, 1968. (*DSSE*)

Vermes, G., *The Dead Sea Scrolls: Qumran in Perspective*, London, Collins, 1977.

Vermes, G., 'Ḥanina ben Dosa', in *Post-Biblical Jewish Studies*, Leiden, Brill, 1975, pp. 178–214. ('Ḥanina')

Walker, W. O., 'Jesus and the Tax-Collectors', in *JBL*, 97 (1978), pp. 221–38.

Weiss, J., *Jesus' Proclamation of the Kingdom of God*, Philadelphia, Fortress, 1971.

Wellhausen, J., *Das Evangelium Marci*, Berlin, G. Reimer, 1903; *Das Evangelium Matthaei*, Berlin, G. Reimer, 1904; *Das Evangelium Lucae*, Berlin, G. Reimer, 1904; *Einleitung in die drei ersten Evangelien*, Berlin, G. Reimer, 1905.

Wernberg-Møller, P., *Manual of Discipline*, Leiden, Brill, 1957.

Wernle, Paul, *Die Synoptische Frage*, Freiburg, Mohr, 1899.

Westerholm, S., *Jesus and Scribal Authority*, Lund, CWK Gleerup, 1978.

Wilson, M., *Religion and the Transformation of Society : A Study in Social Change in Africa*, London, Cambridge UP, 1971.

Worsley, P., *The Trumpet Shall Sound. A Study of 'Cargo' Cults in Melanesia*, London, Paladin, 1970.

Wrede, W., *The Messianic Secret*, Cambridge, Clarke, 1971. (*Secret*)

Wrede, W., 'The Task of New Testament Theology', in R. Morgan, *The Nature of New Testament Theology*, London, SCM, 1973.

Würthwein E., and Preisker, H., art. *misthos*, *TDNT*, vol. iv, pp. 695ff. (*misthos*)

Yadin, Y., *The Scroll of the War of the Sons of Light against the Sons of Darkness*, Oxford, OUP, 1962.

Zeitlin, S., *The Rise and Fall of the Judaean State; a political, social and religious history of the 2nd Commonwealth*, 2nd edn, Philadelphia, Jewish Publication Society of America, 1968.

Zimmermann, H., *Neutestamentliche Methodenlehre*, Stuttgart, KBW, 1967.

Index of Authors Cited

237

Index of Names and Subjects

God's separation of Jew and Gentile 124

Community Rule (Qumran) 96, 104, 119, 127, 157, 159

conventional associations 18, 32, 36, 41; of doing the law 130, 132; of God's justice 36, 39, 74, 113, mercy 113, 135, righteousness 70, 75, 164; of holiness 76, 113, kingdom 42, 57, 87, 91, 100, 128, 175, 210n, kingship 93, 112; of 'not doing as Gentiles' 130, purity 113, 125, 127, 137, 143, righteousness 76; of terms, applied to Jesus 172, in Jesus' language 99, in prophetic-apocalyptic tradition 145–6

Coorgs of South India 25–7, 197n, 218n

core-meaning: of 'black' 34; concept of 18; of God's righteousness 70, kingdom 99–100, retained by Jesus 103; of kingship 91, purity 143, Son of Man 177

corporate personality, concept of 222n

corpse impurity 84, 208n

Daniel 73–6, 93, 173; vision of 92

Darius III Codomanus 62

David, King 85, 92, 172, 209n

Dead Sea Scrolls 67

debts, septennial cancellation of 81

Decapolis, The 207n

Deists 1

Diaspora, importation of Jews from 80

dietary laws rejected by Jesus 136

discipleship sayings of Jesus 107, 134, 175

divorce *see* marriage and divorce

dreams as mode of divine revelation 76

dualism, in Judaism 165, Qumran 157

Ecclesiastes *see* Qoheleth

Ecclesiasticus *see* Ben-Sira

Elijah 85, 172, 174, 181

elthon sayings *see under* Son of Man

End, The, in teaching of Jesus 99, 169, 177; in teaching of Zealots 156

enemies: command to love 24, 98, 133–5, 142; definition of 134, 217n; of God, destruction of 94, 103

Enoch (Ethiopic Enoch) 74, 76, 125, 183, 224n

enthronement psalms 210n

eschatological expectations: and Jewish renewal 83; of Palestinian Church 47, 50

eschatological prophet 174, 222n; expectation of 181; John the Baptist as 180

Essenes 77, 98, 168, 205n; declare Temple cult impure 83; develop alternative sanctuaries 69; portrayed as Stoics 215n; preserve conventions of kingship language 96; programme of resistance 168; use of purity regulations 143

ethnos (national grouping), Jewish, high priest head of 64

evil, problem of 155, 166

Exile, The 65,113

Exodus, The 182

Ezekiel 173; Book of 113, 117

241

4 Ezra 224n

forgiveness: emphasized by Jesus
139; of God 99, 139–40, 169,
184, 186
form-criticism 12, 47, 55, 87,
198nn
Formgeschichte see form-criticism
Fourth Gospel *see* John, Gospel
according to

Galatians, Epistle to the 146
Galilee: conditions in, in time of
Jesus 77–83, 134; forcibly
Judaized by Hasmoneans 84;
social anomie in 98
Genesis, Book of 131
Gentile mission 60
Gentiles, customs of, abhorrent to
Yahweh 115; 'not doing as' 115,
130; outside God's covenant 114
Gnosticism 10
God: and destruction of the wicked
97; as king 37, 93–4; and man
171; new vision of 153; in
teaching of Jesus 145–67
Gospels 67, 85; Hellenistic
influences in 11; theological
motifs in 12 *see also* Synoptic
Gospels
Greek: *koine* 64; spoken in Palestine
59
gymnasium: established in
Jerusalem 65; place of, in
Hellenistic society 64–5

haburah 69, 73, 84, 118, 205n,
208n
halakhoth about tithing and purity a
burden on tenant-farmers 85

Ḥanina ben Dosa 86, 104, 140,
212n
Ḥasidic movement 96, 118
Ḥasidism 205n; as protest against
Hellenism 117–18
Hasmonean dynasty 79
healings and exorcisms: as mark of
Jesus' ministry 107–8; as signs of
the kingdom 104, 159 *see also*
miracles
Hellenism 105, 169, 185; and
counter cultures 76; defensive
response to 175; erosion of
Jewish norms under 83; and the
Herods 78; influence in Gospels
11; influence on Judaism 128;
Jewish distinctiveness from 112,
202n; nature of 14, 62–7; in
Palestine 62–7; programmes of
resistance to 168; relation to
Judaism 59–61; as threat to
Judaism 142, 147, 170
Hellenistic Christianity 57–60, 144,
199n, 202n; christological beliefs
47; pre-Pauline 11;
sacramentalism in 15–16; and
Synoptic tradition 52
Hellenistic mystery religions 10, 46
Hellenistic Reform 76
Herod the Great 78–81
Herod Agrippa *see* Agrippa I
Herod Antipas 78, 80, 99–100,
180, 206n
Herodians, involvement of, with
Roman government 97
Hindu caste system 25, 27
History of Religions School 1,
9–10, 12, 56
holiness, conventional associations
of 76, 113

holy war: concept of 182; in Jesus' teaching 107, 160, 164, 176, 179; Zealot notion of, rejected by Jesus 167

Homer, study of 65

Honi the Circle-Drawer 104, 140

'I' sayings of Jesus 90, 175, 183

ideal settings of Jesus' sayings 103 *see also* apophthegms

immortality, doctrine of, not present in Old Testament 2

Israel, election of 124

Jephta 172

Jerusalem 82; entry into, by Jesus 4–5; ethnarch in 78; gymnasium established in 65; industry in 80, 207n; priesthood 127; principal centre of Judaism 86; settlement of Greek speaking Jews in 202n; walls of, destroyed 182

Jesus: authenticity of sayings 49–52, 170; baptism by John 164, 180; contrasted with Qumran 129–32, 143; crucifixion 6, 55; discrepancies in teaching 46; distinctiveness of teaching 99 entry into Jerusalem 4–5; espousal of pacifist values 99; God's righteousness and mercy already present in 178; healings and exorcisms 104, 107–8, 159; intention and purpose vii, 2, 4, 6–7, 9, 170, 179, 183; and Jewish sectarianism 13

knowledge of God's will 129; life of, material for 45; modifies Zealot concept of discipleship 107; and political situation 6, 23;

preaching 11, 23, 130, 180, 185, 188; preaching of Kingdom *see* preaching of Kingdom by Jesus; as prophet 180–1, 188; and purity regulations 112–44

relation to John the Baptist 12, 99, 105, 158–9, 164, 180, 223n; self-consciousness of 9, 55; self-understanding of 196n; shares meals with social outcasts 101, 109, 168; suffering of 224n; taken for a Zealot 188; teaching about the Law 129–32; teaching contrasted with that of Moses 184; Theism of 145–67; typical actions of 102, 104

Jewish renewal movements 112

Jewish Revolt 81

Jewish upper classes 65

Jewish War (A.D. 66–70), Marxist interpretation of 203n

Job, Book of 225n

Johanan ben Zakkai 175, 216n, 219n

John, Gospel according to 45

John the Baptist 15, 82, 98, 154, 224n; announces imminent judgement 154; as ascetic figure 105, 184; attacks Jewish particularism 97, 107–8; charismatic character of 212n; death of 180; expectations of 103, disconfirmed 180; messianic movement of 80; preaching of the 'stronger one' 39, 161, 177–9; referred to as prophet 180–1; relation to Jesus *see under* Jesus; and term Kingdom of God 96, Son of Man 223n; view of the End 156

243

244

Hellenistic rule 62–7; in time of Jesus 77–83, 134

Palestinian Christianity 57–66, 144, 199n, 202n; eschatological expectations of 47, 50; and Synoptic tradition 52

parables 151–2; as apocalyptic-prophetic sayings 210n

Passover meal 105

Paul, Saint 15–16, 40, 197n

Pentateuch 67–9, 75

Peraea, revolt in 79

Pharisees 2, 59, 66, 68, 77, 121, 158, 208n, 213n; apply priestly laws to consumption of secular food 84; and concept of enemy 134; concerned with purification of everyday life 118; develop alternative sanctuaries 69; and the Essenes 96–8; in Galilee 85; observance of law intensified by 97, 142; offended by Jesus' meals 105; origins of 72; programme of resistance 168; and purity 97, 117; self-understanding of 109

Philip (son of Herod) 78, 206n

Phinehas 85, 172

phylacteries of Pharisees 133

Poleyas (caste of untouchables) 197n

Pompey 78, 81

prayer 150; quality of as opposed to regularity 104

preaching of Kingdom by Jesus 9, 13, 24, 87–111, 128, 145, 159, 168, 172, 175, 184, 210n

predestination in Qumran 157–8, 166

prophetic-apocalyptic, Jewish 48, 145

prophetic-apocalyptic sayings in Gospels 50, 55, 60, 90–1

prosbul 81

Psalms 92; enthronement *see* enthronement psalms

Ptolemies 62–4; rule in Palestine 64; undermine Judaism 147

punishment *see* rewards and punishments

purification: of the elect 158; not automatic in Qumran 127; of the righteous 88; rites of, in Qumran 126

purity: associated with moral purity 100; concept of, in teaching of Jesus 128; conventional associations of 113, 125, 127, 137, 143; core-meaning of 143; in Galilean Judaism 85; integral to Jewish renewal movements 144; linked to holiness 116; origins of, in priestly caste of Israel 113; and Pharisees 117; in post-Exilic community 113; and purity regulations 114; in Qumran 117, 119, 127–8

purity regulations 112–44; Essene use of 143; extended to everyday life 72; and Hanina ben Dosa 86; in Josephus 215n; outside the Temple 214n; in Pentateuch 214n; in Qumran 123, 128; rejected by Jesus 136, 138; related to Israel's election 115; sociological significance of 116; and Temple 124; and Zealots 209n

'Q' 45–6, 57–8, 202n

yaḥad 120, 122, 124, 214n, 220n

Zealots 37, 59, 77, 186, 210n; concept of discipleship, modified by Jesus 107; and concept of 'King' 4, 37, 40, 94; concept of the Kingdom 18, 106; in conflict with Jesus 217m; geographically close to Jesus 93; and holiness 96; and holy war *see under* holy war; and military action 83, 85; and national independence 97, 118; programme of resistance 168; risings of, defeated 99

Index of References

(Covers the Bible, Qumran, Talmud and Midrash, and Greek and Latin Authors.)

250

251

252

253